Heaven and Earth in Little Space

Andrew Burnham is the Bishop of Ebbsfleet in the Diocese of Canterbury.

A musician and liturgist, he served on the Liturgical Commission of the Church of England.

He is the compiler of *A Manual of Anglo-Catholic Devotion* and *A Pocket Manual of Anglo-Catholic Devotion*.

He lives in Oxfordshire.

D1234847

Also by the same author and available from Canterbury Press

A Manual of Anglo-Catholic Devotion
A Pocket Manual of Anglo-Catholic Devotion

www.canterburypress.co.uk

Heaven and Earth in Little Space

The Re-enchantment of Liturgy

Andrew Burnham

CANTERBURY
PRESS
Norwich

© Andrew Burnham 2010

First published in 2010 by the Canterbury Press Norwich
Editorial office
13–17 Long Lane,
London, EC1A 9PN, UK

Canterbury Press is an imprint of Hymns Ancient and Modern Ltd
(a registered charity)
St Mary's Works, St Mary's Plain,
Norwich, NR3 3BH, UK

www.scm-canterburypress.co.uk

British Library Cataloguing in Publication data

A catalogue record for this book is available
from the British Library

978 1 84825 005 5

Typeset by Regent Typesetting, London
Printed and bound in Great Britain by
CPI William Clowes, Beccles, Suffolk

Contents

For in this rose contained was
Heaven and earth in lytle space,
Res miranda.

Alleluia, res miranda,
Pares forma, gaudeamus,
Transeamus.

There is no rose of sych vertu

Anonymous, c. 1420

Acknowledgements

Coming to fruition over several years, *Heaven and Earth in Little Space* was completed not long after the announcement at a Vatican Press Conference on 20 October 2009 of an Apostolic Constitution enabling Anglicans to join 'Personal Ordinariates', and thus belong corporately to the Roman Catholic Church. This surprising gift is, undoubtedly, one of the most significant developments in the relationship between Catholics and Anglicans since 9 October 1845, when John Henry Newman, who had been the Vicar of the University Church of St Mary the Virgin, Oxford, until 1843, was received into the Catholic Church. This book is published, moreover, in 2010, the year in which Cardinal Newman is beatified, that is, recognized as one of the *beati* (blessed ones) of the Church. When, in due course, he is canonized he will be recognized, in all probability, to be a doctor of the Church, so profound has been his influence as a theologian.

Any doubts one might have had about writing this book, in which liturgical matters both Anglican and Catholic are discussed, have disappeared in the new ecumenical context. The question of what constitutes Anglican Patrimony, and is available and suitable for export, have suddenly become pressing and topical: the more so because Anglicans have a liturgical culture which is so similar to, and yet so very different from, the Latin Rite from which it sprang nearly five hundred years ago. Even so, most of *Heaven and Earth in Little Space* is not about Anglicanism, nor about Anglican liturgy, but about the re-enchantment of Catholic liturgy. The force of the obvious objection – why would an Anglican bishop have so much to say about that subject? – has been mitigated by the announcement by the Congregation for the Doctrine of the Faith. That announcement is itself a response to various approaches over the years of Anglicans seeking unity with the Holy See in obedience to the high-priestly prayer of the Lord (John 17), *ut unum sint* (that they may be one).

The ecclesial climate remains delicate and it seemed unfair to ask for help from any of my colleagues who are bishops – Anglican, Catholic, or Orthodox – whose episcopal task, primarily as the focus of unity within their local churches, might be undermined by dreaming the dangerous dreams of ecumenical journeying, or even engaging in the precarious party politics of liturgical re-enchantment. For nearly a decade, I have been entrusted by successive Archbishops of Canterbury with the privilege of serving the parishes, priests, and people of Ebbsfleet – many of them the urban poor for whom the fire of Christ's love blazes especially fiercely. I am grateful to both archbishops for their very light touch: they have allowed me to minister, as seems best, without let or hindrance. They have warmly encouraged programmes of catechesis and evangelism, and the necessarily informal machinery of chapters and deaneries for the pastoral care of God's people, and the furtherance of the gospel. Together the people in the Ebbsfleet parishes have begun to discover what it might be like to be 'an apostolic district', seeking to become a local church, in the full Catholic understanding of that word. It is to these folk that this book is dedicated with thanks for their love, their loyalty, and, in innumerable cases, a holiness to which one can only aspire oneself. Particularly impressive are the new adult Christians, often previously strangers to Christianity, whose commitment and devotion demonstrate true *metanoia*, a radical commitment to Christ and his Kingdom.

Travelling around I have been asked most days 'where's Ebbsfleet?' Meanwhile the little village of Ebbsfleet, a mile or two inland from Richborough Castle on the Isle of Thanet, has been overshadowed by Ebbsfleet International, the train station, higher up in Kent. During the Lambeth Conference 2008, when I visited the Ebbsfleet Cross, marking the spot where St Augustine first preached, there was a temporary sign in Ebbsfleet Lane saying 'No Through Road'. My prayer is that Ebbsfleet will be known in the history books not as a 'No Through Road' but, rather like the train station, serving a mainline route connecting with the continental mainland and its deep and rich Catholic life, nourished by the Petrine ministry, itself long recognized as desirable by the Anglican–Roman Catholic International Commisson.

I gratefully acknowledge advice and help from several sources. I am especially indebted to Fr Aidan Nichols OP for reading the manuscript, for offering encouragement, and for contributing a foreword which expresses a very generous view of the part these reflections may play within what, from almost any vantage point, are important debates about faith and practice, liturgy and church music. I am grateful too to the Revd Dr Jonathan Baker, Principal of Pusey House, Oxford, for writing an introductory essay, for setting the scene so sympathetically, and for his fulsome support throughout the project. The book was first imagined over lunch with Christine Smith of SCM-Canterbury Press.

Christine Smith is justly known for her ability to inspire and guide her authors in appropriate measure. I express my very warm thanks to her.

I am especially indebted to other friends and colleagues who, from a variety of perspectives, have been prepared to offer comment and watch out for errors whether of commission or omission. I acknowledge quiet support from the Rt Revd Dom Aidan Bellenger, Abbot of Downside, who read a draft of the manuscript through. Lucy Gardner, a former colleague at St Stephen's House, and Jill Pinnock, before retirement a teacher of liturgy in Truro and Oxford and secretary of the Ecumenical Society of the Blessed Virgin Mary, were each particularly helpful on the 'Mother or Maiden' chapter. Jessica Rose, herself an author and teacher, kept a eye on what I had to say about Orthodox faith and practice and the Revd John Hunwicke, formerly of Lancing College, second to none in his knowledge of things liturgical and rubrical, lent his learned eye. I am indebted, as well, to Max Kramer for allowing me to quote from a fine sermon of his and to Ole Martin Stamnestrø, formerly my secretary and now at St Eystein presteseminar in Oslo, for scholarly advice at various times. I owe a particular debt to Daniel Lloyd, of St Stephen's House, who not only sorted the manuscript out so that it could be sent on with some confidence to the copy-editor for publishing, but also, with his considerable intellect, watched out for inaccuracies, inconsistencies, and infelicities.

It being well over twenty years since I myself conducted choirs and orchestras and taught music, it seemed sensible to ask for some help from the musicians and I am immensely grateful to Dr Dana Marsh, Assistant Director of Music and Director of Chapel Music at Girton College, Cambridge, for his help on 'Said or Sung'. A contemporary of mine reading music at New College, some forty years ago, was Professor Craig A. Monson, of the University of St Louis, Missouri. Reading 'Said or Sung', he reminded me of things I had long forgotten and told me of things I never knew. None of those mentioned should be held to account for any of the errors, idiosyncracies, opinions, perspectives, and suggestions made in the book.

Finally, I must acknowledge the support of my family, especially my wife Cathy, a psychologist, who persuaded me at last to get 'that book' written, and my grown-up children, Hannah and Dominic, whose own stories have included fruitful encounters with Anglo-Catholic liturgy and the English choral tradition. It is because the secular culture amidst which they and their contemporaries live and work is so assertive that we must learn joyfully to celebrate and proclaim the mysteries of the Kingdom, increasingly confident in the sacrifice of Christ and his sacramental presence. My prayer is that my children's children and their children's children will have ever richer experiences of 'heaven and earth in little space' through the re-enchantment of liturgy.

Omnis spiritus laudet Dominum.
(Let everything that breathes praise the Lord!) Psalm 150

†Andrew Burnham
Bishop of Ebbsfleet
St Charles Borromeo, 4 November 2009

Foreword

It is an honour to be invited to contribute a foreword to this aptly entitled and even more appropriately sub-titled book. The aim of the sacred Liturgy is our union, redemptive and transfiguring, with the Triune God through Jesus Christ in whose person 'heaven and earth' are united in the 'little space' of the humanity he assumed and made and makes his own. The space of the Liturgy, and even the space of the building which houses the Liturgy, is to reflect this extraordinary conjunction which is now the ruling fact about our world. When the Christian imagination is coarsened, or the Christian sensibility dulled, we truncate the full dimensions of this mystery – to our loss. Hence the periodic need for the Liturgy's 're-enchantment' which is rarely more acute than in a pragmatically minded Church, set in a de-sacralized cosmos, in an epoch of cultural de-Christianization.

The Liturgy is always in a given place and time. Specificity of context has to be important. Though, in Eliot's words, there are 'other places/ which also are the world's end, some at the sea jaws,/ Or over a dark lake, in a desert or a city – / . . . this is the nearest, in place and time,/ Now and in England'. Quite rightly, the author of this book, conscious of pastoral and evangelical priorities, seeks to give counsel not for Elk City, Oklahoma, or for those located on the Eastern Ghats, but for Ebbsfleet, and thus for England. In so doing, the path he has to tread follows a delicate line. On the one hand, he accepts the revisionist historiography for which the English Reformation is, frankly, a Protestant affair, and its Catholic survivals a matter of Tudor good order in the State or Stuart decorum in the Church. On the other hand, he by no means wishes to write off the entire history of Anglicanism as, in a Catholic perspective, a failed experiment from which, at best, only cautionary lessons can be learned.

To the contrary, he thinks the Anglican experience of Western Christianity, whether through scholarly retrieval or inspired initiative, has much that can be repatriated to the benefit of the Latin Church. For that Church, for the most part, now uses not a Latin but a vernacular worship, even if the 'typical editions' of its liturgical books remain in the language of Jerome and Leo, and the Papacy no longer – as seemed the case in the immediate aftermath of the Second Vatican Council – wishes to distance itself from the earlier forms of the Roman rite. Where worship in the popular tongue is concerned, Anglican Christians still have things to teach Western Catholics whose learning curve in such matters was cut dangerously short by bureaucratic fiat in the later 1960s and 70s. That is relevant to the linguistic idiom of praise and petition, but Anglo-Catholics in particular, through their century and a half of struggle with sacramental minimalism, anti-ritualism, artistic iconoclasm, and the rupture of historical memory, have many other lessons to give their brethren in union with the Holy See, whose opinion-formers for a good deal of the twentieth century have been seduced by theories, theological, anthropological, and even architectural and musicological, inconsistent with Catholic plenitude of meaning and form.

The election of Joseph Ratzinger as Pope Benedict XVI was, among other things, a confession by the College of Cardinals that all is not well in Western Catholic worship. The notion of a hermeneutic of continuity – logically entailed by the Pope's disparagement, *expressis verbis*, of a logic of 'rupture and discontinuity' – underlined this need for a second look at the liturgical reformation of 1969 onwards. Hence the new seriousness with which Catholic liturgists are now considering – doubtless critically in some cases – the proposal of 'reform of the reform'. *Heaven and Earth in Little Space* can fit effortlessly into this setting.

At the same time, it is an open secret that Cardinal Ratzinger, when Prefect of the Congregation for the Doctrine of the Faith, encouraged territorial bishops – in England, but, presumably, not only here – to show generosity in their dealings with Anglicans of Catholic tradition. Those involved are people who, for reasons, especially, of sacramental order and moral doctrine no longer feel their own Communion to be a secure and lasting ecclesial home, and yet fear to seek a re-configuration of identity which might macerate communities and reduce to a bare common denominator the 'full Catholic privileges' for which clergy and laity of the Catholic movement in the Church of England sacrificed so much. Some of those privileges (one thinks, for instance, of devotion to the reserved Sacrament, or encouragement of monastic vocations) seem, it is hardly too much to say, distinctly under-appreciated in many Western Catholic circles today.

So the voice we hear in this book – the 'we' is the common reader, but I must also confess an interest as an English Roman Catholic sympathetic to the Anglo-Catholic cause – is not only that of an unusually knowledgeable liturgical specialist, equally familiar in the history of Anglican and Roman worship. Much of the book can indeed be read at that level – and quarried for helpful suggestions for diocesan policy or parish worship. But there is more. This book is also the work of someone who wishes to forward, in the domain of worship, the 'Benedictine' hermeneutic of continuity understood as an optimally rich renewal from the best possible sources. And he wishes to do so, not only in the interests of helping the two existing Communions most closely affected – Anglicanism and Rome – but also as a midwife to a babe yet to be born, an embryonic *ecclesia* with an Anglican patrimony 'united not absorbed'. That would be a fine addition (we are learning to call them 'the Anglican Ordinariates') to the circle of churches, Western and Eastern, that make up the Great Church, from whose universally primatial see Gregory once sent Augustine to England, to land on the Ebbsfleet shore.

Aidan Nichols, OP
Blackfriars, Cambridge

Introduction

The fundamental calling of the Church, and therefore of all Christian people, is to offer worship to God; to celebrate the Liturgy. It is in her liturgical worship that the Church becomes most closely what she is intended to be; it is in the liturgy that heaven and earth meet. Nothing – no other activity, no other concern – is more important for Christians. Yet the Liturgy has become disenchanted. *Heaven and Earth in Little Space* asserts with confidence that the Liturgy matters, and matters desperately: for it is not something that Christians do, but rather the essence of who they are. I am grateful to Andrew Burnham for his invitation to contribute this introductory essay: an essay which, I hope, will provide something of a road-map for what follows, while also – I hasten to add – including some material, and many opinions, which are entirely my own.

The book hits the crest of two waves. The first is the renewed enthusiasm, in the Latin Church, for the pre-conciliar liturgical tradition, a movement strengthened and further legitimated (though not initiated) by the *motu proprio Summorum Pontificum* of Pope Benedict XVI. The second is the question of Anglican identity, perennially to the fore in the collective Anglican mind, explored afresh in a host of recent publications,[1] and again accorded special significance by a decree issued in the present pontificate, this time the Apostolic Constitution *Anglicanorum Coetibus* which paves the way for the creation of 'Personal Ordinariates' in order to receive groups of former Anglicans into full communion with the Holy See. Integral to the logic of *Anglicanorum Coetibus* is the notion of 'Anglican patrimony', a term deeply

---

1 See, for example: Duncan Dormor, Jack McDonald and Jeremy Caddick, *Anglicanism: The Answer to Modernity,* London: Continuum, 2003; Edward Norman, *Anglican Difficulties: A New Syllabus of Errors,* London: Morehouse 2004; Rowan Williams, *Anglican Identities,* London: Darton, Longman & Todd, 2004; Alan Bartlett, *A Passionate Balance: The Anglican Tradition,* London: Darton, Longman & Todd, 2007; and now Andrew Shanks, *Anglicans Reimagined: An Honest Church,* London: SPCK, 2010. The variety of possible answers to the question of Anglican identity may be inferred from the sub-titles of some of the foregoing.

bound up with the question of who Anglicans are, and what distinctive and particular gifts they bring to the life of the universal Church.

Liturgy, while by no means the only arena in which we can discern an identifiable patrimony (and arguably not even the most important),[2] is unavoidably a key part of the discussion. We face a fascinating problem. In the Prayer Books of 1549, 1552, 1559 and, finally, 1662, the Church of England possesses a treasury of liturgical texts which exemplify all that is best in 'sacral' language composed in the vernacular: memorable, appropriate for both public worship and private devotion, and spiritually deeply nourishing. The suitability for singing the praises of God in that English idiom generally denoted by the term 'traditional language' is evidenced not only by the Prayer Books of the sixteenth and seventeenth centuries, but by the versions of modern Anglican rites cast into 'Tudor English', 'Rite B' of the Alternative Service Book (1980), and the Traditional Language version of *Common Worship* Order One. Many Church of England parishes which were gently derided for resisting the move to 'modern English' for the liturgy look wiser now; while the Roman Catholic Church is recognizing the limitations of the language of the *Novus Ordo* in English by undertaking a wholesale re-translation of the 1970 Missal of Pope Paul VI.[3]

The problem, of course, is not with the *style* of Anglican liturgical expression, but with its content. We have to face the fact that Cranmer's project in devising and then revising his Prayer Book was one of consciously expunging the theological underpinnings of the Catholic Mass from the new English liturgy, and teaching, through that liturgy, Reformed doctrine. In his recent book *Signs of God's Promise: Thomas Cranmer's Sacramental Theology and the Book of Common Prayer,*[4] Gordon P. Jeanes alerts us to the care which Cranmer took to achieve his aims of ensuring, *inter alia,* that the Communion service could not be understood as a propitiatory sacrifice; that there was no real difference, other than that of function, between the lay person and the priest; and that the Eucharist was instituted by Christ so that his death might be remembered, not offered to the Father.[5] There can be

---

2 A full consideration of this subject would have to include, at the very least: the distinctive nature of Anglican – more particularly, Church of England – parochial ministry and mission; the long experience of a married presbyterate and episcopate; different emphases in moral and pastoral theology; different models of formation for the clergy and lay ministers; and a differently evolved understanding of Canon Law.

3 An exercise not lacking in controversy, the final outcome of which cannot yet be predicted with complete certainty.

4 Gordon P. Jeanes, *Signs of God's Promise: Thomas Cranmer's Sacramental Theology and the Book of Common Prayer*, London: T&T Clark, 2008.

5 Gordon P. Jeanes, *Signs of God's Promise*, pp. 217–20.

no doubt that, plotting the trajectory from 1549, via 1552, to 1559, the Church of England of the Elizabethan settlement was one whose official formularies conveyed a minimalist eucharistic theology. Hence, as Peter McCullough has so ably demonstrated,[6] the sermons preached by Lancelot Andrewes at St Giles, Cripplegate, and at St Paul's Cathedral in the late 1580s and 1590s demonstrate 'a eucharistic theology far more radical for its English context than has ever been appreciated'; and McCullough notes that this is particularly so with respect to the fact that the consecrated eucharistic elements themselves remit sin.

'Catholic or Reformed', the first chapter of the present volume, looks first at Cranmer's texts. Here, Andrew Burnham helpfully 'nails' one of the key movements in Cranmer's project as being the transfer of the 'locus' of the rite from that of standing under the Cross (as in the Catholic Mass) to that, in the Reformed celebration of the Lord's Supper, of being present in the Upper Room where all are gathered for the meal. He continues the analysis of the liturgies of the Church of England through to the present day, and reaches the conclusion, surely supported by the evidence, that the composition of official liturgical texts in the Church of England requires the exclusion, or at best the 'watering down', of a catholic doctrine of the Eucharist, even as the shape and structure of those new rites came closer again to the classic Western model. A paradox here is that this has not inhibited agreement between Anglicans and Roman Catholics on eucharistic theology. The 2007 Report of the International Anglican-Roman Catholic Commission for Unity and Mission (hereafter IARCCUM)[7] contains an impressive summary of what Anglicans and Roman Catholics both affirm about the Eucharist: that it completes the sacramental process of Christian initiation; that it is the memorial *(anamnesis)* of the crucified and risen Christ; that Christ's body and blood become really present and are really given in the consecrated elements, and that only bishops and episcopally ordained priests may preside. Yet these ecumenical agreements – even those which have been received by the authoritative bodies of the two churches – exist alongside the sense that that eucharistic theology continues to be 'felt' in different ways; that the two churches do not, quite, share the same assumptions about what is going on at the altar. Inevitably, the official liturgy of the Church of England has to accommodate a range of emphases in sacramental theology;

6 Peter McCullough (ed.), *Lancelot Andrewes: Selected Sermons and Lectures*, Oxford: Oxford University Press, 2005; see the Introduction, p. xix.

7 *Growing Together in Unity and Mission: Building on 40 years of Anglican–Roman Catholic Dialogue. An Agreed Statement of the International Anglican–Roman Catholic Commission for Unity and Mission*, London, SPCK, 2007. See pp. 25–9.

but there can be little doubt that, whether via the sheer multiplicity of Eucharistic Prayers provided in *Common Worship* (which include some of extreme brevity and even superficiality), or by sheltering under the cover of pastoral necessity,[8] the impression can easily be given that the Church of England is able to sit comfortably with considerable eucharistic 'minimalism'.

A good example of this can be seen in some comments of Archbishop Vincent Nichols, the Roman Catholic Archbishop of Westminster, in an interview in *Standpoint* magazine.[9] The Archbishop, reflecting on the Archbishop of Canterbury's address at the Symposium held at the Gregorian University in Rome on 19 November 2009, in which he – Rowan Williams – challenged the Roman Catholic Church over its restriction of ordination to men, pointed to the link between the Incarnation and the celebration of the Mass as the key to understanding the Roman position on Holy Order. He said this:

> Christ is really and sacramentally present in the Mass. So there's a very strong link between what happens at the altar and the historical events of the life and death of Jesus . . . *As you go into the Anglican experience it's a bit more symbolic. That sense of reality weakens. It becomes more of a ministry and therefore more of a service that is led* [my italics].

Now, the comments of one Roman Catholic Archbishop (however senior) in a monthly journal (however reputable) cannot in themselves overturn an ecumenical consensus hammered out over many years by theologians from both churches. Yet, while in a variety of teaching documents, Anglican authorities have asserted a strong sense of the sacrificial aspect of the Eucharist,[10] it is equally true that Anglican reluctance to equate the Sacrifice of the Altar with the Sacrifice of Calvary (the same sacrifice, but offered under a different form) has made it easier to advance the case for the ordination of women; or, at least, not to have that case derailed by arguments derived from the identification

---

8 The proposed new Church of England Eucharistic Prayers for use with children – still in draft form at the time of writing (February 2010) – are a case in point.

9 In the January/February 2010 issue.

10 See, for example, *Sæpius Officio* (1897), the response of the Archbishops of Canterbury and York to the Bull of Pope Leo XII, *Apostolicæ Curæ*, which condemned Anglican Orders; or, more recently, *The Eucharist: Sacrament of Unity* (2001) (GS Misc 632), an occasional paper of the House of Bishops of the Church of England, issued in response to *One Bread One Body*, a teaching document on the Eucharist issued by the Catholic Bishops' Conferences in Great Britain in 1998.

of the ministerial priest, the sacramental priest, with Christ the High Priest offered at the Eucharist under sacramental signs.

Heaven and Earth in Little Space is not, however, a book about the disputed question of the ordination of women to the priesthood and episcopate, except in so far as that is one development in the life of the Church of England and wider Anglican Communion (by no means the only, but among the more significant) which has provoked with greater intensity than ever uncertainty about the catholicity of Anglicanism. For, as Andrew Burnham rightly emphasizes – and this, in essence, is the matter which stands at the heart of the whole book – *both* Anglicans *and* Roman Catholics have forgotten, or failed sufficiently to remember, what stands at the centre of the liturgical and devotional life of the Catholic Christian; and *both* traditions, having walked apart for 450 years, have particular things to contribute to the rediscovery, renewal, and revivification of the worship of God and that life in Christ which flows from it. So what is it that *has* been forgotten, and which *Heaven and Earth in Little Space* offers a *prospectus* for recovery?

In his review[11] of a book to which Andrew Burnham will often draw the reader's attention in what follows, Laurence Hemming's *Worship as a Revelation: The Past, Present and Future of Catholic Liturgy*,[12] Brian Horne sums up Hemming's thesis like this: '[T]he grace of the liturgy is that which comes to human beings from the heavenly future, and the liturgy itself is a figuration of that future.' Here we have the vital counterpoint to the view expressed (fairly or unfairly) in Vincent Nichols's account of an Anglican understanding of the liturgy of the Eucharist, quoted earlier. The Liturgy is not something which 'we do', it is not an aspect of human creativity or endeavour, through which we expect to conjure God into our view. On the contrary, as Hemming himself writes in an essay which stands alongside the more extensive treatment of the theme in his book,[13]

Each particular Eucharist does not bring God, or the divine presence to us. Rather through the action of the Eucharist we are moved to enter the divine conspection . . . we are made present to the one and single sacrifice of Calvary, a sacrifice which is at the same time the

---

11 In the *International Journal for the Study of the Christian Church*, vol. 9 no. 4, 2009.

12 Laurence Hemming, *Worship as a Revelation*, London: Continuum, 2008.

13 Laurence Hemming, 'The Liturgical Subject: Introductory Essay', in James G. Leachman OSB (ed.), *The Liturgical Subject: Subject, Subjectivity and the Human Person in Contemporary Liturgical Discussion and Critique*, London: SCM Press 2008, pp. 1–16.

heavenly banquet of the eternal Liturgy, of the self-offering of the Divine Lamb to the Father (the Eucharist as such).

He continues:

> Too often the Liturgy has been treated as a set of actions to be manipulated or controlled for specific outcomes or effects (outcomes and effects we believe ourselves exhaustively to understand) . . . The meaning of the Liturgy is not something at the disposal of the modern subject, rather it is something into which the Christian faithful have to grow as we advance in understanding and faith. The meaning of the Liturgy is *primarily* for God, only *secondarily* for us.

Hemming's analysis of the decadence – surely not too strong a word – of much liturgical practice, both Anglican and Roman Catholic, in the last third of the twentieth century and on into the twenty-first, leads very naturally into the wider discussion and many of the conclusions to be found in what follows in Andrew Burnham's work.

A word which sums up Hemming's approach to the Liturgy might be 'givenness'. It is the Liturgy's *givenness* which makes it something which requires the gradual deepening of our understanding; it is its *givenness* which makes it resistant to manipulation by us, makes it refuse to be the means by which to achieve ends of our own devising. Before turning to look at the liturgy itself, however – whether that of the Divine Office or of the Mass – *Heaven and Earth in Little Space* looks at the context in which the rites of the Church are celebrated, and her prayer offered; that is, the liturgical year, with its rhythms and routines (as the title of Chapter 2 suggests) of feast day and fast, plenty and moderation, gold and green. Here, too, we can identify a collapse in what, for almost every generation before this one, might have been taken as 'given': the punctuation of the secular calendar by religious (in our case, specifically Christian) observances of which the larger part of the population – even those who were not themselves especially faithful in worship – would have been aware. When the General Synod of the Church of England met in London for its group of sessions of February 2010, a Private Members Motion was debated calling on the BBC to give Christianity greater prominence. The mover of the motion drew the attention of the Synod, in particular, to the fact that the previous year, on Good Friday, there had been no indication in the television schedules of the day that it was indeed this most holy day in the Christian Year, evidence indeed that the *chronos* of the secular calendar was no longer being intersected by the *kairos* of sacred time.[14] It would be easy to confuse the imperative for the restoration, in contemporary culture and society, of a greater awareness of the seasons, holy days and special observances of the Christian calendar with mere nostalgia, were it not for the fact that so many social ills can be diagnosed as a failure to learn – or to remember – the wisdom of the ages embodied in just such a framework for individual and corporate living. It will not be the last word on the subject, but neither is it inappropriate, to suggest that the spectrum of ills in the West connected with food (from obesity to anorexia to some of the consequences of intensive farming) and drink (alcoholism) share a refusal to embrace that *balance* which the liturgical year necessarily provides over the course of a twelve-month cycle. Few nutritionists would disagree that we should avoid a constant diet of meat. Wine on feast days and solemnities and not on ferias and fasts (with the restriction of spirits to Eastertide, perhaps) would go most of the way to meeting the target of two or three alcohol-free days per week enjoined on us by the health experts. In the Anglican context in particular, we need to remember that the first of the *Tracts for the Times* contributed by Dr Pusey was on fasting.[15] Pusey pointed to four principal benefits resulting from the practice of abstinence: an increase in prayer; an improved ability to recall the things of God when engaged in the pursuit of the ordinary things of life; a more extensive practice of charity; and a heightened public recognition of 'the reality of things spiritual'. None of those benefits would appear any the less urgent today.

But neither is it only a matter of what we eat and drink. The Reformers replaced the medieval array of saints days and holy days with the centrality of Lord's Day (even if that led inexorably to the substitution of the Day of Resurrection with the penitential 'Sabbath day' of the bourgeois Victorian home); now that Sunday is as busy a day for retailers and consumers (and, therefore, for those who have to work to service these activities) as any other, we have lost out twice over. To rediscover the routines – the work and rest – of *kairos* alongside *chronos* would be, surely, to improve our chances of finding that Holy Grail of modern times, the 'work/life balance', and assist also with the safeguarding of family life.

Andrew Burnham's point in 'Fast or Feast' is that the Church itself – and again, we can speak of both the Roman Catholic Church and

---

14 I am grateful to Mr Daniel Lloyd for his sermon at Pusey House on 14 February 2010 for highlighting the relationship between *chronos* and *kairos*. The sermon is available (2010) at www.puseyhouse.org.uk/chapel/sermons

15 E. B. Pusey, *Thoughts on the Benefits of the System of Fasting, Enjoined by our Church, 'Tracts for the Times'*, Number 18.

the Church of England – has not helped in this creeping amnesia about sacred time, through a well-meaning but ultimately misplaced drive away from what appears complex or muddled (but which in fact lives deep in the memory of the Christian community) and towards what – borrowing a term from industry – we can call 'standardization'. Examples of this trend toward the smoothing away of the edges of an earlier and more authentic, if less straightforward, way of doing things include the abolition of the Octave of Whitsun, or Pentecost; the suppression of the pre-Lent -*gesima* season; the restriction of the opportunities available for the commemoration and celebration of the saints; and, most recently of all, the compulsory transfer, in the Roman Catholic Church in England and Wales at least, of the Solemnities of the Epiphany and the Ascension of Our Lord to the nearest or following Sunday. But if the churches, in their institutional reforms, have not helped to foster the daily recollection of sacred time, then 'Fast or Feast' concludes with the hope to be found among committed lay people. Here, rather than seeing their energies further dissipated by a misplaced activism in the parish, the laity are called to model an 'attractive and alternative lifestyle' – which is, of course, not 'alternative' at all, save that it challenges post-modern and secular assumptions, and is in tune with the best and most hallowed instincts of Holy Church.

In Chapter 3, 'Said or Sung', we move from the framework for the celebration of the Liturgy provided by the days, times and seasons of the Church year, to the consideration of one of the primary means through which the Liturgy is offered, namely, music. In his posthumously published intellectual biography of St Augustine,[16] Henry Chadwick reminds us how strongly the African doctor disagreed with those puritan Christians who wished to exclude music from worship. In Book X. 33 of the *Confessions*, as Chadwick notes, Augustine teases out something of the paradox of the influence of church music on the Christian soul: when sacred words are sung, they stir the mind to greater religious fervour, and kindle a 'more ardent flame of piety'[17] than when they are merely said; on the other hand, the mere gratification of the senses, which music can inspire, can also lead the mind astray. Augustine explains further that, now that he is no longer a fresh convert to the faith, 'it is not the singing that moves me, but the meaning of the words when they are sung in a clear voice to the most appropriate tune'. These

---

16 Henry Chadwick, *Augustine of Hippo: A Life* , Oxford: Oxford University Press, 2009; see p. 97.

17 Here I am quoting from the translation by R. S. Pine-Coffin, Harmondsworth: Penguin Books, 1961.

words – particularly the latter part of Augustine's phrase, the need for sacred texts to be sung *in a clear voice to the most appropriate tune* – can serve as a diagnosis of much that has gone wrong with liturgical music in the West in recent decades, and which has been the cause of that 'disenchantment' to which Andrew Burnham refers. For surely (and here I write entirely from the perspective of a non-specialist), it is the chant which provides 'the most appropriate tune', and therefore holds a privileged position, for both the Proper and the Ordinary of the Mass. 'Said or Sung' recalls us to the centrality of the chant, but in a way which is genuinely helpful, setting out as it does a variety of possibilities, varying in complexity and difficulty, with the anxious amateur in mind, yet true to the fundamental principles of this ancient form in which, par excellence, the text fits to 'the most appropriate tune'. Thus do the words become 'internalized', a living aspect of the company of those gathered for worship.

If Anglicans struggle, and need the help which 'Said or Sung' offers, with those parts of the Liturgy which, in some form, require the ability to appropriate the chant,[18] then, as Andrew Burnham rightly points out, the gift which Anglicans can bring comes through hymnody. There is little to add to the theology of the Ascension beyond what is contained in Christopher Wordsworth's hymn, 'See the Conqueror mounts in triumph'.[19] It is interesting that one of the greatest of all Anglo-Catholic theologians, Eric Mascall,[20] draws on hymnody to exemplify an orthodox Christology of the Incarnation. In his contribution to the 'Signposts' series, *The God-Man*,[21] Mascall prefers the words of the nineteenth-century Anglican Henry Ramsden Bramley to those even of Aquinas in giving expression to the means whereby, at the Incarnation, human nature is raised to the level of divinity itself. He quotes three verses of Bramley's hymn 'The great God of Heaven is come down to earth',[22] concluding with this one:

The Word in the bliss of the Godhead remains,
Yet in flesh comes to suffer the keenest of pains;
He is that he was, and for ever shall be,
But becomes that he was not, for you and for me.

---

18 Perhaps the Responsorial Psalm takes first prize here.

19 No. 132 in the *New English Hymnal*, Norwich: Canterbury Press, 1986.

20 He is one of the 'separated doctors' of the Anglican Communion identified by Aidan Nichols OP in *The Panther and the Hind*, London: T&T Clark, 1993; see p. 128.

21 E. L. Mascall, *The God-Man*, London: Dacre Press, 1940; see pp. 48–9

22 No. 37 in the *New English Hymnal*.

Mascall comments: 'The two last lines are an exact summary of the central truth of the Christian Faith; and only two of the words in it are more than one syllable.' With commendations like that, we should not fear for the propriety of continuing to accord the best of theologically literate metrical hymns a place in the celebration of the Liturgy.

What 'Said or Sung' provides for music, Chapter 4, 'Town or Country', does for the celebration of the Divine Office: it suggests a way forward which is both a 're-enchantment' and the means by which such a re-appropriation of the deep waters of the Tradition can be made available to Christians who are really (and not just theoretically) gathered for prayer in the churches and cathedrals of the land. However, in the short space remaining for this Introduction, I want to pass on to Chapter 5 of this book, 'Extraordinary or Ordinary'. Here, the challenge is to offer a synthesis between the opposing sides of what Andrew Burnham calls contemporary Catholicism's 'culture wars': Old Rite or New, Extraordinary Form or Ordinary. The forces ranged behind the opposing colours on the battlefield describe with surprising precision and clarity the different generations: on the one side those who implemented the *Novus Ordo* and who saw it, and continue to see it, as the great leap forward; on the other, a younger generation, who include (though not exclusively) many champions of the older ways, disillusioned by the – as they perceive it – banality of the modern rites, and not just as a matter of preference for a ceremonial both more elaborate and more precisely delineated, but also from a conviction that the 'new mass' fails to teach adequately or with sufficient clarity eucharistic doctrine, notably in the vital matter of the Sacrifice of the Mass.

David Torevell's important book *Losing the Sacred: Ritual, Modernity and Liturgical Reform* (which will be quoted later in *Heaven and Earth in Little Space*) was published[23] in 2000, a little before the 'culture wars' really began to hot up. In it – anticipating almost precisely the issues raised by Laurence Hemming in his essay quoted above, as well as in *Worship as Revelation* – he describes the pre-conciliar Roman Rite as 'a reconfiguration of time and space in relation to the eschaton'.[24] He identifies the crisis – as he sees it – of the new rite to lie precisely in its failure to preserve the analogical relationship between the sacred space of ritual and the heavenly realm; instead, worship was now to be envisaged as being entirely in tune with the secular world. This 'domestication', or secularization, of worship could inevitably lead not only to

---

23 David Torevell, *Losing the Sacred: Ritual, Modernity and Liturgical Reform*, London: T&T Clark, 2000.
24 David Torevell, *Losing the Sacred*, p. 159.

a far-reaching amnesia about what worship is actually *for*, but also a near-total collapse in any sense of the transcendence of God.

If this is the problem – can the answer be, simply the restoration of the pre-conciliar rite? Even if agreement could be reached on precisely *which* version of the 'Old Rite', then the answer – and here I write entirely personally – must surely be 'no'. While it is entirely welcome that the 'Extraordinary Form' should be as 'mainstream' as possible a part of the diet of liturgical worship in the West, it seems unlikely – to the point of wilful eccentricity – that it could become once again the predominant expression of the Liturgy. Rightly or wrongly, regrettably or inevitably, the task of re-converting the entire Catholic population to former ways must be – to say the least – remote. Interestingly, a recent Catholic writer who is no uncritical friend of the *Novus Ordo*, and who takes the 'conservative' changes in the proposed translation of *Missale Romanum editio typica tertia*, the third edition of the Roman Missal, as read, has this to say:

> While some conservative organisations and seminaries are now celebrating the 1962 rite with a certain regularity, and places where it is being celebrated are drawing crowds of young people often out of curiosity for experiencing what they never knew growing up, I do not believe that the 'extraordinary Form of the Roman Rite' poses any significant threat to the Conciliar liturgy or its ongoing renewal ... The Second Vatican Council has set us on a path from which the Church cannot and will not turn back, especially evident within the full breadth of its liturgical life.[25]

The key phrase here, of course – aside from the rather pugnacious defence of the *Novus Ordo* – lies in the words 'ongoing renewal'. How is the 'Ordinary Form' to be renewed? Much has been written about the *authentic* mind of the Council, not least in the matter of the Liturgy,[26] and a great deal more about the so-called 'Reform of the Reform', the search for a more dignified celebration of the *Novus Ordo* (encompassing, for example, celebration *ad orientem,* a greater use of Latin, especially for the Ordinary of the Mass, more use of singing – for example, of the whole of the Eucharistic Prayer and not just the Preface) while remaining faithful to the texts of the new rite. Here, in 'Extraordinary or Ordinary', Andrew Burnham – picking up what he surely correctly

---

25 Keith Pecklers SJ, *The Genius of the Roman Rite,* London: Burns & Oates, 2009.
26 See, for example, Matthew L. Lamb and Matthew Levering (eds), *Vatican II: Renewal within Tradition,* Oxford: Oxford University Press, 2008, chapter 5.

sees as a hint of Pope Benedict XVI's in *Summorum Pontificum* – takes us into newer and more exciting territory, with a programme of well-grounded opportunities for integrating the two rites, not only via Calendar and Lectionary, but at certain points in the Liturgy itself, so that the one may truly enrich the other. Not the least of these suggestions – though it might at first appear minor – is the insertion of the Offertory Prayers from the Extraordinary Form to replace those in the Ordinary; at a stroke, a great recovery would be achieved in setting forth, unambiguously, the theology of the sacrifice of the Mass.

Why end with Mary? If, in the Liturgy, heaven and earth meet, so much the more do they meet in Mary. In 'The Dry Salvages', Part IV of T. S. Eliot's *Four Quartets,* Mary is the one 'whose shrine stands on the promontory'. In words I have used before:

> . . . [S]he is *stella maris,* the Star of the Sea, the one who guides not only seafarers but, figuratively, all humanity through the rough seas of this world; but whose place is also liminal, on the threshold of heaven and earth – the meeting-point of the Incarnation.[27]

As for Our Lady, so with the Liturgy: each *Heaven and Earth in Little Space.*

Jonathan Baker
Pusey House, Oxford

---

27 Jonathan Baker, 'Seeking Holiness: Eliot, Auden, Betjeman', in *Literature and Aesthetics: The Journal of the Sydney Society of Literature and Aesthetics,* June 2008.

Catholic or Reformed

Every priest stands daily at his service, offering repeatedly the same sacrifices, which can never take away sins. But when Christ had offered for all time a single sacrifice for sins, he sat down at the right hand of God . . . For by a single offering he has perfected for all time those who are sanctified.

Hebrews 10.11–12, 14

A persistent counterpoint of this book is the way in which the practice of Anglicanism, and in particular of the Church of England, throws light on the Latin Rite and on issues of revision and reform. Thus, in Chapter 4, 'Said or Sung' (page 106), there is some highlighting from the perspective of Anglican hymnody. In Chapter 5, 'Town or Country' (page 140), similarly, there are contrasts with cathedral Evensong in the English tradition and in what revisers of the Church of England Office, reacting at least in part to the Bugnini reform of the Roman Office, have chosen to do. Whereas in Chapter 2, 'Extraordinary or Ordinary' (page 43), the discussion is focused mostly on the battleground within Catholicism, here we are concerned mostly with Anglicanism. We shall look at what Anglicanism is. Is it nearly 1,500 years old, taking us back to Augustine, landing at Richborough Castle and preaching the gospel to Ethelbert, king of Kent, at Ebbsfleet, or only 500 years old, going back to Henry VIII and the wresting of supremacy from Rome? We shall look too at the specific questions of Anglican liturgical practice and what, for the purposes of ecumenical export or ecclesial emigration, may constitute 'Anglican patrimony'.

What is Anglicanism?

When it comes to the claim of Anglicanism to be both Catholic and Reformed, there are whole areas of study, historical, ecclesiological, and ecumenical, making and refuting this claim. In the end, the claim stands or falls not on evidence, nor yet on its interpretation, but on the aspirations – and sometimes the prejudices – of those making or refuting the claim. Broadly speaking, within a Western framework, the Anglican reader will make the claim and, usually, the Roman Catholic[1] reader will not. Whether from the Anglican or the Catholic perspective, liturgical comparison is fruitful. Anglicans can see thereby the sources and origins of their own traditions, and where modern revisions are derivative (and, by contrast, therefore, where such revisions are creative or merely eccentric). Catholics, regardless of their view of the Anglican enterprise, can similarly see where a more established vernacular tradition has flourished and where it has stumbled. And there are comparisons facilitated by different scale too: something rather similar has happened in the two traditions in the last half century in the adopting of innovation, the recovery of, what for a time, seemed lost, and the lament by some for what seems to have been irrecoverably lost. The Prayer Book Society and the Latin Mass Society have many similarities, not least their ability to encourage innovators to attend to radical conservative concerns.

Lex Orandi est Lex Credendi

One of the things that we shall be doing is bringing the eucharistic liturgy of the Church of England into the foreground, against a wider backdrop of the Latin Rite – the opposite perspective from other chapters. Looking at the *lex orandi* (literally 'the law of what is to be prayed') of the Church of England we shall see what we can infer definitively from that about the *lex credendi* ('the rule of what is to be believed'). There are dangers in this exercise: Anglicanism is not confessional in the sense that, say, Lutheranism is. The Declaration of Assent,[2] required by the Church of England's Canon C 15 speaks primarily of 'the faith uniquely revealed in the Holy Scriptures and set forth in the Catholic creeds' and only secondarily of 'its historic formularies, the Thirty-nine Articles of Religion, The BCP and the Ordering of Bishops, Priests and Deacons'.[3]

---

1 The convention is adopted of using 'Roman Catholic' only when it is necessary to avoid ambiguity or make a particular point. Otherwise the word 'Catholic' – the way Roman Catholics normally describe themselves and the Church – is used.

2 See *Common Worship: Services and Prayers for the Church of England*, London: Church House Publishing, 2000, p. xi.

3 Secondarily because the claim is no longer made that these documents are true, merely that 'led by the Holy Spirit' the Church 'has borne witness to Christian truth' through them. The *lex orandi* as contained in Prayer Book and Ordinal cannot but develop: the same is not

Given that, to date, there is not yet a binding covenant amongst Anglicans about what to believe and how to behave, still less a touchstone of doctrinal authority for the Church of England itself, beyond what is stated in the Declaration of Assent, one danger is that the *lex orandi* will not give us much clarity about the *lex credendi*. Another danger is that the *lex orandi* is sometimes honoured in the breach as much as the observance. To give a simple example: the so-called Athanasian Creed, the *Quicunque vult*, has fallen into almost complete disuse even though the BCP requires it to replace the Apostles' Creed on thirteen mornings of the year. There was a new version of the text in the 1928 Prayer Book, and a shorter and gentler extract for responsorial use in *Common Worship: Services and Prayers*.[4] Its use, however, remains as rare as the reading of the exhortations in Cranmer's Communion Order, and there is some doubt as to how far many Anglicans would give it their assent if they knew what it said. 'Whosoever will be saved: before all things it is necessary that he hold the Catholick Faith', the opening, would cause problems for some; 'and they that have done evil into everlasting fire', for others. Most, meanwhile would be mystified by its discussion of 'uncreate', and 'confusion of Substance'.

There has always been evidence that the Catholic Church's prayer in Breviary and Missal reflects its teaching in Catechism and Creed, rather than the other way round. Pope Pius XII had this to say in *Mediator Dei* (1947):

> if one desires to differentiate and describe the relationship between faith and the sacred liturgy in absolute terms, it is perfectly correct to say: *Lex credendi legem statuat supplicandi* – let the rule of belief determine the rule of prayer.[5]

A well-known example of that is the Office and Mass for Corpus Christi: though their traditional attribution to St Thomas Aquinas cannot be substantiated,[6] the propers certainly set out to celebrate and precisely enunciate the Catholic Church's Thomistic teaching on the

---

true of Scriptures, Creeds or Articles of Religion. No one suggests so much as rearranging the order of the books of the Bible. Few are going to suggest that the Thirty-nine Articles are revised, still less base their views on capital punishment on what Article XXXVII *Of the Civil Magistrates* tells them.

4 See *CW: Services and Prayers &c.*, p. 145. The 1662 and 1928 versions are printed after the Orders for Morning and Evening Prayer in the respective editions of the BCP.

5 Pope Pius XII, *Mediator Dei*, London: Catholic Truth Society, 1947, p. 26.

6 See Archdale A. King, *Liturgy of the Roman Church*, London: Longmans, 1957, p. 198.

Holy Eucharist. But sometimes the opposite happens too: the articulation of doctrine emerges from the Church's faith and its tradition of prayer. An example of that is the dogma of the Assumption of the Blessed Virgin Mary, proclaimed by Pius XII in 1950 in response to an age-old practice of prayer and devotion. Here, one might say, it is not so much *lex credendi legem statuat supplicandi* as *lex supplicandi legem statuat credendi* – let the rule of prayer determine the rule of belief. Or, as one might say more simply, *lex orandi est lex credendi* (loosely, what you pray is what you believe). John Wetherell, in a considered attack on the *Novus Ordo* of Pope Paul VI, the Mass of 1970, makes much of the notion that people will believe what they get used to praying: one of the chapters of his short monologue is called 'Turning Catholics into Protestants'.[7]

Unable to modify its Prayer Book between 1662 and 1928,[8] except in small ways, the Church of England was freed by the Prayer Book (Alternative and Other Services) Measure 1965, and the Worship and Doctrine Measure 1974, when it gained some independence from Parliament in these matters, to authorize and commend new liturgies. This new facility far exceeds its ability successfully to articulate or re-formulate its *lex credendi*. In short, it remains a body where, in the view of many,[9] *lex orandi est lex credendi*, what you pray is what you believe. Just as the 1662 Prayer Book showed the attempts of the Caroline Church gently to modify the books of the Edwardian Church (virtually untouched by the Elizabethans) – a delicate matter – the Church of England since the mid-1960s has been attempting to broker liturgical agreements between Anglo-Catholics, liberals and evangelicals. It has produced, first, compromise texts that show all the brilliance – as well as the limitations – of committee work, and then, second, rather less brilliant, but synodically agreed, versions of these texts. The General Synod of the Church of England has shown for nearly forty years the continuing vitality of the three sub-traditions of Anglicanism, shrewdly analysed by Fr Aidan Nichols OP in *The Panther and the Hind*[10] but, as we shall see, the tradition of 'Common Prayer', in a church whose faith and unity is expressed and maintained by agreed texts, has never been so shaky.

---

7 John Wetherell, *Lex Orandi, Lex Credendi*, Cambridge: The Saint Joan Press, 2005. For the chapter referred to, see pp. 51ff.

8 The 1928 Deposited Book did not receive parliamentary approval but, with the encouragement of the bishops, many of its texts made their way into the liturgical life of the Church of England.

9 But see p. 31 below.

10 Aidan Nichols OP, *The Panther and the Hind*, London: T&T Clark, 2000.

Historical Background

Before looking in more detail at the liturgical texts, we need to briefly survey, for the benefit of the general reader, something of the historical, and ecclesiological and ecumenical background.[11] Scholars such as Heiko A. Oberman[12] and Eamon Duffy[13] have shown that medieval Catholicism was not as the Reformers sought to portray it – putrescent and unpopular – and Diarmaid MacCulloch[14] has established beyond peradventure that Thomas Cranmer was what in modern parlance would be called an evangelical. The arguments of a previous generation that Cranmer was really a Catholic, bringing in essential reforms amidst a careful continuity,[15] have had to give way to the frank admission that the Edwardian and Elizabethan Church were much closer, doctrinally, to continental Protestantism than the mainly High Church prejudices of twentieth-century Anglicanism used to allow. More has had to be invested in the Catholic sympathies of William Laud and the Caroline Divines and their impact on the 1662 BCP, as well as on what was revolutionary in the Tractarian movement, though, as Peter Nockles has conclusively demonstrated,[16] there was more continuity between the Tractarians and the eighteenth-century Church than was once thought. Even so, John Henry Newman was not alone in the feeling of having been 'taken in' by the Caroline Divines and their supposed Catholic credentials.[17]

One of the most startling innovations of the Reformed Church of England is what would later be called Erastianism. The King is head of the Church, as is shown by the Collect for the Monarch in the Communion Order, even more so in 1552 and thereafter, when that prayer is placed first, before the Collect of the Day. More than that, as the Prayer

---

11 This work is done expertly by Aidan Nichols OP not only in *The Panther and the Hind* but also concisely in *The Realm*, Oxford: Family Publications, 2008, especially Chapter 2.

12 Heiko A. Oberman, *The Dawn of the Reformation; Essays in Late Medieval and Early Reformation Thought*, Edinburgh: T&T Clark, 1986.

13 Eamon Duffy, *The Stripping of the Altars: Traditional Religion in England c1400–c1580*, New Haven: Yale University Press, 1992.

14 Diarmaid MacCulloch, *Thomas Cranmer: A Life*, New Haven: Yale University Press, 1996.

15 C. W. Dugmore, *The Mass and the English Reformers*, London: Macmillan, 1958. See also A. G. Dickens, *The English Reformation*, London: Fontana, 1964; second edition, London: B. T. Batsford, 1991.

16 Peter Nockles, *The Oxford Movement in Context: Anglican High Churchmanship, 1760–1857*, Cambridge: Cambridge University Press, 1997.

17 Peter Nockles, 'Survivals or New Arrivals?', in Stephen Platten (ed.), *Anglicanism and the Western Christian Tradition*, Norwich: Canterbury Press, 2003, see especially p. 181.

for the Church in the Communion Order shows, the King is assisted by 'hys whole counsayle, and . . . all that be putte in aucthoritie under hymn and by 'all Bisshops, Pastours, and Curates'.[18] The clergy are servants of the King and servants of the state.

Ecclesiological Background

Recent ecclesiological studies of the Catholic and Reformed claims of Anglicanism have included those of Stephen Sykes[19] and Paul Avis.[20] Anglicanism, as Avis sees it, is a distinctive, if provisional, group of churches, independent and interdependent, part of the One, Holy, Catholic and Apostolic Church, with a witness to the continuing vigour of conciliarism,[21] and astride the three-legged stool of Scripture, Tradition and Reason. This is rather different from how the founders of the Oxford Movement saw things. 'As a Christian nation', said John Keble in his 1833 Assize Sermon, England 'is also a part of Christ's Church, and bound, in all her legislation and policy, by the fundamental rules of that Church.'[22] No wonder the admission of non-conformists, atheists, and Jews to Oxford and Cambridge and to the House of Commons would prove so problematic for the nineteenth-century Church of England. Essentially, Keble's view of Christian England was the view that Cranmer or Hooker would have taken in Tudor times, though, for both Cranmer and Hooker, the national character of the Church of England was more important, and the distinction between the episcopal ordering of the Church of England and the presbyterian ordering of some continental Reformation churches rather less important. Keble and the Oxford Fathers already had a deeper, more mystical view of the visible Church than that, and regarded bishops, the 'Successors of the Apostles', as necessary, but it was the Anglo-Catholics who took things

---

18 1552 wording: 1549 spelling and wording is slightly different. For the texts, see *The First and Second Prayer Books of Edward VI*, London: Dent, 1910, last reprinted 1968.

19 Stephen W. Sykes, *The Integrity of Anglicanism*, London: Mowbray, 1978 (1984 printing); Stephen W. Sykes, John Booty, and Jonathan Knight (eds), *The Study of Anglicanism*, London: SPCK, revised edition 1998.

20 Paul Avis, *The Identity of Anglicanism: Essentials of Anglican Ecclesiology*, London: T&T Clark, 2008.

21 Conciliarism, prevalent in the thirteenth and fourteenth centuries, is the view that the final arbiter in matters of doctrine is not the Pope but a General Council. Gallicanism – the French version of this view – persisted within a Roman Catholic context into the nineteenth century.

22 John Keble, *Assize Sermon on National Apostasy*, Steventon: The Rocket Press, 1983, p. 16.

further. Hurrell Froude, pioneered this view, accepting the doctrine of transubstantiation and refusing to 'abuse the Roman Catholics as a Church for anything except excommunicating us'.[23] He was realizing that Anglicanism was a fragment of the Latin West. A high view of the Church and its episcopal ordering arguably first gained official recognition from the Church of England through *Sæpius Officio* (1897), the response of the Archbishops of Canterbury and York to the apostolic letter of Pope Leo XIII, *Apostolicæ Curæ*, the previous year.[24] It seems clear that it was this view of itself – which is not the view that either Cranmer or Hooker would have taken, for both of whom the national character of the Church of England would have been more important and the distinction between the episcopal ordering the Church of England and the presbyterian ordering of some continental Reformation churches less important – that informed Church of England – and hence Anglican – contributions to ecumenical theology for most of the twentieth century, about which we shall have more to say.

It has been Rowan Williams's job, as Archbishop of Canterbury and the leading contemporary apologist and theologian of Anglicanism, to make a similarly robust claim, but he does not always sound such a confident note. In the introduction to his *Anglican Identities*, a collection of lectures, he admits that 'the word "Anglican" begs a question at once':

> I have simply taken it as referring to the sort of Reformed Christian thinking that was done by those (in Britain at first, then far more widely) who were content to settle with a church order grounded in the historic ministry of bishops, priests and deacons, and with the classical early Christian formulations of doctrine – the Nicene Creed and the Definition of Chalcedon. It is certainly *Reformed* thinking, and we should not let the deep and pervasive echoes of the Middle Ages mislead us: it assumes the governing authority of the Bible, made available in the vernacular, and repudiates the necessity of a central executive authority in the Church's hierarchy. It is committed to a radical criticism of any theology that sanctions the hope that human activity can contribute to the winning of God's favour, and so

---

23 See Ian Ker, *John Henry Newman: A Biography*, Oxford, New York: Oxford University Press, 1988 (reissued 2009), p. 113.

24 See R. William Franklin (ed.), *Anglican Orders, Essays on the Centenary of Apostolicæ Curæ*, London: Mowbray, 1996, and Christopher Hill and Edward Yarnold, SJ (eds), *Anglican Orders: the Documents in the Debate*, Norwich: Canterbury Press, 1997.

is suspicious of organized asceticism (as opposed to the free expression of devotion to God which may indeed be profoundly ascetic in its form) and of a theology of the sacraments which appears to bind God too closely to material transactions (as opposed to seeing the free activity of God sustaining and transforming certain human actions done in Christ's name).[25]

We note the deference to the Reformed tradition in this 'generous definition', deference paid by one who would be described as a 'Catholic Anglican'.

A rather more confident expression of what the Church of England is and what she teaches was memorably articulated by one of Rowan Williams's predecessors, Geoffrey Fisher (Archbishop of Canterbury 1945–61), not known for 'advanced' churchmanship, nor, indeed, profundity of thought:

> We have no doctrine of our own – we only possess the Catholic doctrine of the Catholic Church enshrined in the Catholic Creeds, and those Creeds we hold without addition or diminution ... The Church of England was in existence long before the Reformation, and while it was deeply affected by the travails of the Reformation, it emerged from them in all essential respects the same Church as before within the One Catholic and Apostolic Church.[26]

Two of Fisher's successors, Ramsey and Runcie (both, like Williams, at the Catholic end of the churchmanship spectrum), were heard to admit that there is something provisional about the Anglican project. Ramsey, for instance, had this to say:

> [T]he Anglican Communion is not a body seeking to be attached to the See of Rome. It has always looked in other directions as well ... [I]f the Anglican Communion were to disappear because of its good and great service in the reconciliation of all Christians, then its disappearance would be something in which we should rejoice.[27]

---

25 Rowan Williams, *Anglican Identities*, London: Darton, Longman and Todd, 2004, pp. 2f.

26 The quotation comes from a speech at the Central Hall Westminster on 30 January 1951 which Geoffrey Fisher made on returning from his tour of Australia and New Zealand. It was reported in the *Church Times*, 2 February 1951, and is referred to by Colin Podmore in *Aspects of Anglican Identity*, London: Church House Publishing, 2005.

27 In Michael Ramsey, *The Anglican Spirit*, London: SPCK, 1991, a posthumous collection of addresses edited by Dale Coleman, pp. 141–2.

All Fisher's successors – including Dr Coggan and Dr Carey, both from the evangelical wing of the Church – have had to come to terms with the emergence of the Church of England as, more and more, one amongst many Christian denominations and, less and less, the natural religious habitat of the English.

Ecumenical Background

One would expect a family of churches which claims to be both Catholic and Reformed to play a special role in ecumenical theology. For that reason, the Anglican–Roman Catholic International Commission (hereafter ARCIC) statements[28] have particular significance, not only in an ecumenical context, but also in the discussion of what it might mean to be 'Catholic' *or* 'Reformed', as well as what 'Catholic *and* Reformed' might mean. What we have in the various statements is what might be called a maximalist expression of what Anglicans believe – that is, in the words of Fr Edward Yarnold SJ, 'a statement falls within an agreed comprehensive spectrum of Anglican doctrines', itself, as he goes on to say, a 'minimalistic interpretation'.[29] For Roman Catholics, however, the statements are indeed minimalist expressions: whatever the Catholic Church teaches, it must insist at the very least on these things. It is not uncommon to hear these statements described as Southern European theology done in a Northern European way or theology originally framed within a cultural context of Roman Law, re-expressed within a Common Law tradition. Other Anglican ecumenical dialogues – with Lutherans, Methodists, Moravians and French Reformed – have been careful hitherto not to contradict the ARCIC statements, though Porvoo (signed in 1994, ratified in 1996)[30] entailed some ambiguity over the necessity for the historic succession of bishops and episcopal ordination. One presumes that, like the merging of presbyterian and episcopal ordering in the creation of the Church of South India (1947), different histories, variously interpreted, would merge to form a common future. The Anglican–Orthodox Theological Dialogue began in 1973, not long

---

28 The first Commission met from 1969 to 1981 and the second Commission from 1982 to 2005. The first set of documents was published in Christopher Hill and Edward Yarnold SJ (eds), *Anglicans and Roman Catholics: The Search for Unity*, London: SPCK, Catholic Truth Society, 1994. The documents of the second Commission have appeared separately.

29 Christopher Hill and Edward Yarnold SJ (eds), *Anglicans and Roman Catholics &c.*, p. 336.

30 Conversations between the British and Irish Anglican Churches and the Nordic and Baltic Lutheran Churches.

after ARCIC. Its third and longest phase produced the document *The Church of the Triune God – The Cyprus Agreed Statement*.[31] Just as Roman Catholics within the ARCIC process made clear their unease about the Anglican practice of admitting women to holy orders, so the Cyprus Statement revealed considerable unease among the Orthodox. For the Catholics this sharply poses the question of authority and, for the Orthodox, the question of whether the ordination of women constitutes a heresy.[32] These bilateral ecumenical discussions have taken place against a backdrop of wider multilateral ecumenical discussion and it is hard to read such documents as the World Council of Churches Lima Text (1982), *Baptism, Eucharist and Ministry*,[33] without thinking how very Anglican they sound. Catholic *and* Reformed.

How Catholic is Anglicanism?

We have spent some time on the ecumenical background, because it is clear that Anglicanism has been seen ecumenically – and has seen itself – as a bridge between Catholic and Reformed. We can leave to others the question of how 'Reformed' Anglicanism really is.[34] What concerns us here is to what extent it can be called 'Catholic', beyond the obvious sense that its members, with all who are baptized in the name of the Holy Trinity, receive the Catholic sacrament of baptism. We shall discover that, though many Anglican liturgical texts, used repeatedly in the formal liturgical worship of the cathedrals and parish churches of England, possess what Rowan Williams, in the passage quoted earlier, referred to as 'deep and pervasive echoes of the Middle Ages', they have been purged of – or have avoided – Catholic doctrinal content. This is true not only of Cranmer's clever work (where the unwary can mistake reformulation for translation) but also of the modern service books which betray what the late Michael Vasey, an evangelical liturgist, used to refer to in conversation as something of a 'Laudian takeover', an ornateness which deftly avoids doctrinal controversy. Perhaps

---

31 *The Church of the Triune God – The Cyprus Agreed Statement 2006*, London: Anglican Communion Office, 2006.

32 *The Church of the Triune God*, p. 88.

33 Available (2009) online as *Baptism, Eucharist and Ministry* (Faith and Order Paper no. 111, the *'Lima Text'*).

34 The boycotting of the Lambeth Conference of 2008 by some bishops of the Global South and the specific disputes about whether 'The Episcopal Church' (as 'The Episcopal Church in the USA' now styles itself) is drifting into liberalism and jettisoning traditional teaching on faith and morals is not, in any sense, an accusation that a 'Catholic' bias is replacing a 'Reformed' one.

Newman's critique of the Caroline divines, referred to earlier,[35] comes in handy here: there may be votive candle stands and reservation of the Blessed Sacrament in almost every cathedral, and in many parish churches, but that does not mean that particular doctrines of the Holy Eucharist or of the Communion of Saints are being promoted, any more than Cranmer, preserving saints days in the Prayer Book Calendar to Martin Bucer's dismay, was advocating the intercession of the saints.

First Prayer Book of Edward VI: Collects

In a brief examination of liturgical texts, we shall look, first, at a couple of features of the First Prayer Book of Edward VI (hereafter 1549), prepared by Archbishop Cranmer, and then, having briefly considered what is going on in the meantime, jump 450 years to what has emerged recently. In the last half-century the Church of England has added to the provision of the BCP the resources of what were, first, experimental 'Alternative Services'. Then, in more settled form, we will look at what is generically called 'Common Worship' (hereafter CW). One of the treasures of the BCP is the thesaurus of collects, many of them apparently translations of Latin originals. Ostensibly Cranmer was faithfully translating many of the collects of the Sarum Use, the dominant Pre-Reformation rite. Geoffrey Cuming, discussing the 84 collects in Cranmer's version of the Proper, notes that Advent begins with new compositions, whereas all the collects for Sundays after Trinity are adaptations or translations. This suggests, says Cuming, that 'either time or enthusiasm for new composition seems to have run out'.[36] Cuming's remark is drawn to our attention by Bridget Nichols who herself usefully shows us something of how Cranmer adapts original texts.[37] It is too easy to show, despite Bucer's early fears, how seeking the intercession of the saints has been avoided.[38] It is not much

---

35 See above p. 5.

36 Geoffrey Cuming, *The Godly Order*, London: Alcuin Club-SPCK, 1983, p. 56.

37 Bridget Nichols, 'An Anglican Experiment in Appreciating the Liturgy: the Easter Day Collect (First Holy Communion) in the First Prayer Book of Edward VI', in James G. Leachmann OSB and Daniel P. McCarthy OSB (eds), *Appreciating the Collect*, Farnborough: St Michael's Abbey Press, 2008, pp. 141ff.

38 The collects for St Andrew, St Thomas, St Matthias, St Mark, SS Philip & James, St Barnabas, St John the Baptist, St Peter, St James, St Matthew, St Luke, SS Simon & Jude, and All Saints were all new compositions for 1549. In the rest of the *Sanctorale*, only the collects for the Conversion of St Paul, the Presentation, the Annunciation, St Bartholomew, and St Michael and All Angels are Sarum adaptations. The prayer 'to follow' the saints 'in all virtues and godly living', as 1549 puts it, is a thoroughly Reformed sentiment.

harder to see how, when he is engaged in new composition, Cranmer struggles to capture the terse style of the Roman collect. The masterly compositions for Advent Sunday and Ash Wednesday are neither brief nor understated: memorable and beautiful, but not terse. More subtly, in the adaptations we find ancient Latin texts carrying new theological freight. As Nichols says:

> Again and again, it is not the surrender of the independent will, but the positive discovery of the will that desires to work in harmonious obedience with the God who wills good things for his creation, that emerges in these collects.[39]

As well as the collect for Easter Day, which her article analyses, she cites the collects for the Second Sunday in Lent, the Fourth Sunday after Easter, the Fifth Sunday after Easter, the First Sunday after Trinity and the Fourteenth Sunday after Trinity.[40] Of these she says:

> All of these prayers, when compared with their Sarum predecessors, appear at first sight to be faithful translations. Yet closer inspection shows how subtle changes have altered the original emphasis, ruling out any possibility of an independent impulse to good, or of personal merit. Instead, they show a progressive movement from faith to the love of God that readily co-operates in a divinely directed course of action.[41]

To point out the theological changes made, and to discuss their appropriateness within the new Augustinian emphases of Reformation theology, is to underline what Cranmer himself was doing. He was not simply translating the Catholic liturgy into the vernacular: he was reforming it theologically, as best he could. Most particularly he was writing good works as a means of earning salvation out of the script. He could not remove all the ambiguities of the liturgy: 'O God, make speed to save us', a verse from Ps. 69(70), is retained in Morning and Evening Prayer, despite the obvious objection that, in Christ, the salvation of the believer is already assured. And yet he could remind the believer, as he does at the end of the Prayer of Thanksgiving following

---

39 Bridget Nichols, 'An Anglican Experiment &c.', p. 153.

40 Martin Dudley (comp. and ed.), *The Collect in Anglican Liturgy, Texts and Sources 1549–1989*, Collegeville: Liturgical Press, 1994, conveniently provides the Sarum originals (pp. 45ff.) and the English versions (pp. 66ff.), including notes of where 1549 texts differs from those in later Prayer Books.

41 Bridget Nichols, 'An Anglican Experiment &c.', p. 153.

Holy Communion, that whatever 'good works' we do are such as God has 'prepared for us to walk in' (Eph. 2.10).

First and Second Prayer Books of Edward VI: Communion Services

It is in the service of Holy Communion that Cranmer effects the greatest of changes. Diarmaid MacCulloch records Bucer, having met Cranmer in 1549, reporting back to Strasbourg Cranmer's assurance that vestments, candles, commemoration of the dead and the use of chrism were all temporary concessions 'to the infirmity of the present age'.[42] Cranmer is making haste slowly: 'The supper of the Lord and the holy communion, commonly called the mass', as it was known in 1549, was no longer the Mass in 1552. What Cranmer had somewhat incautiously referred to in 1549 as 'the canon'[43] was no longer intact in 1552. Furthermore, the words of administration had changed, as we shall see. The 'canon' of 1549 had 'deep and pervasive echoes' of the Sarum Canon of the Mass, so much so that F. E. Brightman[44] and a whole generation of Anglo-Catholic liturgists regarded it as quintessentially Catholic in doctrine and defended it as such, much as Bishop Stephen Gardiner had done at the time. Indeed it was Gardiner's argument that the 1549 rite was patient of a Catholic understanding which most clearly demonstrated the urgent need for the 1552 version.[45]

If we look at the 1549 'canon' we see that the Preface, *Sanctus* and *Bendictus qui venit* are followed by prayer 'for the whole state of Christes churche', including 'high praise, and heartie thankes' for the lives of the Blessed Virgin and the saints, and commending the faithful departed, praying that they may be among the chosen at the great assize (Matt. 25.34). What became later known as the Prayer of Consecration

---

42 Diarmaid MacCulloch, *Thomas Cranmer*, p. 410.

43 Whenever we refer to Cranmer's usage we therefore use the word 'canon', that is, with a lower case C and in inverted commas. Referring to the Roman Canon we use the word Canon, that is, with an upper case C.

44 An accessible introduction to F. E. Brightman is Bridget Nichols's essay in Christopher Irvine (ed.), *They Shaped Our Worship, Essays on Anglican Liturgists*, London: SPCK, 1998.

45 See Gregory Dix, *The Shape of the Liturgy*, London: Dacre Press, 1945, new edition, London: Continuum, 2005, p. 657. Gardiner, according to MacCulloch (*Thomas Cranmer*, p. 492) 'faced the dilemma of later Anglo-Catholics, and might even at this stage of his career be termed the first Anglo-Catholic'. Later Gardiner was to serve under Queen Mary and, challenged by Cardinal Pole, supported the return to Roman obedience. (See Eamon Duffy, *Fires of Faith*, New Haven and London: Yale University Press, 2009, pp. 41–3.)

followed, with an *epiclesis* (invocation of the Holy Spirit) and the sign of the cross over the bread and cup, and a rubric saying that the priest takes the bread and cup into his hands during the institution narrative, recalling the words of Jesus at the Last Supper. The third section is what later became known as the Prayer of Oblation. We do well to compare this 'canon' both with what went before (the Sarum Missal) and what comes after (the Second Prayer Book of Edward VI).

Conveniently, we have an English version of the Roman Canon from the time, though it is probably not, as sometimes thought, a version translated by Miles Coverdale,[46] the sixteenth-century Bible translator, whose version of the psalter remains embedded in the BCP. The Roman Canon itself begins with what is essentially a Prayer for the Church. Yet, apart from subject matter, there are virtually no similarities of wording so far. The Roman Canon has no explicit *epiclesis* (invocation of the Holy Spirit) but there are close similarities between the Roman Canon and Cranmer's 'canon' with regard to actions and words at the institution narrative. The Roman Canon has 'the day before he suffered' and Cranmer 'the same nyght that he was betrayed': we are not standing under the Cross but gathered in the Upper Room. Thus, in the Roman Canon the consecrated sacrament is elevated and shown to the people (an allusion to the 'lifting up' of John 3.14–15) whereas the 1549 'canon' prohibits 'any eleuacion, or shewing the Sacrament to the people'. Despite the verbal differences and ceremonial changes, what has happened so far is superficially similar. If anything, Cranmer has recovered something that the Latin Rite had lost: mention of the activity of the Holy Spirit. He has looked East and West – 'with thy holy spirite and worde, vouchsafe to bl+esse and sanc+tifie these thy gyftes, and creatures of bread and wyne' – and recovered the emphasis of the Liturgy of St John Chrysostom on the activity of the Spirit and Martin Luther's insistence on the transformative power of the Word.[47] We may be worried by the loss of the elevation and the showing, but many a priest in his 'white Albe plain, with a vestement or Cope'[48] would

---

46 The so-called Coverdale Canon is printed in *The English Missal*, Norwich: Canterbury Press, 2001, a reissue of the fifth (1958) edition of W. Knott & Son. Had Coverdale translated it, he would have done so for polemical purposes, being himself a convinced evangelical. The Sarum Use of the Roman Canon is different only in that it includes the name of the monarch after the name of the Pope.

47 St John Chrysostom himself, however, says that it is the words of Christ, pronounced by the priest, in the role of Christ, that transform 'the things offered', *Catechism of the Catholic Church* (hereafter CCC), para. 1375.

48 The cope, prohibited in 1552, was allowed once more in 1559 but not the 'vestement' (chasuble) permitted in the 1549 rubric. See Eamon Duffy, *The Stripping of the Altars*, p. 567.

feel that he was offering the Mass and many congregations, however alarmed and excited by the use of the vernacular, would feel likewise reassured.

It is what happens next which worries us more, despite the many resonances and similarities in the two versions of the rest of the Eucharistic Prayer. It concerns the meaning of *anamnesis* – remembering. The Roman Canon says that, 'remembering the blessed passion . . . resurrection . . . and ascension', we 'do offer unto thine excellent majesty of thine own gifts and bounty, the pure victim &c'. 1549 says:

> according to the Instytucyon of . . . Jesu Christ, we thy humble seruauntes do celebrate, and make here before thy diuine Maiestie, with these thy holy giftes, the memoryall whyche thy sonne hath wylled us to make, hauyng in remembraunce his blessed passion . . . resurreccyon, and gloryous ascencion.

It is a subtle change but the medieval Canon has the priest and the people offering Christ the victim, a supertemporal event, whereas Cranmer's 'canon' makes a 'memoryall' in 'remembraunce' of a historical event. Eucharistic sacrifice has not quite gone: though it is 'by the merites and death of . . . Jesus Christ, and through faith in his bloud' that we 'obteigne remission of our sinnes, and all other benefites of hys passyon', we nonetheless 'offre and present unto thee (O Lorde) our selfe, our soules, and bodies, to be a reasonable, holy, and liuely sacrifice'. There are other similarities and differences too: the Roman Canon prays that God's 'Angel'[49] bring these offerings to the heavenly altar that all who receive 'the most sacred Body and Blood . . . may be fulfilled with all heavenly benediction and grace'. Cranmer, however, asks that 'these our prayers and supplicacions, by the Ministery of thy holy Angels . . . be brought up into thy holy Tabernacle' and, yes, mentions 'grace and heauenly benediccion' but as what is there to be received by the worthy partaker of Holy Communion. In short, just as with the collects mentioned earlier, Cranmer has taken the familiar words and phrases and reworked them to suit his theological agenda.[50] As John Hunwicke puts it:

---

49 This reference is sometimes thought to be to Christ himself, God's Messenger, 'the Lord' whose coming to the temple was prophesied (Mal. 3.1). See Joseph Jungmann, *The Mass of the Roman Rite: Its Origins and Development (Missarum Sollemnia)*, vol. 2, Benziger Brothers Inc., 1951, pp. 231ff. See also Enrico Mazza *The Eucharistic Prayers of the Roman Rite*, New York: Pueblo, 1986, pp. 81–2.

50 For further discussion of Cranmer's theology, see Geoffrey Cuming, *The Godly Order*, pp. 91–107; Colin Buchanan, *What did Cranmer think he was doing?*, Bramcote:

Only the occasional phrase from the Canon survived the Zwing-
lian prism of Cranmer's mind, but how those survivors whet one's
appetite; such as *not weighing our merits but pardoning our offences*
for *non aestimator meriti sed veniae . . . largitor*. And if *It is very
meet, right, and our bounden duty . . .* is not quite a literal translation of *Vere dignum et justum est . . .* how exquisitely it echoes the
majestic Latin syllables with which the Roman rite begins the Great
Eucharistic Prayer.[51]

The subtlety of these changes was lost on many, no doubt, but the
policy of making haste slowly enabled Cranmer within three years to
complete his work. Comparing the 1549 'canon' with the material in
the 1552 book, we notice some stark changes. What is now a prayer for
'the whole state of Christes Church *militant here in earth*' (my italics)
is sited after alms and offerings have been made, and is quite separate
from the 'canon'. It was not until 1662 that the English Prayer Book
had the rubric at this point that, after receiving the alms for the poor,
'the Priest shall . . . place upon the Table so much Bread and Wine as
he shall think sufficient'. The faithful departed are omitted from the
Prayer for the Church Militant, as is any mention of the Blessed Virgin
and the saints. We notice that what we were calling the 'canon' no
longer begins with the salutation,[52] the *Bendictus qui venit* is omitted
after the *Sanctus* – no Host is offered and no Guest expected. What is
usually called 'the Prayer of Humble Access' is brought forward from
just before Communion and said by the priest 'kneling down at Goddes borde', before he stands and says what is certainly not called, but
in 1662, when the High Churchmen have had their say, will be called,
'the Prayer of Consecration'. There are no manual acts in the Prayer
and immediately after the institution narrative all receive Holy Communion, which is distributed with the new, unambiguously receptionist phrases: 'Take eate this, in remembraunce that Christ dyed for thee
. . .'; 'drinke this in remembraunce that Christ's bloude was shed for
thee, and be thankefull'. As for the Prayer of Oblation, that becomes
the first of two prayers, given as alternatives after Holy Communion,
and the anamnetic words of 1549, 'hauyng in remembraunce his blessed
passion . . . resurereccyon, and glorious ascencion', are no longer rele-

---

Grove Liturgical Study 7, 1976; republished in Colin Buchanan, *An Evangelical &c.*,
London: SPCK, Alcuin Club Collections 84, 2009, pp. 71ff.; and Diarmaid MacCulloch,
Thomas Cranmer, pp. 351ff.
51 John Hunwicke, 'Hunwicke on Sacral Language', 2009, an unpublished essay.
52 'The Lord be with you: and with thy spirit.'

vant. In so far as we offer anything, then, it is 'our selfes, our soules, and bodies' (Rom. 12.1) in response to God's gift of salvation in and through Calvary. This is the Reformed Communion Service and, notoriously, 'yf any of the bread or wyne remayne', said the 1552 rubrics, 'the Curate shal haue it to hys owne use'.

450 Years of Liturgical History

To tell the tale properly, we should have to look carefully at the modifications of the Elizabethan Prayer Book of 1559: the removal of the 'Black Rubric' (which had anyway been added at the last minute to deal with John Knox's objection to receiving communion kneeling),[53] the provision that 'the minister at the time of Communion ... shall use such ornaments in the church as were in use ... in the second year of the reign of K. Edward VI',[54] and the combining of the two sets of words used at the delivery of the Sacrament to communicants, that is, the 'Body and Blood' formulæ of 1549 and the receptionist formulæ of 1552. This definitely marked a certain recovery of ground and it is not incidental that a royal injunction of 1559 suppressed the rubric allowing leavened bread, and that the Latin Prayer Book of 1560 permitted the taking of communion to the sick – that is, Holy Communion outside the Eucharist – and the celebration of Holy Communion at funerals.

We should also have to look carefully at the output of the Caroline period before and after the Civil War – the 1637 Scottish BCP (substantially a reversion to the 1549 Order) and the 1662 BCP. 1662 was a conservative recension of 1559 and not of 1637: the priority for Cosin and Wren, High Church bishops from the time of Archbishop Laud, was the re-establishing of episcopacy and the BCP at the Restoration of the Monarchy. That said, Cosin's notes on what needed to be revised and strengthened – notes contained in the Durham Book[55] – were con-

---

53 See below, p. 23. See also Roger Beckwith, 'The Anglican Eucharist: from the Reformation to the Restoration', in Cheslyn Jones, Geoffrey Wainwright, Edward Yarnold, SJ, and Paul Bradshaw (eds), *The Study of Liturgy*, revised edition, London: SPCK, 1992, pp. 313f.

54 see above, p. 14, and note 48.

55 See Geoffrey Cuming (ed.), *The Durham Book*, London: Oxford University Press, 1961. This was a copy of the 1559 Prayer Book, annotated by Cosin both before the Civil War and in connection with the Savoy Conference of 1661, when 12 bishops and 12 Presbyterian leaders met in the Strand, in London, to discuss whether the Prayer Book could be further adapted to meet Puritan objections. The Presbyterians were unsuccessful and, with the restoration of episcopacy and the Prayer Book, some 2,000 clergy were deprived of their livings.

siderable and influential, especially in the provision of rubrics, which advanced some High Church positions and protected others, as we shall see.

Finally we should have to have regard to the complex history of liturgical reform in the nineteenth and twentieth centuries. We should begin with the challenge of the Ritualists, met first by the Public Worship Regulation Act (1874) and then hardly more successfully by the attempt in 1927 and 1928 to replace the 1662 BCP. To do justice to Anglicanism – though our focus here has been the Church of England – there is also the gamut of rites and uses emerging from the evolving Anglican Communion: those based on the 1662 English Prayer Book and those developing from the 1637 Scottish Prayer Book – the 1764 Scottish eucharistic rite, and the United States of America BCP (1789).[56] There are the preferences and prejudices of the missionary societies, High Church and Low Church, which established overseas provinces and spawned distinct liturgical usages, and there is the increasing importance of inculturization and indigenization. As well as the textual history, there is the story of what was and is actually said and done. For much of the twentieth century, for example, a copy of the BCP would have been a very misleading guide as to what was said and done in many English parish churches during the celebration of Holy Communion.

Even confining ourselves to England, there is the unleashing of the liturgical reforms permitted by the Prayer Book (Alternative and Other Services) Measure 1965, passed by the Church Assembly, and the Worship and Doctrine Measure 1974, passed by the General Synod, then in its first quinquennium. Endorsed by Parliament, the measures permitted 'alternative and other services', that is, services 'alternative to' or 'other than' those provided in the BCP of 1662[57] to be authorized without further resort to Parliament. The outworking was three sets of 'alternative services' – Series 1, Series 2 and Series 3 – each authorized for a short period of time and culminating in the Alternative Service Book 1980 (hereafter ASB),[58] itself authorized for twenty years. After a

56 Sources include Bernard Wigan (ed.), *The Liturgy in English*, London: Oxford University Press 1962; Colin Buchanan (ed.), *Modern Anglican Liturgies 1958–1968*, London: Oxford University Press 1968; and Colin Buchanan (ed.), *Further Anglican Liturgies*, 1968–75, Bramcote: Grove Books, 1975.

57 'Alternative' neatly side-stepped the whole question of reform of the BCP, which remains standard. The methodology of the 1927/28 Book had been to provide 'alternative' orders.

58 *The Alternative Service Book 1980*, jointly published by Oxford: Oxford University Press and Mowbray, and Cambridge: Cambridge University Press, Colchester: William Clowes, and London: SPCK.

generation of upheaval – services in little booklets – *Common Worship* emerged at the turn of the millennium, as a library of resources in book and electronic form, a library so diverse that the very phrase 'Common Worship' seems ironic. We have come a long way since Thomas Cranmer complained that

> the nōbre and hardnes of the rules called the pie, and the manifolde chaunginges of the seruice, was the cause, yᵗ to turne the boke onlye, was so hard and intricate a matter, that many times, there was more business to fynd out what should be read, then to read it when it was founde out . . . Furthermore by this ordre, the curates shal need none other bookes for their publique seruice, but this boke and the Bible; by the means wherof, the people shall not be at so great charge for bookes, as in tyme past they haue been.[59]

1662: Progress or Stasis?

The importance of the 1662 BCP is not that it remains the customary use of the Church of England or of churches of the Anglican Communion – its eucharistic rite has not been customary in most places for quite some time – but that it remains the doctrinal norm. In this respect, we can leave aside the question of collects, the subject of the first of our liturgical enquiries. There has been no significant doctrinal evolution of their contents beyond the cautious decision of the 1958 Lambeth Conference (Resolution 79) to allow Anglican Calendars to expand to include heroes of the Christian Church: such as Lancelot Andrewes, Josephine Butler, Edward King, and C. S. Lewis.[60] Commemorating names of this kind remains controversial amongst Anglo-Catholics because there is no formal canonization process but, needless to say, none of the collects actively invokes the intercession of these or other figures.

What we cannot leave aside, as we look at 1662, are the crucial issues of eucharistic doctrine exposed by our examination of the development of the Communion Service of the first two Prayer Books. There is a deceptive image of Anglicanism as a religion of moderation

---

59 The Preface to *The Booke of the Common Prayer and Administracion of the Sacramentes, and other Rites and Ceremonies of the Churche after the Use of the Churche of England*, 1549.

60 See *The Commemoration of Saints and Heroes of the Faith in the Anglican Communion; the Report of a Commission appointed by the Archbishop of Canterbury*, London: SPCK, 1957.

and reason. Certainly the battles between the Puritans and the High Church Party in the seventeenth century, reaching a bloody climax in the Civil War, belie this. There are not dissimilar tensions in the nineteenth century between Kensitites and Tractarians, and, in recent times, between evangelicals and liberals, modernizers and traditionalists. It can scarcely be disputed that the liturgical centre of gravity in the second half of the sixteenth century was what we would now call evangelical. Queen Elizabeth shared many of the Catholic tastes of her half-sister, Mary, but we are speaking of decent music and ornaments, and liturgical good order in the Chapel Royal of a Protestant Queen. Whereas the 1559 Prayer Book was little more than a reissue of 1552, the theological climate of the seventeenth century was influenced first by the High Church convictions of Archbishop Laud and then, after the Commonwealth, by the restoration of a court not only influenced by its exile at the French royal court, but by a heightened awareness of the link between revolutionary church order and revolutionary political order. To this day Scotland remains a place where the English – we would now say 'the British' – experiment with new political and social ideas. Through the Prayer Book of 1637, Archbishop Laud was certainly hoping to re-introduce into Scotland the riches of the 1549 Use, an ecclesiological and political advance which, because of the abiding presence of the Puritans in a deteriorating political climate, could not be contemplated at that point in England.[61]

After the Restoration of 1660, though politically the 1662 BCP could not be the reversion to 1549 which Laud was attempting in 1637, there was nonetheless a good deal of tidying up. From a Catholic perspective, the enormities of 1552 had included the omission of the faithful departed from the Prayer for the Church, and the omission of any mention of the Blessed Virgin and the saints. There is now careful, and doctrinally sensitive, mention of the faithful departed, who, in Reformed thinking, are indistinguishable from the saints. We bless God's holy name for those of his servants 'departed this life' in God's 'faith and fear' and we ask 'to follow their good examples' so that, come the general resurrection of the quick and the dead, we shall be 'with them partakers of' God's 'heavenly kingdom'. Similarly, what are now called 'oblations' (the bread and the wine) are placed on the Table before, and mentioned in, the Prayer for the Church Militant. The 'canon' still does not begin with the salutation, the *Bendictus qui venit* is still omit-

---

61 The 1637 Prayer Book did not become established in Scotland but it became the basis of the 1764 Scottish eucharistic rite, which in turn influenced the first American BCP of 1789.

ted after the *Sanctus*, and what is usually called 'the Prayer of Humble Access' is still said kneeling by the priest before he stands and says what, in 1662, is now called 'the Prayer of Consecration'. There are manual acts in the Prayer too – including breaking the bread (this being a point on which Puritans and High Churchmen agreed). The Prayer of Oblation remains the first of two prayers, given as alternatives after Holy Communion, and the only offering we do remains of 'ourselves, our souls, and bodies', but the Curate has for his own use only unconsecrated Bread and Wine remaining: 'if any remain of that which was consecrated, it shall not be carried out of the Church, but the Priest . . . shall, immediately after the Blessing, reverently eat and drink the same'. There was a general strengthening of rubrics: the singing of the Creed and of the *Sanctus* is permitted, as is the consecration of further supplies, first found in the 1637 Scottish Order. Firmly denoting boundaries between what is unconsecrated and what is consecrated was a High Church victory and settled what had been a matter of great contention between High Churchmen and Puritans for over a century.[62] There are some stalemates too: 'it shall suffice that the Bread be such as is usual to be eaten; but the best and purest Wheat Bread that conveniently may be gotten' says one of the rubrics at the end of the 1662 service, without outlawing either leavened or unleavened bread.

There is indeed a maddening ambiguity at the heart of Anglican eucharistic theology, an ambiguity preserved by this service of 'The Lord's Supper or Holy Communion', the 1662 title. A High Church trajectory takes us from the Sarum Use Preparation of the Lord's Prayer and Collect for Purity, through the Decalogue (effectively an extended *Kyrie eleison* litany) and a Collect for the Monarch and a Collect of the Day. The Epistle and Gospel are duly read – by ordained ministers, with the people standing for the Gospel. The Nicene Creed is said and the sermon or homily preached. So far – in broad detail – the ancient liturgy of East and West has been celebrated. An Offertory – alms and oblations – follows, and a Prayer for the Church, a recovery of the Prayer of the Faithful, the practice of the Church of the first centuries.[63] The exhortations – of which there are three – are nowadays almost universally omitted. There is then an invitation and confession and absolution and some 'comfortable words' drawn from Archbishop Herman's *Con-*

---

62 On a second consecration, see Francis Procter and Walter H. Frere, *The Book of Common Prayer*, London: Macmillan, 1901 (Third Impression with corrections and alterations, 1961), p. 495.

63 See, for example, Joseph Jungmann, *The Mass of the Roman Rite*, pp. 480ff.

sultatio of 1543. Then come the *Sursum corda*,[64] the Preface, *Sanctus*, Prayer of Humble Access, Prayer of Consecration, administration, Lord's Prayer and Prayer of Oblation. This could almost be the Canon of the Mass with the breaking and the distribution incorporated into the narrative. Filled with the Bread of Life, and after a Post-communion (the Prayer of Thanksgiving), the congregation says or sings the *Gloria in excelsis*, transposed in 1552 into a post communion pæan of praise, and with real flair incorporating the *Agnus Dei* into itself.[65] Reconciliation having been wrought through Holy Communion, this is celebrated in the blessing – a form of 'The Peace' – which, because of the rubrics about ablutions, is pronounced in the presence of the Blessed Sacrament, much as in the Orthodox Liturgy the final blessing amounts to Benediction with whatever remains of the Blessed Sacrament. Loyal High Churchmen reassured themselves that this rite – eccentric though it be – was nonetheless a version of the Western Rite, but have never ceased to attempt to remedy its inconsistencies and inadequacies, by addition, revision and substitution. Battles would be fought in due course to restore the *Kyries*, the position of the *Gloria* at the beginning of the Eucharist, to remove the Collect for the Monarch[66] from its position as principal oration, to recover the shape of the eucharistic prayer, and to restore the *Bendictus qui venit* and *Agnus Dei*, but none of these details seemed to be crucial.

A no less convincing Low Church trajectory, however, takes us through the Lord's Supper, celebrated at the North End of the Lord's Table, originally placed lengthways in the midst of the chancel (so that the minister is still standing at one of the longer sides of the table). There is the proclaiming of the Word and the preaching – which perhaps take place at Morning or Evening Prayer with a 'stay behind' by the faithful few on 'Communion Sunday' for the Communion. The invitation, confession, absolution and 'comfortable words' – like the Ten Commandments earlier and the Prayer of Humble Access a little later – add to the devout reception enjoined by the exhortations. The Prayer of Consecration incorporates the scriptural mandate required by the Reformers, essentially the reading of 1 Corinthians 11.23–25, and, as communi-

---

64 'Lift up your hearts &c.', in the Latin Rite the second versicle and response in the introduction to the Preface but in 1552, 1559 and 1662 the first.

65 In 1552 Cranmer had moved the *Gloria* from near the beginning of the service to near the end and introduced the repeated phrase 'that takest away the sinnes of the world, haue mercye upon us' thus incorporating what amounted to the threefold *Agnus Dei* which had been sung by 'the Clarkes' at 'the Communion tyme' in 1549.

66 Which in 1549 had succeeded, rather than, as in 1552, preceded the Collect of the Day.

cants receive devoutly and reflectively, they are conscious of the graciousness of God, and the generosity of his redeeming love on Calvary. Thus they are inspired once more to pray as Jesus teaches his disciples to pray. If they do not say 'thank you' in the Prayer of Thanksgiving, they offer themselves once more to God in the Prayer of Oblation. Such an offering is a response to God's free gift and, because of its position in the liturgy, clearly not a mechanism for exciting God's generosity. A hymn of praise – the 'Glory be to God on high' – and the assurance of God's Peace (Phil. 4.7) send them out joyfully into the world. If they have been somewhat discountenanced by the vivid language of body and blood, they have been encouraged by the 'Black Rubric' at the end of the service which reassures those who kneel to receive Communion that 'no Adoration is intended, or ought to be done, either unto the Sacramental Bread or Wine there bodily received, or unto any Corporal Presence of Christ's natural Flesh and Blood . . .'[67]

The Twentieth Century

The Tractarians – and more particularly the Ritualists – tackled the inconsistencies and inadequacies of the 1662 rite partly by rediscovering the romance of Sarum ceremonial – the Percy Dearmer 'British Museum Rite', as it was affectionately nicknamed[68] – and partly by wholesale adapting of ultramontane liturgy and practices, about which we shall have more to say shortly. We catch a glimpse of these tensions at the first Anglo-Catholic Priests' Convention in 1921, S. R. P. Moulsdale, founder of St Chad's, Durham, and later Vice-chancellor of the University of Durham issued this challenge:

Would it not be a great triumph for this priests' convention if we could agree firmly upon some broad but definite guiding principles of uniformity in the conduct of worship, if we could put an end to the jarring arguments between the adherents of the Sarum Use, the West-

---

67 The word 'corporal' was substituted for 'real and essential' when the 1552 'Black Rubric' was reintroduced in 1662. The point was that 1552 seemed to exclude any notion of sacramental presence whereas 1662 was content simply to exclude transubstantiation. 'Black' because of the colour of the ink: rubrics, as the word suggests, are written in red.

68 See Cyril E. Pocknee, *The Parson's Handbook, the Work of Percy Dearmer*, London: Oxford University Press, 1965, the thirteenth edition of Percy Dearmer's 'practical directions . . . according to the Anglican Use, as set forth in the BCP'. The twelfth edition, prepared by Dearmer himself, was published in 1932, the first in 1899. All but the first were published by Oxford University Press.

ern Use, and the 'English' Use? Cannot we do something to secure that at least so far as Catholics are concerned 'now from henceforth all the whole realm shall have but one Use'?

Later, he says: 'what would Cranmer have said (to say nothing of St Augustine) had he lived in our day and seen every parish priest a law unto himself?'

Moulsdale insists that 'uniformity must be based upon the BCP *so far as it goes*' (his italics). 'One rule laid down at the Tridentine reformation of the Missal was that a new Missal should not be made, but that the existing one should be restored "according to the custom of the holy Fathers".' 'Any rite could be kept that could show a prescription of at least two centuries.' For Moulsdale, the crucial feature of the BCP – 'it is our low gear; it is not our speed limit' – was 'the great principle of our worship in the vernacular must be admitted'. Liturgical reform was in the air in the Church of England of the 1920s – as indeed in the Protestant Episcopal Church of the USA – and both Anglican bodies were to produce 1928 Prayer Books, the one defeated in Parliament, the other established as the new American Use. In 1921 Moulsdale is saying that

> the modern revisers of the Prayer Book have exhibited a singularly timid reluctance to agree to the very modest suggestion that our first vernacular Canon of the Mass, that of the Prayer Book of 1549, should be restored to us.

This concession, he said,

> would have supplied a centre of unity to Catholics. Is the time not ripe for us to ask that our branch of the Church Catholic should authoritatively give us back the rock from which the Canon of 1549 was hewn, I mean that grand possession of Western Christendom, the Gelasian Canon of the Mass?

The establishment – neither as romantic as Dearmer and Moulsdale, nor as anarchic as the Ritualists – sought to achieve what was generally thought to be necessary by pursuing Prayer Book Revision. The 1927/1928 Book suited no one: the evangelicals rejected its praying for the departed, for others a pastoral necessity following the massive slaughter of the Great War; the Anglo-Catholics scorned its wordy conformity and its adopting of a eucharistic prayer of Eastern shape, that is, a prayer with the *epiclesis* (invocation of the Holy Spirit on the people and the gifts) after the institution narrative (and therefore, for Anglo-Catholics, after the climax of the prayer, the consecration and elevation of host and chalice). Defeated in Parliament, the Bishops eventually – and slightly bravely – encouraged the less controversial parts of the Deposited Book to be used in the parishes, and the hugely popular *Shorter Prayer Book* was published in 1948, with sections of 1928 material placed alongside 1662 material in a twin column format. Meanwhile, use of the 'interim rite' spread, urged by Bishop Chandler in 1931. The 'interim rite' described the practice of using the Prayer of Oblation immediately after the Prayer of Consecration, as in the 1637 Scottish Prayer Book. Timid users of the 'interim rite' mumbled the Prayer of Oblation silently. Braver spirits read it aloud and brought the Lord's Prayer forward to the classical position before Communion.[69] In this complete 'canon', the salutation almost always preceded the *Sursum corda* and the *Bendictus qui venit* was inserted after the *Sanctus*. Few dared to omit the Prayer of Humble Access, or even move it, as in 1549 and CW, to just before Communion. Even in parishes where the priest mumbled much of the Roman Canon during the singing of a choral *Sanctus*, and went on to say the rest of the Roman Canon, whilst the choir, in Tridentine fashion, sang the *Benedictus qui venit*,[70] the central narrative that the congregation heard was usually the 1662 Prayer of Consecration, which *The English Missal*, the pre-conciliar Roman Missal in Prayer Book English,[71] obligingly printed.

The twentieth century saw the flowering of the Liturgical Movement in the Roman Catholic Church: the work of Dom Prosper Guéranger (1805–75), the first Abbot of Solesmes, was given impetus by the reforms of Pope Pius X and, thereafter, the revival of the popular use of plainsong, and the facilitation of lay participation in, and understanding of, the Mass developed steadily. Something not entirely different was happening in the Church of England but one of the paradoxes was that some of those most influential in the Church of England's Liturgical Movement were those least obedient to its liturgical forms. Thus, Dom Gregory Dix, monk of Nashdom, E. C. Ratcliff, a linguist, expert

---

69 Thus investing 'Give us this day our daily bread' with liturgical meaning.

70 According to custom in the Latin Mass, the *Bendictus qui venit* was either said or sung to plainsong immediately after the *Sanctus* or, in polyphonic settings, sung after the elevation of the chalice.

71 The fifth and last edition (London: W. Knott & Son, 1958) of the altar version was reissued in 2001 by the Canterbury Press, Norwich. Unlike some liturgical reprints, the publishers took the trouble to recalculate the Table of Moveable Feasts, in this case from 2001 to 2030.

in classical and Semitic languages, and Geoffrey Willis, the scholarly Vicar of Wing, were all enthusiasts for the Roman Canon. Dix used the Roman Canon more or less every day of his priestly life.[72] It would not be unfair to say that their view – shared by other 'separated doctors' (as Aidan Nichols calls them),[73] such as Austin Farrer, Kenneth Kirk, and Eric Mascall[74] – was that *Ecclesia Anglicana*, 'in existence long before the Reformation', as Archbishop Fisher put it, taking the 1,500 year view,[75] had been saddled with a Reformed liturgy which disguised and undermined, rather than proclaimed, the claim of the Church of England to be the ancient Catholic Church of the land – as they themselves undoubtedly believed it to be. Fisher, of course, would not have accepted that argument and, for him, as for most bishops, Anglicans who used the Roman liturgy – its use in England for 1,000 years before the Reformation notwithstanding – were lawbreakers, scoundrels who did not honour the oath made at ordination and licensing, to 'use only the forms of service which are authorized or allowed by canon'.[76]

Series 1 and Series 2 in the 1960s set out to regularize these anomalous practices and Series 3, somewhat daringly, took us into the whole culture of modern liturgical English, at a time when the Roman Mass was beginning to be celebrated in the vernacular. Much was made of shared ecumenical texts for the Ordinary. Yet the same old eucharistic controversies continued to be fought out, despite the repeated point that the eucharistic shape, popularized by Dom Gregory Dix, had achieved

72 See John Hunwicke, 'Which one this morning?', *New Directions*, March 2005. See also Simon Bailey, *A Tactful God*, Leominster: Gracewing, 1995, pp. 258ff.

73 Aidan Nichols, *The Panther and the Hind*, p. 128.

74 These theologians were nonetheless conscious of the limitations of the medieval rite: see Eric Mascall, *Corpus Christi*, London: Longmans, 1953, pp. 79–80. Nevertheless, when he was not constrained by the conventions of the Cathedral (Christ Church), Mascall would celebrate the Roman Rite.

75 See above, p. 8.

76 The words of the Declaration of Assent: the older form of subscription (when only the BCP was authorized) was: 'in public prayer and administration of the Sacraments I will use the Form in the said Book prescribed, and none one other, except so far as shall be ordered by lawful authority'. For reference to the newer wording, see above, p. 2. John Hunwicke, classicist and liturgist, referring to Gregory Dix, *The Shape of the Liturgy*, pp. 587ff., challenges the *ius liturgicum* of the bishop. Dix himself makes the case, pp. 716f., for the Pre-Reformation rite to have equal standing in the Church of England with those of more recent times. Hunwicke's own argument, made over the years and set out most recently in his *Order for the Eucharist 2009*, London: Tufton Books, in introductory notes 10 (p. xv) and 19 (p. xviii), is that, even granted that bishops have the right to legislate, the ruling of the Church of England House of Bishops in 1984 and 1990 that services whose authorization has technically lapsed may still be used would apply, if only the bishops realized it, to the Pre-Reformation rite. The point might be made that this would cover the Sarum Missal, and the *Missale Romanum* as used by Dix, but not any translation of the Roman Mass into English, such as the English Missal.

ecumenical consensus and that the language of *anamnesis* and offering had proved acceptable to various Protestant communities. Evangelicals appeared divided on the first of these issues – the shape of the Eucharist. Scholars such as Colin Buchanan were happy to go with a eucharistic prayer which joined consecration and oblation (provided that one was careful about how these concepts were expressed).[77] Roger Beckwith[78] and others continued to insist that the 1552 (and 1662) separation of consecration and oblation should be maintained to ensure that there was absolutely no misunderstanding about eucharistic offering.

The result of this was that the ASB 1980, for its modern language 'Rite A' Order for Holy Communion, had 'The Order following the pattern of the BCP' as a variant (p. 146). That was part of the price paid for synodical approval. The remaining part of the price was a good deal of linguistic ambiguity in the eucharistic prayers. Is the phrase 'holy things' too prosaic? What about 'holy gifts': too redolent of sacrifice?[79] 'Rite B' in the ASB 1980 was the form of the Eucharist preferred by parishes that had welcomed Series 1 and Series 2 – traditional language versions of the Eucharist – because they combined the new consensual ('Catholic') ecumenical eucharistic shape with the language of the BCP, or at least, in the case of Series 2, with the traditional archaisms for addressing God preserved. Those who wished to preserve the Prayer Book shape and traditional language, it was argued, were provided for by the 1662 BCP.[80]

---

77 Colin Buchanan battled against the notion of Offertory as promoted by Dix. With regard to the text of the eucharistic prayer, he was content for the full shape to be used in a form acceptable to all schools of Anglican thought but clear that such a prayer should not contain words which suggest that the gifts are in any sense offered to God. See Colin Buchanan, *The New Communion Service – Reasons for Dissent*, London: Church Society, 1966, republished in Colin Buchanan, *An Evangelical &c.*, pp. 3ff.

See also Colin Buchanan, *The End of the Offertory*, Bramcote: Grove Liturgical Study 14, 1978, republished in Colin Buchanan, *An Evangelical &c.*, pp. 114ff.

78 See for example R. T. Beckwith and J. E. Tiller (eds), *The Service of Holy Communion and its Revision*, Abingdon: Marcham Manor Press, 1972.

79 A phrase from 1549, it allowed Colin Buchanan to make a joke about *missa tombola* in his monthly *News of Liturgy* tracts, in which information and opinion were mixed somewhat polemically.

80 In the ASB 1980 the difference between 'Rite A' (which was available in two shapes) and 'Rite B' (which was available only in one) was mainly use of modern language in the one and archaisms in the other, hardly a basis for discerning between rites. The ASB Propers, somewhat illogically, were in modern language only.

Anglican Ambiguities

By the time CW was produced, in 2000, it had become policy to incorporate Prayer Book texts and 'alternative' material in a complementary way and to permit a good deal more mixing of idioms. Thus the twin-tracks – the consensual 'Catholic' eucharistic shape and the Prayer Book 'Reformed' shape – were embedded. More than that – by including in Order One, Eucharistic Prayers of both Eastern and Western shape – the Church of England seemed to be suggesting that the external logic of the Eucharistic Prayer itself, as well as its doctrinal interpretation, is a matter of preference and taste.[81]

It is a common Anglican view that 'it is the whole Prayer which consecrates' – a view fashionable amongst liturgists and not unknown in Rome during the Bugnini reforms – but the notion that there is therefore no moment of consecration goes against both the teaching of the Catholic Church (a *sententia catholica*) – that the use of the words of the Lord within the Eucharistic Prayer is what consecrates[82] and the psychology of the worshipper, that there needs to be, in any sacramental action, a clear, performative moment. The underplaying of the dramatic importance – and hence the spiritual and theological energy – of the eucharistic action must inevitably lead to a collapse of eucharistic spirituality, an observation made by Brian Harrison which we shall examine in greater depth in Chapter 2 but which is pertinent here too.[83]

English Anglican style is nowadays superficially more 'Catholic': the Calendar has 15 August as the feast of the Blessed Virgin Mary; the three-year Mass lectionary of the Catholic Church, rejected as a model by the General Synod in the run up to the ASB 1980, is the basis for the Revised Common Lectionary, which the Church of England has adapted for its purposes. Many parish churches, often enough led by 'open evan-

---

81 In the appendix to this chapter, see p. 40, the CW Eucharist is discussed, together with some of the ambiguities and complexity of Orders One and Two, each available in both traditional and contemporary language, rather than the one being contemporary and the other traditional.

82 CCC, para. 1353. It was Pope Pius VII in 1822 who finally, in a *sententia catholica*, confirmed that the repetition of the Lord's words at the Last Supper were what effected consecration. See Archdale A. King, *Liturgy of the Roman Church*, p. 323.

83 See Chapter 2, p. 63. Brian W. Harrison OS, 'The Postconciliar Eucharistic Liturgy: Planning a Reform of the Reform', an address to the St Thomas Aquinas Society Eucharistic Conference, Colorado Springs, 26 March 1995 and printed in editions of *Adoremus* Bulletin serially from November 1995 to January 1996. Reprinted in Thomas Kocik, *The Reform of the Reform? A Liturgical Debate: Reform or Return*, San Francisco: Ignatius Press 2003, p. 157.

gelical' clergy, nonetheless wear eucharistic vestments and have candles on what they are content to refer to as 'the altar'. They light Advent wreaths, bless Christmas cribs, impose ashes on Ash Wednesday, bless palms on Palm Sunday and collect chrism on Maundy Thursday. They wash feet that holy night and incorporate what is called 'The Proclamation of the Cross' the following day in their Good Friday service. They light the Paschal Candle at the Easter Vigil – or 'sunrise service' – and may even celebrate 'The Day of Thanksgiving for the Institution of Holy Communion (Corpus Christi)' on the Thursday after Trinity Sunday. Whereas the insights and ecclesiology of the Tractarians seemed to be winning the day – and the excesses of the Ritualists were held in disrepute – it seems now that much of the theological infrastructure of Tractarianism has fallen away and the instincts of the Ritualists – hyperbole and sensuality – have finally begun to commend themselves. The influence of the charismatic movement has been such that a whole generation of liberal evangelicals, not fully schooled in the controversies of the sixteenth century, has seen the good sense of what are not so much sacramentals as visual aids. There has also been an almost desperate search for whatever is diverting or entertaining, in order to grab the attention of an increasingly uninterested general public. A movement called 'Fresh Expressions' has sought to find new, and on the whole non-eucharistic ways, of 'being Church' in the early years of the twenty-first century.[84] It was Archbishop George Carey[85] who famously enunciated the sound-bite that the Church of England used the music of BBC Radio 3 – classical – and the discourse of Radio 4 – talk-radio for the educated – to speak to the masses who listen to pop music on Radio 1 or light music and conversation on Radio 2. The Anglican equivalents of the Catholic culture wars, in England at least, are not liturgical rivalries, even in a Communion in which liturgical rivalries have been rampant. They are found rather in the dichotomy described by the English theologian, Martin D. Stringer: 'those churches that put a primary emphasis on the shared meal of the Eucharist are seldom those that place an emphasis on Spirit-filled worship, although there are notable exceptions'.[86]

The battle, in Anglicanism – in England and internationally – is nowadays, therefore, between a liturgically decorous, if doctrinally deviant,

---

84 *Mission-shaped Church: Church Planting and Fresh Expressions of Church in a Changing Context*, GS 1523, London: Church House Publishing, 2004.

85 Archbishop of Canterbury from 1991 to 2002.

86 Martin D. Stringer, *A Sociological History of Christian Worship*, Cambridge: Cambridge University Press, 2005, p. 235.

liberalism (which sometimes describes itself as 'liberal Catholic', but is more notably 'liberal' than 'Catholic'), and a more orthodox evangelicalism, usually more pneumatic (though there are plenty of neo-Calvinists too). It must be confusing to some that those whose worship seems most conservative are best described as 'liberal' and those whose worship seems most experiential and free are most accurately described as 'conservative'. It is this latter group that has given most energy to, and derived most energy from, the Alpha phenomenon, and the phenomenal success, in Western European terms, of Holy Trinity, Brompton, a church in London. And huge numbers of Roman Catholic parishes throughout the world are buying into Alpha too, 'Catholic Alpha', notwithstanding that the Alpha course itself is non-eucharistic and implicit of a non-regenerative view of the sacrament of Baptism. (More precisely, it is pre-eucharistic, being usually based on a shared meal of those helpful symbols pasta [wheat flour] and wine, and implicit of a doctrine of 'baptism in the Spirit' which suggests the importance of *glossolalia* [speaking in tongues].) As institution and licensing services in the Church of England often show,[87] there is indeed a very inadequate symbology underlying Anglican religious life nowadays. New ministers ring bells and receive keys, maps and terriers (that is, inventories) of varying usefulness, they are presented with water with which they will not be baptizing, bibles from which they will not be reading, oil with which they will not be anointing, and leavened loaves and flagons of wine which, at least in Anglo-Catholic parishes, will never be put to eucharistic use. The Church of England Liturgical Commission has been aware of these difficulties and, having given its mind to the task of liturgical formation in the wake of CW, has encouraged a new generation of liturgists in producing suitable resources, as the work of Benjamin Gordon-Taylor and Simon Jones, for example, shows.[88]

Catholic or Reformed?

The point here is not to lampoon – let alone criticize – the Church of England and its ways: despite the 'Catholic makeover' this is very much the Church from which John Henry Newman finally took his leave when he was received into the Roman Catholic Church on 9 October

---

87 Services to inaugurate the new ministry of a parish priest: such services are devised on a diocesan basis.

88 See the Bibliography in Christopher Irvine (ed.), *The Use of Symbols in Worship*, Alcuin Liturgy Guides 4, London: SPCK, 2007; and for the Alcuin Liturgy Guides written by Gordon-Taylor and Jones.

1845. The reasons for Anglo-Catholics staying and going then, one suspects, were very much the same as the reasons for staying and going now. Those who stay will stay because the Church of England, as they perceive it, is 'Catholic and Reformed': those who go will go because the Church of England, as they perceive it, may be 'Reformed' but it is not in a sufficiently intelligible sense 'Catholic' within the trajectory of the Catholic tradition. In the ordination of priests, in the CW Ordinal (2007), the Bishop asks the ordinands,

Bishop Will you faithfully minister the doctrine and sacraments of Christ as the Church of England has received them, so that the people committed to your charge may be defended against error and flourish in the faith?[89]

For some Anglo-Catholics, it is more than sufficient to commit to what the Church of England 'received': the tradition of the first millennium and the vigorous life of the medieval Church. Referring back to the earlier point about the Declaration of Assent, we should say that these are they who, in answer to the Declaration of Assent, promise to 'use only the forms of service which are authorized or allowed by Canon',[90] but mean by that that, in company with all faithful Catholic priests, they are ministers of the Catholic liturgical tradition, obedient to its forms and doctrines, and not, like non-conforming ministers or self-appointed pastors, free agents, choosing and inventing what should be said, sung and preached. They would have more difficulty if the Declaration specified The Canons of the Church of England[91] and specifically excluded the *Codex Juris Canonici* (The Code of Canon Law 1983).[92]

The conflict between different eucharistic theologies, of which we have been aware throughout this chapter, has created for us, at best, a distinct liturgical dialectic and, at worst, have confirmed one's prejudices as to whether Anglicanism, finally, is 'Catholic' or 'Reformed'. These ambiguities beset the *lex orandi* ('the law of what is to be prayed') from which we have been attempting to infer the *lex credendi* ('the law of what is to be believed'). What is clear from any reading of Cranmer that takes into account his writings on the Eucharist, as well as his

---

89 *CW, Ordination Services*, 2007, London: Church House Publishing, p. 38.

90 *CW: Services and Prayers &c.* p. xi. Also *CW, Ordination Services*, p. 6.

91 *The Canons of the Church of England*, London: Church House Publishing. The current edition (sixth edition, 2009) and additions and corrections are available online through the Church of England website.

92 *The Code of Canon Law in English Translation*, 1983, London: Collins Liturgical Publications.

compilations, texts and translations, is that he was setting out to teach folk what they should believe about the communicant's encounter with Christ's true presence in the heart of the believer. He was teaching them to prepare for that encounter not least by a proper emphasis on penitence, and a proper emphasis on the 'one oblation . . . once offered', the full, perfect and sufficient sacrifice, oblation and satisfaction achieved on the Cross. He sought to consecrate the congregation and not the eucharistic elements. In that sense he would be one with Pius XII's admonition: *lex credendi legem statuat supplicandi*, let the rule of belief determine the rule of prayer (p. 3). It has fallen to later generations to re-introduce more Catholic ideas, working with, or avoiding, Cranmer's Communion Order. As we have seen in this chapter, studied ambiguity – or appealing to ancient or ultramontane practice – have been the ways of going beyond Cranmer's theology. Characteristically, an over-preoccupation with what is said has led to an under-preoccupation with what is done. Anglo-Catholics have been as obsessed as anyone else with changes to wording and structure but meanwhile it has been through ceremonial and doctrinally rich hymnody that they have inspired eucharistic devotion and taught eucharistic theology.

Rowan Williams's definition of 'Anglican' in *Anglican Identities*, mentioned earlier in the chapter (pages 7–8), reminds us that Anglicanism is critical of 'any theology . . . that human activity can contribute to the winning of God's favour', but sees 'the free activity of God sustaining and transforming certain human actions done in Christ's name'. It is '*Reformed* thinking', says the Archbishop of Canterbury, Thomas Cranmer's successor. This is borne out by Bridget Nichols's demonstration of Archbishop Cranmer's amendments of medieval material as he compiled a vernacular Common Prayer (pages 11–12). So, if we must say 'Catholic' or 'Reformed', then perhaps we shall have to say 'Reformed'.

Secession to Rome

Anglo-Catholics who have become convinced that the Anglican tradition is 'Reformed' rather than 'Catholic' in the end have sought reconciliation with Rome (and occasionally with Orthodoxy). Individuals, moving from one ecclesiastical body to another, take their own history with them – just as people moving from one town to another, or one country to another, do so. When this happens with large numbers – patterns of immigration, for example – there is the transmission, informally or formally, of customs, ways of life and ways of think-ing. Similarly, there is experience of Anglicans moving in small but dis-tinctly ecclesial groupings to the Catholic Church. One is the famous conversion of Aelred Carlyle, the Abbot of Caldey and his community, a group of Anglican Benedictines. Founded in 1906, this group 'went to Rome' in 1913. Less well known is the conversion of other communi-ties, as Petà Dunstan relates:

> A branch house of the Society of St Margaret in Bloomsbury had gone over to Rome in 1908. A small Franciscan order in the Epis-copal Church of the United States had converted in 1909. Most of the fledgling Community of St Francis in London had followed their Reverend Mother to Rome in 1910.[93]

And there were other communities associated with Aelred Carlyle: a community at Baltonsborough in Somerset and a community which moved from Malling Abbey in Kent to Milford Haven in Wales in 1911. Led by Abbess Scholastica Ewart, the nuns converted to Rome at the same time as the Caldey monks, giving rise to speculation as to whether Scholastica had led or been led by Aelred. What is striking, in the subsequent history of the Anglican Benedictines is that there are many stories of individuals wrestling with submission to Rome, and constant talk of the corporate journey of Anglicanism to corporate re-union with the great Communions of East and West, but little evidence of particular communities, such as those already mentioned, discussing corporate secession.

A more recent example of corporate secession from Anglicanism, is the establishing of the 'Pastoral Provision' in 1980, under the Vatican's Congregation for the Doctrine of the Faith, whereby married Anglican and Episcopalian priests could be received and ordained as priests, and they and convert laity, within existing diocesan structures, as members of 'personal parishes' could maintain 'certain liturgical elements proper to the Anglican tradition', as the American website puts it (2009). The adapted liturgies are collected in *The Book of Divine Worship*.[94] Whilst we are talking much larger numbers than the communities of a century

---

93 Petà Dunstan, *The Labour of Obedience: The Benedictines of Pershore, Nashdom and Elmore: A History*, Norwich: Canterbury Press, 2009, p. 6.

94 *The Book of Divine Worship*, Mt Pocono: Newman House Press, 2003, 'for use by Roman Catholics coming from the Anglican tradition', is also available online. 'The Holy Eucharist: Rite One' (that is, the traditional language version) also has the Roman Canon in an 'Old English Translation' which is included also in the 2001 reprint of *The English Missal* by the Canterbury Press, Norwich (see note 46). At the time of writing (2009) a

earlier, the numbers in the first thirty years in America have been quite small: not much more than seven parishes and seventy priests.

Febrile speculation about present and future Anglican secession to Rome was dramatically increased by the announcement by the Congregation for the Doctrine of the Faith, at a Vatican press conference on 20 October 2009, of an Apostolic Constitution establishing 'Personal Ordinariates', a new canonical instrument, for Anglicans who wished to become reconciled with the Holy See. It seems that the stimulus to corporate submission, which began in the late 1970s with the ordination of women in the Episcopal Church, may be set to continue indefinitely. It would not be an over-simplification to see the ordination of women as the second of two major stimuli for group conversion, the first being the discovery by some of the early religious communities that the restoration of monastic life entailed – for them – becoming reconciled with the entire Western monastic tradition. As regards the ordination of women – issues of human sexuality are another, and according to one view, more critical matter – some have taken the view that innovations of this kind may be decided by provincial synods, such as the General Synod of the Church of England, or the General Convention of The Episcopal Church; others that they must be determined ecumenically or by a magisterium. Indeed there were signs at the 2008 Lambeth Conference, and in the protracted discussion of an Anglican Covenant, of the realization that, for any Reformed international denomination that seeks to maintain cohesion and organic development, something like a 'liberal magisterium' has to be invented. For many Anglicans, living the religious life or seeking to preserve the faith and order of the Church and the guaranteed catholicity of her sacraments, submission to Rome, individually or corporately, has become – is becoming – will become for the foreseeable future, inescapable. Individuals come and go as they please, taking their luggage with them – and there is, of course, 'two-way traffic'.[95] How the story of the Personal Ordinariates unfolds will be told elsewhere and, no doubt, in a decade or two's time. Meanwhile we are here concerned not with emerging ecclesiological structures but with what Anglicans corporately take with them, what, so to say, is in the Anglican knapsack.

---

successor to *The Book of Divine Worship* (2003) was being prepared by the Congregation for Divine Worship and the Discipline of the Sacraments.

95 Joseph P. Cassidy, Principal of St Chad's College, Durham (2009), and formerly a Jesuit, is a modern example. Dewi Morgan (ed.), *They became Anglicans*, London: Mowbrays, 1959, includes the stories of two monks, the Hungarian, Emod Brunner, (pp. 36ff.), and the Belgian, Emmanuel Amand de Mendieta (pp. 94ff.) who became Anglican out of conviction.

Anglican Patrimony

Though a small Prayer Book lobby continues to exist, and there is even the occasional parish which still uses English Missal, the BCP tradition that Moulsdale urged Anglo-Catholics to rally round has now very largely gone, in England at least. (America is different: Anglo-Catholic churches in the United States show a continued fondness for the language of the Prayer Book and Americans often cannot understand the rather distinctive, and liturgically anarchic, 'Anglo-papalism'[96] of English Anglo-Catholicism). And Moulsdale's point about the vernacular is no longer a matter of dispute between those inside and outside the Roman obedience. The Church of England has nearly 500 years' experience of using the vernacular liturgically but its experience of a modern liturgical vernacular, though different stylistically from that of English-speaking Catholic hierarchies, is from almost the same date: it was in 1971 that Series 3 burst upon the Church of England and that was when Catholic parishes were beginning to use the *Novus Ordo*, using temporary leaflets as they awaited publication of the missals. One reason that English Anglo-Catholics are not, as one might say, 'Prayer Book people' is that the excitement about convergence generated by the ARCIC discussion, encouraged English Anglo-Catholics in the 1970s and 1980s to adopt the new English Mass and the three-year lectionary as fully as they could. Many Anglo-Catholic parishes – and it is frustrating that there are no statistics for these variants (not least because the information obviously would not be revealed to and through episcopal and archidiaconal visitations) – transferred entirely to the *Novus Ordo*. They took the view that Anglican–Roman Catholic convergence, thought highly likely after Pope John Paul's 1982 visit to Canterbury Cathedral, was assisted by not doing differently that upon which it was thought agreement had been reached.[97] It was the closest Anglo-Catholics got to the Lund Principle: the Lund Principle, agreed by the 1952 Faith and Order Conference of the World Council of Churches held at Lund, Sweden, stated that churches should act together in all matters except those in which deep differences of conviction compel them to act separately. It has been a popular principle in

---

96 For a discussion of Anglo-papalism, see Michael Yelton, *Anglican Papalism: An Illustrated History 1900–1960*, Norwich: Canterbury Press, 2005.

97 The final report of ARCIC I, the first Commission (1969–81), emerged in 1982. It included the agreed statement on Eucharistic Doctrine (1971). The official Roman Catholic response was not to appear until 1991 which requested clarifications on Eucharist and Ministry, to which ARCIC II responded in 1993. See Christopher Hill and Edward Yarnold SJ (eds), *Anglicans and Roman Catholics &c.*

relations between English Anglicans and the free churches – leading to local ecumenical projects, shared posts and shared training – and here were Anglo-Catholics practising their very own version of it, looking to the rock from which they were hewn.

More moderate Anglo-Catholics used ASB 'Rite A' with the ASB Third Eucharistic Prayer or, using the *Missa Normativa* (as *Novus Ordo* was usually known) in full midweek, substituted the ASB Third Eucharistic Prayer for the Roman Eucharistic Prayers on Sundays. Whatever the arrangement, the *Novus Ordo*, especially on Sundays, was often disguised by preserving the Anglican (and Ambrosian) place for the Peace,[98] that is, before the Offertory, and including the occasional evocative Anglican phrase or prayer – 'For thine is the kingdom &c' at the end of the Lord's Prayer, or 'We break this bread &c' at the Fraction. Some parishes used 'Rite A' for everything *except* the Eucharistic Prayer: congregations never knew that what they were hearing, Sunday by Sunday, was not an authorized Anglican Eucharistic Prayer at all but Roman Eucharistic Prayer II or Roman Eucharistic Prayer III (with or without mention of the name of the Pope). The intention here was to ensure that the eucharistic action was properly understood by being properly prayed (despite the view that Roman Eucharistic Prayer II, the Hippolytan Prayer, is an inadequate vehicle of eucharistic theology). We see something similar in the 'Pastoral Provision' in the United States, where *The Book of Divine Worship* 2003 incorporated the four Roman Eucharistic Prayers within what is essentially the liturgy of the Episcopal Church, adapted from the 1928 and 1979 versions of the American BCP.

The disadvantage of the enthusiastic application of the Lund principle for a generation or more is that younger clergy, and newer and younger members of congregations, often have little experience of, and no instinctive feel for the language of Cranmer. There are considerable cultural differences between the way Anglo-Catholics and Catholics worship – and not just that Anglo-Catholics include everything they can get away with and Catholics miss out anything they can get away with – but the differences are elusive and to attempt to describe them is to deal with quicksilver. A further problem is created by the new translation of mass by the International Commission on English in the Liturgy (hereafter ICEL): unlike its predecessor, forged in the high summer of ecumenism, it has within it now no ecumenically agreed contemporary texts. Within ten years of the appearance of CW, with its texts 'based

---

98 See also Chapter 2, p. 69, note 114, on the papal initiative in *Sacramentum Caritatis* to consider the position of the Peace in the Roman Rite.

(or excerpted) from *Praying Together*', the English Language Liturgical Consultation (ELLC) anthology published in 1988,[99] the ICEL English translation of *The Order of Mass I*,[100] appeared, with its own texts of the Ordinary of the Mass, making the fight of the Church of England bishops in General Synod to retain the ELLC Creed in its entirety seem particularly piquant, given that the ecumenical reason for its use in CW has now disappeared.[101] The divergence of vernacular translations – Anglican and Catholic – especially where they concern the congregational texts, the Ordinary, pose a particular problem for those who would seek still to apply the Lund principle to liturgical celebration.

It follows from this that, since they no longer share a common contemporary vernacular text with Catholics – and ICEL have shown little sign apparently of wanting to buy into modern Anglican, or other ecumenical texts, working instead, and understandably, within the parameters of *Liturgiam authenticam*[102] – Anglo-Catholics bring to the table, in terms of texts, only the inherited liturgical language of their tradition. This language is what *Liturgiam authenticam* itself calls 'a sacred style, which is also to be recognized as the correct dialect for worship (*sermo proprie liturgicus*)'. Quoting this phrase, John Hunwicke goes on to say:

> What, of course, any Christian brought up in the Anglican tradition will want to point out is that Anglicanism developed just such a sacral dialect in the sixteenth century. The age was propitious; liturgical Latin had owed a fair part of its genius to the Roman passion for legal precision and completeness, and Tudor English had many of the same legalistic characteristics.[103]

This sacral language is no mean possession. There are perhaps three liturgies – Morning Prayer, Evening Prayer and the Litany, complete texts, which have proved their value as vehicles of public worship and which need only a little editing: requiring the use of *Benedictus* and

---

99 The English Language Liturgical Consultation (ELLC) was the ecumenical successor of the International Consultation on English Texts (ICET) whose work is used and acknowledged in the English version of the Roman Missal of 1975.

100 English translation of *The Order of Mass I* © 2006, 2008, ICEL Inc. All rights reserved.

101 The word 'excerpted', in the acknowledgement of *Praying Together*, indicates the problem that the Church of England has had synodically, for a generation, in using ecumenical texts word for word.

102 *On the Use of Vernacular Languages in the Publication of the Books of the Roman Liturgy*, London: Catholic Truth Society, also available (2009) at www.vatican.va

103 John Hunwicke, 'Hunwicke on Sacral Language', 2009, an unpublished essay.

Magnificat, for example, and permitting the omission of the Litany on Sundays. To these should be added the Coverdale Psalter, as classical and irreplaceable in its way as the Clementine Vulgate Psalter is in its way, the thesaurus of collects, and various prayers which, individually commend themselves. Clearly related to this body of texts are three other categories of material. One is the tradition of English Bible translation of which the Revised Standard Version[104] is the finest example, that is, if criteria of accuracy, clarity, grandeur, meaning, and style are allowed to topple the Authorized Version from its perch. (There are passages in the King James Bible, however, which a sheer sense of occasion demand to be used: the Festival of Nine Lessons, 1 Cor. 13 at a wedding). The second is the tradition of hymnody, a store which the Catholic Church has raided but, so far, carrying off only the most accessible and obvious items. The third is less defensible (because it does not meet the Tridentine criterion of two centuries' usage): the rich quarry of texts which Anglicanism has acquired. Obvious examples include *My God, my Glory* (1954),[105] the work of Eric Milner-White (1884–1963), and some of the felicitous adaptations of Prayer Book material for wedding and funeral services, published in the 1928 Prayer Book and resurrected, and subsequently re-authorized as 'Series One' of the Alternative Services. If this material is admitted then various similar resources are available: the *English Missal* translations, for example, the excellent *Monastic Breviary* (published in 1961)[106] and the *Monastic Diurnal* (last printed in 1963),[107] both of which exhibit a handsome Anglican register of language in a Benedictine framework, much as Cranmer does in his BCP offices, and *The Anglican Breviary* (1955),[108] a translation of the office of Pius X. In any corporate recep-

104 A recent edition of the RSV (*Revised Standard Version of the Bible*, Second Catholic Edition, San Francisco: Ignatius Press, 2006) lightly removes archaisms (albeit from an American perspective) and thus makes this classical translation very accessible. *The New Revised Standard Version of the Bible* draws impressive amounts of praise and, though sometimes clearer than the RSV, does not conform to the conventions of *Liturgiam Authenticam* (for details of which, see the Bibliography for 'Extraordinary or Ordinary', for instance using inclusive language where the Greek of the New Testament does not.

105 Eric Milner-White, *My God, my Glory*, London: SPCK, 1954, published again in 1994.

106 *Monastic Breviary: Matins according to the Holy Rule of Saint Benedict*, Tymawr, Lydart, Monmouth: The Society of the Sacred Cross, Glendale, Colorado: Lancelot Andrewes Press, 1961, reprinted 2007.

107 *The Monastic Diurnal*, last printed in 1963, London: Oxford University Press (not to be confused with the equally excellent Latin–English Diurnal of Abbot Alcuin Deutsch (1877–1951) of St John's Abbey, Collegeville, the sixth edition of which was published in 2004 by St Michael's Abbey, Farnborough.

108 *The Anglican Breviary*, Mt Sinai, Long Island, NY: Frank Gavin Liturgical Foundation, Inc., 1955, reprinted 1998.

tion of Anglican Patrimony, the Roman congregations would have much work to do, doctrinally and liturgically, if they were to extract and secure the finest materials.

By plundering the 1662 BCP and incorporating within its own anthologies most of what is commonly used in the Prayer Book tradition, to the fury of some in the Prayer Book Society lobby no doubt, CW made the Prayer Book itself, as a publication, less useful than it was in 1980. Supposing, as we have suggested, that the Church of England, because of its smallness, completed these changes very much more quickly, willingly influenced by the times in which we live. Supposing it managed to integrate, within a culture hospitable to heritage, things both new and old, managing to be like St Matthew's scribe trained for the kingdom, a good householder (Matt. 13.52), then perhaps the Catholic Church too will manage, over a longer period of time, not only to integrate the Extraordinary and the Ordinary, the Latin and the modern vernacular, but also the archaic sacral language of Anglicanism and some of its riches.

Meanwhile, as we shall discuss in Chapter 2, Klaus Gamber says that 'most people in our time cannot relate to the liturgical forms of the baroque'.[109] Much the same can be said of traditional Anglo-Catholic liturgy. If Anglo-Catholic parish priests have wondered at the lack of response of the population to the splendours of High Mass, they have forgotten (though they have almost certainly read) the sad conclusion of Colin Stephenson, one time Administrator of the Anglican Shrine of Our Lady of Walsingham, in his memoirs, *Merrily on High*:

> I do not now believe there was ever any hope of converting the Church of England as a whole to baroque Catholicism, but I am glad to have lived at a time when for a moment it seemed a dizzy possibility. I am glad that I experienced something of the splendour of its worship and the tortuous complexities of its disciplines . . .[110]

There was a time when the glories of Anglo-Catholicism seemed set to dominate the Church of England, if not also much of the Anglican Communion. That time has passed, and Anglo-Catholics who conclude that the church they belong to is 'Reformed' and not 'Catholic', and

---

109 See Chapter 2, p. 69. Klaus Gamber, (tr.) Klaus D. Grimm, *The Reform of the Roman Liturgy: Its Problems and Background*, San Juan Capistrano, California: Una Voce Press, 1993, p. 52.

110 Colin Stephenson, *Merrily on High*, London: Darton, Longman & Todd, 1972, republished by London: SCM-Canterbury Press, 2008.

that they need to join the Catholic Church should take heart that they do not journey empty-handed. There is the whole hinterland of Anglican pastoral ministry, a way of relating to, and serving, the community in which one is set, beyond the congregation one serves – and all of that, though considerable, is beyond the scope of this chapter. As we have seen, there is a language and a literature, a liturgy or two and, last of all, a fine musical tradition which need not, and should not, be abandoned just because the textual underlay comes from what we finally decide is not the 'Catholic' but the 'Reformed' tradition.

Appendix

The Common Worship Eucharist

As the Church of England Liturgical Commission field-tested its work on the Common Worship Eucharist, it was recognized that 'Rite' was far too grand a term when, arguably, every bit of Anglican liturgy worldwide amounted to no more than a 'Use' of the Western Rite. Thus the eucharistic orders in CW, the main Sunday volume for which appeared in 2000 (*CW Services and Prayers*),[111] called 'Rite One' and 'Rite Two' at the experimental stage, were re-named 'Order One' and 'Order Two', with both orders available in both contemporary and traditional language and the difference between 'One' and 'Two' amounting to the difference between the consensual ecumenical eucharistic shape ('Order One') and the traditional Cranmerian shape ('Order Two'). In short, it was recognized that the battle between 'Catholic' and 'Reformed', in this respect at least, could not be resolved, especially since the Calvinist constituency in the Church of England was manifestly growing. A small sign of this is that detailed comparison of Eucharistic Prayer 3 of the ASB 1980[112] and its revised version, Eucharistic Prayer B of CW, sees the disappearance of the sentence 'We pray you to accept this our duty and service, a spiritual sacrifice of praise and thanksgiving'. Similarly

---

111 A useful guide to CW is Paul F. Bradshaw (ed.), *A Companion to Common Worship*, London: SPCK, 2001 (vol. 1), 2006 (vol. 2), see especially Paul Bradshaw, Gordon Giles and Simon Kershaw, 'Holy Communion', vol. 1, pp. 107ff.

112 This Eucharistic Prayer is always known as the Beckwith-Brindley prayer because its wording was hammered out by Roger Beckwith, the conservative evangelical scholar (who, as we have seen, was himself opposed to the Prayer of Consecration and the Prayer of Oblation being joined), and Brian Brindley, the flamboyant and ultramontane sometime Vicar of Holy Trinity, Reading, whose story is told in Damian Thompson (ed.), *Loose Canon*, London: Continuum, 2004. Brindley, then a Roman Catholic, died in 2001 at his 70th birthday dinner party, held at the Athenaeum.

detailed comparison of Eucharistic Prayer 4 and the new Eucharistic Prayer C – that is, the 'interim rite' eucharistic prayer – sees the re-instating of the Cranmerian phrase 'by his one oblation of himself once offered a full, perfect and sufficient sacrifice, oblation and satisfaction'. Prayer C had substituted for this 'a full atonement for the sins of the whole world, offering once for all his one sacrifice of himself', which, from a Protestant point of view is less satisfactory in more senses than one. These changes represent not only an increased recognition of disparate opinions within the one Church of England but also a move towards accepting the increasing diversity of a 'choice' (not to say 'post modern') culture.

Other ambiguities about what is truly held in common also remain. The Eucharistic Prayers A to H are of differing architecture. Prayers A, B and C derive from the First, Second, Third and Fourth Eucharistic Prayers of the ASB (Eucharistic Prayer A combining elements of the First and Second, Eucharistic Prayer B evolving from the consensual Brindley-Beckwith Prayer, and Eucharistic Prayer C deriving from the 'interim rite'[113] prayer that appeared first of all in 'Series 1', then as the fourth prayer in 'Rite A' and the first of 'Rite B'). These Eucharistic Prayers – A, B and C – are all of the shape used in the Catholic *Novus Ordo* Mass: that is, the *epiclesis*, asking for the Holy Spirit to come upon the gifts, happens before the institution narrative, which may be thought, therefore, to be performative, and the *anamnesis* – the remembering – happens thereafter, as the prayer moves towards the doxology. Eucharistic Prayer E, a new composition, has a similar logic. In Eucharistic Prayers D, F, G and H, however, the *epiclesis* – the invocation of the Spirit – happens after the institution narrative and we find ourselves taking a different journey, rather in the fashion of the Byzantine liturgies. Prayer F, indeed, is a version of the Eucharistic Prayer of St Basil the Great (as are Roman Eucharistic Prayer IV and Eucharistic Prayer D of the Episcopal Church's 1979 BCP).[114] Adding to a sense of indifferentism, CW Prayer D (with its constant response

---

113 'Interim rite' because, following the defeat of the 1928 Prayer Book, many 'Prayer Book Catholics' – English Anglicans who used the Prayer Book rather than the English Missal – combined Cranmer's Prayer of Consecration with his (post communion) Prayer of Thanksgiving, to form an interim Eucharistic Prayer of 'Catholic' shape.

114 Bernard Botte describes his involvement with the Alexandrine *anaphora* of St Basil and the defeat of his translation (preserving the Eastern shape) by a version tailored by Dom Vaggagini with epiclesis before the institution narrative. See Bernard Botte OSB, (tr.) John Sullivan OCD, *From Silence to Participation*, Washington: The Pastoral Press, 1988, pp. 149ff. 'The Egyptian Anaphora of St Basil' is available in R. Jasper and G. Cuming (eds), *Prayers of the Eucharist: Early and Reformed*, third edition, Collegeville: Liturgical Press, 1990, pp. 67ff.

'This is our story. This is our song. Hosanna in the highest') feels like a Scripture lesson, and Prayer H, a short prayer with constantly changing responses and culminating in the *Sanctus*, feels like a fresh attempt to write a 'Reformed' Prayer of Consecration (and is used frequently – even normally – by those evangelicals who are not so conservative that they feel they must use Order Two).

2

Extraordinary or Ordinary

From the rising of the sun to its setting my name is great among the nations, and in every place incense is offered to my name, and a pure offering; for my name is great among the nations, says the LORD of hosts.

Malachi 1.11

Something extraordinary about the discussion in this chapter is that it is written from a position immeasurably sympathetic to the debate but essentially from outside it: an outsider is attempting to describe and contribute to what is, in most senses, an internal Roman Catholic debate. It is a debate in which Anglo-Catholics are interested – indeed it is one in which they have a vested interest, in that they have made a habit of closely imitating the style of the day, whether the ultramontane Catholicism of the late nineteenth century, an inspiration to the Ritualists, or the 'post-Vatican II' style of celebrating the Mass in modern English, facing the people and perhaps using only the Catholic liturgical books. As imitators, of course, they give themselves away by doing it too well: anything too convincing, apparently perfect, arouses suspicion. A Roman Catholic priest, attending High Mass in Pusey House, Oxford, was heard to remark privately that the liturgy had been superb – the ceremonial, the music, the preaching, the rite – 'but it isn't the Church': and that is probably what most conservative Catholics would say in similar circumstances. In Chapter 1 the focus was on the issue of Anglican identity and its consequences for Anglo-Catholics. In this chapter we shall examine the 'Extraordinary or Ordinary' debate, mostly as it is taking place in the Catholic world.

The Progressives' Alibis

The culture wars of contemporary Catholicism have encouraged an energetic debate about the Mass, what should be said – rite – and how it should be done – ceremony. As has been often observed, Catholics have discovered 'churchmanship', where different styles of worship seem to be built on different doctrinal assumptions. Whatever the vantage point, there has been decline and disenchantment. The progressives know from the statistics that all is not well but have various alibis in place. One, pleaded by Archbishop Piero Marini, former Master of Pontifical Liturgical Celebrations, 1987–2007, is the suppression of the Congregation for Divine Worship in 1975 after a mere six years' existence, 'one of the first signs of a tendency to return to a pre-conciliar mindset that has for years now characterized the Curia's approach'.[1] Another, which an Anglican, Richard Giles, would say of buildings,[2] and others, Anglican and Catholic, would say of catechesis, of preaching, of liturgical performance, of music, of daily prayer, and of committed outreach, is that the quality of celebration and proclamation – indeed of priestly formation itself – has been inadequate to the task. Some such as Paul Wilkes's *Excellent Catholic Parishes*, tell us what works in the States and why it works:

> The liturgy ends with an upbeat version of 'Awesome God', and congregants continue to sing and clap after the choir and five-piece Christian rock band (two CDs to their credit so far) have stopped. Lights are turned out to gently encourage the last people to leave.[3]

The same parish (a 2,400-family church, a size scarcely imaginable in Britain) auctions off a dinner 'prepared by the two priests'. For $5,000, the priests 'served the meal dressed in togas, laurel leaves around their heads'.[4]

Martin D. Stringer puts this challenge towards the end of *A Sociological History of Christian Worship*:

1 Piero Marini and Mark R. Francis *et al.* (eds), *A Challenging Reform: Realizing the Vision of the Liturgical Renewal*, Collegeville: Liturgical Press, 2007, p. 157. The present Congregation for Divine Worship and the Discipline of the Sacraments derives from the Sacred Congregation for the Discipline of the Sacraments (1908–69). In 1975 this Congregation was renamed 'Congregation for the Sacraments and Divine Worship' and incorporated the tasks of the Congregation for Divine Worship which had been created in 1969 to take over from the Congregation of Rites (1588–1969). From 1984–88 it was re-divided into the Congregation for the Sacraments and the Congregation for Divine Worship under the same Cardinal Prefect.

2 Richard Giles, *Re-Pitching the Tent: Reordering the Church Building for Worship and Mission*, Norwich: Canterbury Press, revised and expanded edition, 1997.

3 Paul Wilkes, *Excellent Catholic Parishes: The Guide to Best Places and Practices*, New York: Paulist Press, 2001, p. 144.

4 Paul Wilkes, *Excellent Catholic Parishes &c.*, p. 147.

Aidan Kavanagh, in his book *On Liturgical Theology*, argues that many contemporary Western eucharistic services have become more like respectable suburban dinner parties than the inner-city butcher's slab on which the paschal lamb is sacrificed for all.[5] . . . I have noticed, in both England and the United States, an increasing sense of comfortableness and intimacy in contemporary worship that stretches across the traditions: carpets on the floor, a crèche for the children, power point technology providing reassuring images, language that does not offend, and music aimed to speak to our emotions and calm us down. This clearly reflects contemporary, global society and the discourses of consumerism and individual well-being that dominate it, but is this truly Christian?'[6]

The Conservatives' Alibis

Elsewhere, the conservatives in the Catholic Church, surveying the decline and disenchantment of the last generation, have better alibis than the progressives. Passing over the immense socio-cultural differences, they can point to the resurgence of the Orthodox Church in post-Communist Russia, whose liturgy makes no concessions to modernity, whose ceremonial is prolix and unfathomable, and whose rite is celebrated in Church Slavonic. They can argue not only that the loss of a shared Latin liturgical text has been a catalyst of fragmentation and decline, but also, because they are now being dumped, that the 'dynamic equivalent' English translations of the 1970s, intended to convey meaning vividly and immediately, have been a failure both catechetically and doxologically. Furthermore – moving from matters of rite to matters of ceremony – they can argue too that the whole action has shifted from something God-ward to something man-ward. Hence the furious debate about orientation, whether the priest should celebrate facing East or preside facing the people.[7] One memorable, but untraceable and therefore unfortunately unattributable, description of the change from *ad orientem* (towards the East) to *versus populum* (facing the people) was that the mysterious sauce chef had been replaced by

---

5 Aidan Kavanagh OSB, *On Liturgical Theology*, New York: Pueblo, 1984.

6 Martin D. Stringer, *A Sociological History of Christian Worship*, pp. 228f.

7 See particularly, Uwe Michael Lang, *Turning Towards the Lord: Orientation in Liturgical Prayer*, San Francisco: Ignatius Press, 2004 (with its Foreword by Joseph Cardinal Ratzinger) and Part II of Klaus Gamber, (tr.) Klaus Grimm, *The Reform of the Roman Liturgy: Its Problems and Background*, San Juan Capistrano, California: Una Voce Press, 1993.

a dismal singing waiter. Cardinal Heenan said something of the sort in a letter to Evelyn Waugh in 1964:

> The Mass is no longer the Holy Sacrifice but the Meal at which the priest is the waiter. The bishop, I suppose, is the head waiter and the Pope the Patron.[8]

Hence, more important here than the aesthetics – if the distinction between aesthetics and orthodoxy can be sustained – is the observation of Laurence Hemming that

> Each particular Eucharist does not bring God, or the divine presence, to us. Rather through the action of the Eucharist are we moved to enter the divine conspection.[9]

Hemming is picking up a distortion which he ascribes to Dom Odo Casel OSB and the Liturgical Movement, a virus of the Enlightenment as it were,[10] and, though he does not make this particular link here, we are seeing a dangerous reversal of a prayer in the Roman Canon. We risk, to be exact, paying God the favour of looking at him, presuming to look at him with our not-so-serene and not-so-kindly countenance, instead of asking him to 'be pleased to look upon [the holy Bread of eternal life and the Chalice of everlasting salvation] with serene and kindly countenance and to accept them'.[11] Jonathan Robinson describes something similar in his account of the influence of Hegel:

> God did not disappear, but the God who remained was a God who had been recast in the light of the community. . . . Catholic theology has always been wary of this rewriting of the idea of God, but Catholics do live in the world the new mentality has created . . .[12]

---

8 Scott M. Reid (ed.), *A Bitter Trial: Evelyn Waugh and John Carmel Cardinal Heenan on the Liturgical Changes*, Curdridge: The Saint Austin Press, 1996, p. 48.

9 Laurence P. Hemming, 'The Liturgical Subject: Introductory Essay', in James G. Leachman OSB (ed.), *The Liturgical Subject: Subject, Subjectivity and the Human Person in Contemporary Liturgical Discussion and Critique*, London: SCM Press, 2008, p. 2.

10 He explores and explains this more fully in Laurence P. Hemming, *Worship as a Revelation: The Past, Present and Future of Catholic Liturgy*, London: Burns & Oates, 2008, pp. 57ff.

11 English translation of *The Order of Mass I*, ICEL Inc.

12 Jonathan Robinson, *The Mass and Modernity: Walking to Heaven Backwards*, San Francisco: Ignatius Press, 2005, p. 139.

It follows that, if Catholics are to be enabled to remain faithful to the tradition that roots them in the apostolic Church, they must be able to be at home when they go to Mass. Robinson elsewhere says 'the old rite of Mass is like the country house. That is, in many ways it needed refurbishing and even some reconstruction, but it did fulfil its stated function'.[13] For Victor Turner, writing as long ago as 1976, the destruction of the pre-conciliar Mass marked the loss of 'a magnificent objective creation, a vehicle for every sort of Christian interiority':

> One advantage of the traditional Latin ritual was that it could be performed by the most diverse groups and individuals, surmounting their divisions of age, sex, ethnicity, culture, economic status or political affiliation.[14]

Professor Baldovin's Response to the Critics

Turner writes as an anthropologist and is one of many critics quoted by the Jesuit professor, John F. Baldovin, in his 'response to the critics', *Reforming the Liturgy*.[15] Another, quoted by Baldovin, is the sociologist Kieran Flanagan, who notes 'the marginal position of liturgists within theology, and their clerical place on the edge of society' which make them

> poor judges of what will convince in contemporary cultural circumstances. They managed to back modernity as a winning ticket, just at the point when it became converted into postmodernism. They found a solution in modern culture just when it failed in sociology.[16]

Or, as Aidan Nichols puts it, 'as Flanagan would see things, the Second Vatican Council simply took place too early so far as the history of sociology is concerned'.[17]

---

13 Jonathan Robinson, *The Mass and Modernity &c.*, p. 300.

14 Victor Turner, 'Ritual, Tribal and Catholic', *Worship* 50 (1976), pp. 504–26.

15 John F. Baldovin SJ, *Reforming the Liturgy: A Response to the Critics*, Collegeville: Liturgical Press, 2008, pp. 91f.

16 Kieran Flanagan, *Sociology and Liturgy: Re-presentations of the Holy*, New York: St Martin's Press, 1991, p. 10, quoted in John F. Baldovin, *Reforming the Liturgy &c.*, pp. 96f.

17 Aidan Nichols OP, *Looking at the Liturgy: A Critical View of Its Contemporary Form*, San Francisco: Ignatius Press, 1996, p. 56.

Baldovin also quotes C. S. Lewis's trenchant criticism of trendy vicars, made in the early 1960s, just as the round of liturgical change was beginning in the Church of England:

It looks as if they believed people can be lured to go to church by incessant brightenings, lightenings, lengthenings, abridgements, simplifications, and complications of the service.[18]

As he takes on the principal critics of the liturgical reform that followed the Second Vatican Council, and even though he is speaking from a different vantage point, Baldovin approvingly cites a template of Francis Mannion.[19] Following 'a methodology of agenda differentiation' learnt from his tutor, Avery Dulles, Mannion had listed 'five identifiable liturgical movements in the English-speaking world':

1 Advancing official reform.
2 Restoring the pre-conciliar.
3 Reforming the reform.
4 Inculturating the reform.
5 Recatholicizing the reform.

Baldovin's instinct – and he cannot be alone in this – is to find himself wanting to tick four of the five boxes, and one might argue that all five could be ticked if the agendas were purely liturgical. Few would argue that the official liturgical reforms which occurred throughout the twentieth century are yet complete. Most would see some place for the pre-conciliar rite, especially since the publication of *Summorum Pontificum*,[20] Pope Benedict's *motu proprio* of 7 July 2007, to which we shall return shortly. Baldovin has to cope with the fact that one of the principal critics of liturgical reform whom he is taking on in argument became Pope and he is writing also in the wake of *Summorum Pontificum* on which he comments.[21] 'Reforming the reform' suggests that mistakes have been made: things have been added that should not have been added and things have been obscured or lost that need to be

---

18 C. S. Lewis, *Letters to Malcolm, Chiefly on Prayer*, London: G. Bles, 1964, pp. 4f., quoted in John F. Baldovin, *Reforming the Liturgy &c.*, p. 98.

19 M. Francis Mannion, 'The Catholicity of the Liturgy: Shaping a New Agenda', was read at a conference of the Centre for Faith and Culture in Oxford in 1996 and is published in Stratford Caldecott (ed.), *Beyond the Prosaic: Renewing the Liturgical Movement*, Edinburgh: T&T Clark, 1998, pp. 11ff.

20 This document is available on www.vatican.va

21 John F. Baldovin SJ, *Reforming the Liturgy &c.*, p. 130ff.

burnished or recovered: that too would be hard to disagree with. The work of inculturation goes on and it is hard to see that it can ever be complete. As for 'recatholicizing the reform', when Mannion says:

> Recatholicization means a renewal of the doxological, praise-filled character of worship capable of rescuing present-day liturgical practice from its excessively pragmatic, didactic and functional conceptions.[22]

It would be hard to disagree, especially when he locates 'the fundamental impulses for doxology' in 'eschatological and cosmic conceptions'. Theological 'motherhood and apple pie', one might say.

To take on the critics of liturgical reform, Baldovin develops 'a kind of typology of the critique',[23] grouping them into 'extreme traditionalists', 'proponents of "reforming the reform"' and those who maintain that 'the reform was poorly implemented'. The first group, says Baldovin, includes the Society of St Pius X,[24] Alcuin Reid,[25] Didier Bonneterre,[26] and some of the French monasteries. The second group includes Klaus Gamber,[27] Pope Benedict before[28] and after his election, James Hitchcock,[29] Kieran Flanagan,[30] and the contributors of appendices to Thomas Kocik's, *The Reform of the Reform?*[31] The third group includes Denis Crouan[32] and Francis Mannion and it is this group to

---

22 John F. Baldovin SJ, *Reforming the Liturgy &c.*, p. 29.

23 John F. Baldovin SJ, *Reforming the Liturgy &c.*, p. 134.

24 See *The Problem of the Liturgical Reform: A Theological and Liturgical Study*, Kansas City: Angelus Press, 2001.

25 This is not a fair description of Alcuin Reid's position. In the Introduction to *The Organic Development of the Liturgy*, Farnborough: St Michael's Abbey Press, 2004, pp. 8f., he explains his desire to contribute to the discussion by establishing 'the principles of liturgical reform operative in the history of the Roman rite' not least by seeking to 'know the mind of Guéranger, St Pius X, Beauduin, Guardini, Parsch, Casel, and others'. 'Only then', he says, 'can discussion of the legitimacy of any "reform of the reform", or of its possible shape, be sufficiently informed.'

26 See Didier Bonneterre, *The Liturgical Movement: from Dom Gueranger to Annibale Bugnini*, Kansas City: Angelus Press, 2002.

27 See Klaus Gamber, *The Reform of the Roman Liturgy &c.* See also Klaus Gamber, (tr.) Henry Taylor, *The Modern Rite: Collected Essays on the Reform of the Liturgy*, Farnborough: St Michael's Abbey Press, 2002.

28 See Joseph Ratzinger, (tr.) John Saward, *The Spirit of the Liturgy*, San Francisco: Ignatius Press, 2000.

29 See James Hitchcock, *The Recovery of the Sacred*, New York: Seabury, 1974.

30 See K. Flanagan, *Sociology and Liturgy: Re-presentations of the Holy*.

31 See Thomas Kocik, *The Reform of the Reform? A Liturgical Debate: Reform or Return*, San Francisco: Ignatius Press, 2003.

32 See Denis Crouan, STD, (tr.) Marc Sebanc, *The Liturgy Betrayed*, San Francisco:

which Baldovin's own position comes closest. Earlier in *Reforming the Liturgy* Baldovin also engages with Catherine Pickstock,[33] an Anglican philosopher, Jonathan Robinson,[34] an Oratorian and philosopher, and David Torevell,[35] who 'while not an anthropologist, employs anthropological concepts'.[36] Baldovin also acknowledges the weighty contributions of Aidan Nichols,[37] Uwe Michael Lang,[38] and László Dobszay.[39]

We have spent as long as we have with Professor Baldovin because, as is already apparent, the onslaught from the mostly conservative lobby is intense and sophisticated and he does us the favour of gathering together the criticism for comment. The value of the book, not least his own suggestions for a way forward[40] is that we not only get to meet most of the outlaws and hear something of what they say, but have chance to size up as we go their significant and weighty conservative arsenal. Baldovin beleaguredly sets about defending the liturgical reforms that followed the Second Vatican Council, rather like a lone ranger cornered in a gulch by outlaws. We began with 'culture wars' and we cannot but notice that the anthropologists, liturgists, monastics, musicologists, philosophers, sociologists and theologians – that is, broadly speaking, the 'intellectuals' – are waging war on the way that bishops, priests and parishioners, parish musicians and worship committees – the hierarchy and *hoi polloi* – interpret, plan, and perform the *Novus Ordo*, the new Order of Mass, the 'ordinary form', usually known as *Missa normativa*. Referring to earlier remarks about decline and disenchantment, one might almost say that one group – the 'intellectuals' – is seeking to explain why the practice of the Faith has lost so much ground amongst the educated classes whereas the other group – 'the hierarchy and *hoi polloi*', that is the parish practitioners – is looking for ever more ingenious – and even entertaining – ways to draw in new recruits, engage with the population and re-engage

---

Ignatius Press, 2000 and Denis Crouan, STD, (tr.) Michael Miller, *The History and the Future of the Roman Liturgy*, San Francisco: Ignatius Press, 2005.

33 See Catherine Pickstock, *After Writing: On the Liturgical Consummation of Philosophy*, Oxford: Blackwell, 1998 and Catherine Pickstock, 'A Short Essay on the Reform of the Liturgy', in Paul F. Bradshaw and Bryan Spinks (eds), *Liturgy in Dialogue*, London: SPCK, 1993.

34 See Jonathan Robinson, *The Mass and Modernity &c.*

35 See David Torevell, *Losing the Sacred: Ritual, Modernity and Liturgical Reform*, Edinburgh: T&T Clark, 2000.

36 John F. Baldovin SJ, *Reforming the Liturgy &c.*, p. 92.

37 See Aidan Nichols, *Looking at the Liturgy.*

38 See Uwe Michael Lang, *Turning Towards the Lord &c.*

39 See László Dobszay, *The Bugnini-Liturgy and the Reform of the Reform*, Front Royal VA: Catholic Church Music Associates, 2003.

40 John F. Baldovin, SJ, *Reforming the Liturgy &c.*, pp. 134ff.

with the lapsed. To put it another way, the conservatives see authentic and organic development of the liturgy as an urgent concern for orthodoxy and orthopraxy as well as being fundamental to mission and evangelization; the progressives deny that they are allowing bright ideas and engaging presentation to take precedence over a concern for the authentic celebration of the eucharistic mysteries by the priestly People of God, and see authentic corporate eucharistic celebration threatened by a return to a clerically dominated church in which the laity are auditors and spectators.

The Spirit of the Liturgy

Though, as we have seen, Baldovin is writing in the wake of Pope Benedict's *motu proprio, Summorum Pontificum*, of 07-07-07 (and there were those who saw that as a date with mystic symmetry), the conservatives whose concerns he was addressing were writing in anticipation of – and even campaigning for – some such papal initiative. The author of *The Spirit of the Liturgy* was unlikely to renege on the perspectives and views he propagated and upheld whilst Prefect of the Congregation for the Doctrine of Faith. He had pointed out that 'in the Old Testament there is a series of very impressive testimonies to the truth that the liturgy is not a matter of "what you please"'.[41] For Ratzinger 'the historical liturgy of Christendom is and always will be cosmic, without separation and without confusion, and only as such does it stand erect in its full grandeur'.[42] Christian worship 'is the worship of an open heaven. It is never just an event in the life of a community that finds itself in a particular place'.[43] He insists that to 'describe the Eucharist, in terms of the liturgical phenomenon as "an assembly", or in terms of Jesus' act of institution at the Last Supper, as a "meal"' is to fail to grasp 'the great historical and theological connections'[44] – Incarnation, Cross and Resurrection – for 'in liturgical celebration there is a kind of turning around of *exitus* to *reditus*, of departure to return, of God's descent to our ascent'.[45] This is the theologian who has said that 'the liturgy is *parousia* . . . Every Eucharist is *parousia*, the Lord's coming, and yet the Eucharist is even more truly the tensed yearning that He would reveal his hidden Glory.' From this it follows that 'the

41 Joseph Ratzinger, *The Spirit of the Liturgy*, p. 22.
42 Joseph Ratzinger, *The Spirit of the Liturgy*, p. 34.
43 Joseph Ratzinger, *The Spirit of the Liturgy*, p. 49.
44 Joseph Ratzinger, *The Spirit of the Liturgy*, p. 50.
45 Joseph Ratzinger, *The Spirit of the Liturgy*, p. 61.

parousia is the highest intensification and fulfilment of the liturgy'.[46]
Uwe Michael Lang makes the same point:

> The arrangement of the altar in such a way that the celebrant and
> the faithful face eastward brings to light the 'parousial' character of
> Eucharist, for the mystery of Christ is being celebrated *donec veniat
> in caelis*' (until he come in the heavens).[47]

For Ratzinger accordingly 'the eucharistic celebration proper takes
place in the apse, at the altar, which the faithful "stand around". Everyone joins with the celebrant in facing East, toward the Lord who is to
come'[48] and, as compared with synagogue worship,

> though the public Liturgy of the Word was not entrusted to women,
> they were included in the liturgy as a whole in exactly the same way
> as men. And so now they had a place – albeit in separation from men
> – in the sacred space itself, around both the *bema* and the altar.[49]

He is concerned too with the place of the cross: 'Moving the altar cross
to the side to give an uninterrupted view of the priest is something I
regard as one of the truly absurd phenomena of recent decades.'[50] The
tabernacle too, 'takes the place previously occupied by the now disappeared "Ark of the Covenant" . . . It is the tent of God, his throne'.[51] 'If
the presence of the Lord is to touch us in a concrete way, the tabernacle
must also find its proper place in the architecture of our church buildings.'[52] *The Spirit of the Liturgy* meditates on 'sacred time' and 'the
question of images', concluding that:

> sacred art stands beneath the imperative stated in the Second Epistle
> to the Corinthians. Gazing at the Lord, we are 'changed into his like-
> ness from one degree of glory to another; for this comes from the
> Lord who is the Spirit (3.18).[53]

---

46 Joseph Ratzinger, *Eschatology*, Washington DC: Catholic University of America
Press, 1988, p. 203. He is quoted by Scott Hahn, *Letter and Spirit: From Written Text to
Living Word in the Liturgy*, London: Darton, Longman and Todd, 2006, p. 116. Hahn is
writing here extensively on Proclamation and *Parousia*, skilfully popularizing.
47 Uwe Michael Lang, *Turning Towards the Lord &c.*, p. 109.
48 Joseph Ratzinger, *The Spirit of the Liturgy*, p. 72.
49 Joseph Ratzinger, *The Spirit of the Liturgy*, p. 73.
50 Joseph Ratzinger, *The Spirit of the Liturgy*, p. 84.
51 Joseph Ratzinger, *The Spirit of the Liturgy*, p. 89.
52 Joseph Ratzinger, *The Spirit of the Liturgy*, p. 91.
53 Joseph Ratzinger, *The Spirit of the Liturgy*, pp. 134f.

It is well known that it is a musical Joseph Ratzinger who is writing, and that his elder brother, Georg, was director of the *Regensburger Domspatzen*[54] (Regensburg Cathedral Choir). 'After the cultural revolution of recent decades', he says, 'we are faced with a challenge no less great than that of . . . the Gnostic temptation, the crisis at the end of the Middle Ages and the beginning of modernity, and the crisis at the beginning of the twentieth century, which formed the prelude to the still more radical questions of the present day.'[55]

Musically speaking, 'there is the cultural universalization that the Church has to undertake if she wants to get beyond the boundaries of the European mind'[56] – in other words inculturation. 'Then there are two developments in music . . . that for a long time have affected the whole of mankind.' He refers to the way 'so-called "classical music" has manoeuvred itself, with some exceptions, into an elitist ghetto' whereas 'the music of the masses has broken loose'. Pop music

> is industrially produced, and ultimately has to be described as a cult of the banal. 'Rock' . . . is the expression of elemental passions, and at rock festivals it assumes a cultic character, a form of worship, in fact, in opposition to Christian worship.[57]

Having examined the essence of the liturgy, time and space, art and music, Ratzinger moves on, in the fourth and final part, to look at 'liturgical form'. Beginning with 'Rite' he makes the point that different rites are 'not . . . just the products of inculturation', but 'forms of the apostolic tradition and of its unfolding in the great places of the tradition'.[58] He examines the rupture between East and West 'which allowed hardly any cross-fertilization' thereafter and, in the West, 'the Pope more and more clearly took over responsibility for liturgical legislation'.[59] In a veiled criticism of Pope Paul VI, he says 'After the Second Vatican Council, the impression arose that the Pope really could do anything in liturgical matters, especially if he were acting on the mandate of an ecumenical council',[60] but 'the authority of the Pope is not unlimited; it is at the service of sacred tradition'. In a phrase

---

54 Literally, the 'Regensburg Cathedral Sparrows'.
55 Joseph Ratzinger, *The Spirit of the Liturgy*, p. 147.
56 Joseph Ratzinger, *The Spirit of the Liturgy*, p. 147f.
57 Joseph Ratzinger, *The Spirit of the Liturgy*, p. 147f. A slightly different view is offered respectfully in Chapter 4, p. 131.
58 Joseph Ratzinger, *The Spirit of the Liturgy*, p. 164.
59 Joseph Ratzinger, *The Spirit of the Liturgy*, p. 165.
60 Joseph Ratzinger, *The Spirit of the Liturgy*, p. 165.

prophetic of the catchphrase on conservative blog-sites – 'say the black, do the red' – the then Prefect for the Congregation for the Doctrine of the Faith said 'The greatness of the liturgy depends – we shall have to repeat this frequently – on its unspontaneity *(Unbeliebigkeit)*.'[61]

Moving from 'Rite' to 'the Body and the Liturgy', Ratzinger discusses the phrase *participatio actuosa*,[62] and is quite clear that 'external actions – reading, singing, bringing up the gifts' are 'quite secondary here. *Doing* really must stop when we come to the heart of the matter: the *oratio*'[63] – and, in this context, *oratio* – the prayer – is 'the Eucharistic Prayer, the "Canon"'.

> In it . . . the human *actio* (as performed hitherto by the priests in the various religions of the world) steps back and makes way for the *actio divina*, the action of God. In this *oratio* the priest speaks with the I of the Lord – 'This is my Body', 'This is my Blood'.[64]

The future Pope recalls that he annoyed many liturgists in 1978 by suggesting that sometimes the Canon might be said silently, and he repeats and underlines the point, citing the importance of the tradition in Jerusalem, and in the West.[65] He is similarly conservative about kneeling and other bodily gestures, such as making the sign of the cross and striking the breast, about vestments, and about the matter of the sacraments: it is through the specifically Mediterranean elements – olive oil, wheaten bread, wine – as well as water 'that Christ comes to us' and it is 'precisely through what is particular and once-for-all, the here and now' that 'we emerge from the "ever and never" vagueness of mythology'. Thus does Christ 'make us brethren beyond all boundaries. Precisely thus do we recognize him: "It is the Lord" (John 21.7)'.[66]

Discontinuity, Rupture and Reform

We have stayed with the argument of *The Spirit of the Liturgy* for several pages not simply because its author became Pope but because there is here – as in other writings – something of a liturgical manifesto. It will help us to examine whether the co-existence of 'extraordinary'

---

61 Joseph Ratzinger, *The Spirit of the Liturgy*, p. 166.
62 Joseph Ratzinger, *The Spirit of the Liturgy*, pp. 171ff. See also Chapter 4, p. 120.
63 Joseph Ratzinger, *The Spirit of the Liturgy*, p. 174.
64 Joseph Ratzinger, *The Spirit of the Liturgy*, p. 174.
65 Joseph Ratzinger, *The Spirit of the Liturgy*, p. 214.
66 Joseph Ratzinger, *The Spirit of the Liturgy*, p. 224.

and 'ordinary' forms of the Roman rite, as sometimes said, is a concession to those who mourn the loss of the pre-conciliar Mass, or whether it is providing oxygen for two legitimate forms of the Western Rite to breathe, grow and live. If it is the latter then there is also the question of cross-fertilization, parallel to the liturgical exchange between East and West in the first millennium. No less fascinating is whether we shall see a convergence of the two forms in another major revision of the *Missale Romanum* (Roman Missal), as the Catholic Church attends to the hermeneutic of rupture – to which the Pope alluded in his first Christmas address as Pope to the Roman Curia, and to which we shall now turn.[67] That speech – along with Pope Benedict's previous writings, principally *The Spirit of the Liturgy* and the apostolic exhortation *Sacramentum Caritatis* of 2007[68] – is the key to understanding *Summorum Pontificum* and the question of 'Extraordinary or Ordinary' that we are addressing. Taking these contributions to the liturgical debate as a whole, we can surely discern not only some common themes but also the course on which Pope Benedict XVI intended from the first to set sail.

From the Christmas address, with its rich and complex themes, we select two, both concerned with continuity. The first, following a reflection on the Synod of Bishops and the Year of the Eucharist, just ended, draws attention to the Congregation for Divine Worship's Instruction *Redemptionis Sacramentum*[69] 'as a practical guide to the correct implementation of the conciliar constitution on the liturgy and liturgical reform'. As we see from *The Spirit of the Liturgy*, this is more than the headmaster saying 'obey the rules': the Pope as guardian of the tradition is teaching once more, as he will in *Sacramentum Caritatis*, that 'the greatness of the liturgy depends . . . on its unspontaneity'.[70] As the piano teacher might say to the pupil struggling over a piece of Mozart and over-confident of his ability, 'let's get the notes right first'. More significantly, Benedict proceeds to a discussion of what he calls 'the correct interpretation' of the Second Vatican Council 'or – as we would say today – on its proper hermeneutics, the correct key to its interpretation and application'.

On the one hand, there is an interpretation that I would call 'a hermeneutic of discontinuity and rupture'; it has frequently availed itself

---

67 The Address of His Holiness Benedict XVI to the Roman Curia offering them his Christmas Greetings, Thursday 22 December 2005, is available on www.vatican.va

68 This document, following the Synod of Bishops in Rome (2–23 October 2005) is available on www.vatican.va

69 This document is available on www.vatican.va

70 See above, p. 54.

of the sympathies of the mass media, and also one trend of modern theology. On the other, there is the 'hermeneutic of reform', of renewal in the continuity of the one subject-Church which the Lord has given to us. She is a subject which increases in time and develops, yet always remaining the same, the one subject of the journeying People of God.[71]

There is no space here for a lengthy reflection on this crucial theme of authentic organic growth. It is one that has appeared in several contexts: Alcuin Reid had it in mind, self-evidently,[72] as did Klaus Gamber, when he declared starkly that 'the reform introduced by St Pius V' (in 1570) 'was simply a comprehensive review' which 'meant that liturgical forms, as they had developed up to that point, had now been made permanent, making further, organic development impossible'.[73] Aidan Nichols spoke of the 'blank cheque, enabling [the professionals] to redesign the liturgy in just that inorganic way against which . . . reflective commentators on the Enlightenment experience . . . had warned'.[74]

For the Pope, however, the option of inveighing against post-conciliar liturgies is, *ex officio*, an impossibility. Instead the Catholic Church's supreme liturgist, pastor and teacher notes that 'the hermeneutic of discontinuity risks ending in a split between the pre-conciliar Church and the post-conciliar Church'. Here we can see his pastoral heart extending towards those who have become separated from the Church for liturgical and doctrinal reasons, that is, those who see the post-conciliar Church as radically discontinuous with the Church of Pope Pius XII and his predecessors. How all that has been playing out – from the forming of *Ecclesia Dei* Commission in 1988 to its incorporation in the Con-

---

71 The Address of His Holiness Benedict XVI to the Roman Curia, see footnote 67. Laurence Hemming discusses 'the hermeneutic of continuity' in Laurence P. Hemming, *Worship as a Revelation*, p. 150. Pope Benedict himself subsequently uses the phrase 'hermeneutic of continuity' to explain what he had meant by 'hermeneutic of reform' in his 2005 Christmas Address. See the footnote on p. 5 of the official edition of *Sacramentum Caritatis*, Liberia Editrice Vaticana, MMVII. (See also London: Catholic Truth Society, 2007; also available [2009] at www.vatican.va)

72 Alcuin Reid, *The Organic Development of the Liturgy*.

73 Klaus Gamber, *The Reform of the Roman Liturgy &c.*, p. 16. He is speaking here of the rite as a whole: he later approves of readings in the vernacular from a wider bank of Scripture, though not of the new Lectionary (pp. 50f.), and of the 'Prayer of the Faithful' though not of extemporaneous petitions (pp. 52f.). He cannot quite disapprove of the congregational recitation of the Lord's Prayer aloud but would have preferred this change, it seems, to have been inspired by the Oriental and Gallican rites rather than by the 'dialogue Masses of the 1920s' (pp. 56f.).

74 Aidan Nichols, *Looking at the Liturgy*, p. 48.

gregation for the Doctrine of the Faith, announced amidst the storm of March 2009, when the Pope lifted the excommunications of the four bishops of the Society of St Pius X – shows that the issues are doctrinal, and, as we already know from the Pope's writings, liturgical celebration is far more than a matter of style and taste. Nevertheless, we should notice that the Pope speaks not only of continuity but renewal: the 'subject-Church' remains the same 'but increases in time and develops'. Moreover, in speaking of the 'journeying People of God', the quintessential image of the Church in *Lumen Gentium*,[75] he is indicating that he is not himself moving away from, let alone abandoning, the spirit of the Second Vatican Council. That said, *Sacrosanctum Concilium*,[76] the Constitution on the Sacred Liturgy produced by the Council, is one thing, and the Bugnini Reforms[77] are another. As we approach *Summorum Pontificum* we can assume that the Joseph Ratzinger who wrote *The Spirit of the Liturgy* and the Pope who addressed the Church *motu proprio* (on his own initiative) in *Summorum Pontificum* saw discontinuity – not rupture – between *Sacrosanctum Concilium* and its outworking in the liturgical reforms that followed the Council. Renewal requires that a correct hermeneutical understanding of *Sacrosanctum Concilium* is applied. That begins with getting the *Novus Ordo*, the 'ordinary form', right – being faithful to text, rubric and General Instruction. It continues with the two forms, the *Novus Ordo* and the extraordinary (pre-1962) form, also known as the Gregorian rite, informing one another's development and reform. It may lead – surely should lead – eventually to the two streams converging.

Summorum Pontificum

In the apostolic letter of 07-07-07, Pope Benedict saw himself as following in the footsteps of his predecessors – particularly Clement VIII, Urban VIII, St Pius X, Benedict XV, Pius XII and Blessed John XXIII – in up-dating liturgical books and clarifying rite and ceremony. He makes special mention of Paul VI and his reforms, and of Pope John Paul II, in whose papacy the third *editio typica* of the Roman Missal

---

75 This document, the Second Vatican Council Dogmatic Constitution on the Church, is available on www.vatican.va

76 This document is available on www.vatican.va

77 See Annibale Bugnini CM, (tr.) Matthew J. O'Connell, *The Reform of the Liturgy 1948–1975*, Collegeville: Liturgical Press, 1990. Also Piero Marini, *A Challenging Reform &c.*

was published.[78] He acknowledges the continuing adherence and love 'in some regions' of 'no small numbers of faithful' to 'earlier liturgical forms' and mentions the provision, *Quattuor Abhinc Anno* of 1984, whereby Pope John Paul II gave permission for restricted use of the 1962 Missal. After prayer and consultation he declares that, though the Missal of Paul VI is 'the ordinary expression of the *lex orandi* (law of prayer) of the Catholic Church',

> nonetheless, the Roman Missal promulgated by St. Pius V and reissued by Blessed John XXIII is to be considered as an extraordinary expression of that same *lex orandi*, and must be given due honour for its venerable and ancient usage. These two expressions of the Church's *lex orandi* will in no any way lead to a division in the Church's *lex credendi* (law of belief). They are, in fact two usages of the one Roman rite.

A whole set of regulations follows, together with an explanatory letter to the world's bishops, and the new dispensation came into force on Holy Cross Day, 14 September 2007. For present purposes, there are a few points which are particularly noticeable. One is that for Masses celebrated without the people – and including those which people specifically choose to attend, but excluding the Easter Triduum – any priest in good standing may celebrate from either rite, without recourse to the Holy See or episcopal authority. Another is that 'where there is a stable group of faithful who adhere to the earlier liturgical tradition, the pastor should willingly accept their requests to celebrate the Mass according to the rite of the Roman Missal published in 1962'. Here there is an appropriate place for the bishop's counsel and guidance with regard to 'the ordinary pastoral care of the parish'. Such Masses may happen on working days and once on Sundays and feasts. (It is not hard to see that the nuancing of these two provisions – the difference between Masses arranged to be celebrated without the people but voluntarily attended by people and Masses providing for 'a stable group of the faithful who adhere to the earlier liturgical tradition' – has already been troublesome.) Another regulation permits the 'extraordinary form for special

---

78 The first edition of the Missal of Paul VI was available in 1970, though sometimes dated 1969. The second, with some minor alterations, mostly corrections, came out in 1975, during the same papacy. The third, sometimes dated 2000, was available from 2002, and included a new version of the *General Instruction of the Roman Missal* (GIRM), some calendrical additions, and some rubrical and textual changes. For details of the changes, see Dennis C. Smolarski SJ, *The General Instruction of the Roman Missal: A Commentary, 1969–2002*, Collegeville: Liturgical Press, 2003.

circumstances such as marriages, funerals or occasional celebrations, i.e. pilgrimages'. Also permitted – at the priest's discretion – is the use of the 1962 Breviary and the older form for baptism, marriage, penance and anointing. The bishop may decide to confirm in the older form.[79] Religious communities and societies may make their own appropriate decisions about which should be their usage and 'the ordinary' may constitute a personal 'extraordinary form' parish.

There is at least one clue in the *motu proprio* that the Pope would like to see the two forms enriching one another:

> In Masses celebrated in the presence of the people in accordance with the Missal of Blessed John XXIII, the readings may be given in the vernacular, using editions recognized by the Apostolic See.

From this one may infer that 'convergence of the two rites, the classical and the modern', as Aidan Nichols puts it, is not impossible. Indeed, Nichols says that:

> The historic Roman rite can only be enriched by the incorporation of the best aspects of the reform – a fuller cycle of readings, the wonderful Prefaces of the new rite, and the possibility, where opportune, of concelebration and the administration of the chalice to the laity – and these are the only terms on which Rome will be able to convince the episcopate that general access to the classical rite and the training of ordinands in its celebration are desirable.[80]

Convincing the episcopate is unlikely to be an easy or speedy process (the Pope's explanatory letter speaks of 'very divergent reactions, ranging from joyful acceptance to harsh opposition, about a plan whose contents were in reality unknown') and he therefore offered a review after three years. The troublesome question, to which we have just referred, of judging when and where the bishop should take an interest is one issue, and the traditionalist blogosphere has vigorously policed episcopal utterances on the subject, denouncing those thought to be tepid, unenthusiastic, or wrong. Another question is whether the bishops are ultimately convinced by the Pope's reasoning, in his explanatory

---

79 There is an interesting issue here: Pope Paul VI arguably changed the form of Confirmation in *Divinae consortium naturae* 15 August 1971 from signing with chrism to laying on of hands and signing.

80 Aidan Nichols OP, 'Salutary Dissatisfaction: An English View of "Reforming the Reform"', in Thomas Kocik (ed.), *The Reform of the Reform? &c.*, p. 203.

letter, that the *usus antiquior*[81] (the more ancient use) is – and should be encouraged to be – a suitable tool for the formation of the young:

> Immediately after the Second Vatican Council it was presumed that requests for the use of the 1962 Missal would be limited to the older generation which had grown up with it, but in the meantime it has clearly been demonstrated that young persons too have discovered this liturgical form, felt its attraction and found in it a form of encounter with the mystery of the Most Holy Eucharist, particularly suited to them.

Consistent with his liturgical manifesto, Benedict XVI makes the point that, not only is the liturgical reform decided upon by the Second Vatican Council not being called into question, 'the Missal published by Paul VI and then republished in two subsequent editions by John Paul II, obviously is and continues to be the normal Form – the *forma ordinaria* – of the eucharistic liturgy'.

Speaking of the 1962 Missal, published with the authority of Pope John XXIII in 1962 and 'used during the Council', this, says Pope Benedict, is the

> *forma extraordinaria* of the liturgical celebration. It is not appropriate to speak of these two versions of the Roman Missal as if they were 'two rites'. Rather, it is a matter of a twofold use of one and the same rite.

The Pope goes on to explain to the bishops that the 1962 'was never juridically abrogated and, consequently, in principle, was always permitted'. The lack of regulation at the time was because it was expected that the old form would die away. Commentators have pointed out that this seems to be a re-writing of history: why did Pope Paul VI not make regulation for the continued used of a rite that was never juridically abrogated and why did Pope John Paul II in *Quattuor Abhinc Annos* present permission for use of the older form as a concession rather than a normal option? What would happen if this were cited as a precedent for rejecting future liturgical revision?

We need to be continually reminded of the then Cardinal Ratzinger's warning that to 'describe the Eucharist, in terms of the liturgical

---

81 A biannual journal, *Usus Antiquior*, edited by Laurence P. Hemming and published by the Society of St Catherine of Siena and Maney Publishing, was launched in January 2010.

phenomenon as "an assembly", or in terms of Jesus' act of institution at the Last Supper, as a "meal"' is to fail to grasp 'the great historical and theological connections'[82] of Incarnation, Cross and Resurrection. Indeed, elsewhere in *The Spirit of the Liturgy*, the future Pope draws attention to the density of the notion of sacrifice whilst speaking of the aptness of seasonal imagery for both Northern and Southern Hemispheres:

> I have already pointed out that, in interpreting the Passion of Jesus, St John's Gospel and the Epistle to the Hebrews do not just refer to the feast of Passover, which is the Lord's 'hour', in terms of date. No, they also interpret it in light of the ritual of the Day of Atonement celebrated on the tenth day of the seventh month (September–October). In the Passover of Jesus there is, so to speak, a co-incidence of Easter (spring) and the Day of Atonement (autumn).[83]

Margaret Barker, a Protestant biblical scholar with affinity to the Orthodox and a following amongst Catholics, similarly makes much of the link between the Eucharist and the Day of Atonement.[84]

Convergence of Extraordinary and Ordinary

It remains to see what might emerge were the Congregation for Divine Worship and the Discipline of the Sacraments (together with the Congregation for the Doctrine of Faith which has responsibility for those who maintain the 'extraordinary form' for what they would regard as doctrinal reasons) to attempt to bring together the 'extraordinary' and the 'ordinary' forms. In some ways the *usus antiquior* and the *usus recentior* (more recent use) are as different from one another as the stone, slate and brick buildings we have inherited in our cities are different from the glass, steel and concrete buildings we now erect. Whereas, a generation ago, these media were very distinct (the new church extension was glass, steel, and concrete), we now build on more congruently, with a feel for heritage, and the aim of concealing within traditional building materials the best, and most up-to-date facilities, constructed with the most ecologically and technologically efficient

---

82 Joseph Ratzinger, *The Spirit of the Liturgy*, p. 50. See also p. 51, above.

83 Joseph Ratzinger, *The Spirit of the Liturgy*, p. 104.

84 Margaret Barker, *The Great High Priest: The Temple Roots of Christian Liturgy*, London and New York: T&T Clark International, 2003, reprinted 2004, pp. 74ff.

materials. We may wonder what a fourth edition of the Roman Missal, attempting to include – perhaps even synthesize – 'extraordinary' and 'ordinary' forms, might look like. Those whom Professor Baldovin called 'extreme traditionalists', like those in the Prayer Book Society for whom the smell and feel, the format and typeset of the book itself is fundamental, would be unappeased. Those whom he called 'proponents of "reforming the reform"' and those who maintain that 'the reform was poorly implemented',[85] might find, however, most – if not all – of their concerns met.

Given that, because of its international importance, English is increasingly going to be the main – if not the official – *lingua franca* of the Church, and given that the watching brief of the *Vox Clara* Committee of the Congregation for Divine Worship and the Discipline of the Sacraments is complete, and the principles of *Liturgiam Authenticam*[86] are judged to have been applied satisfactorily and well in the most recent English translation of the *Missale Romanum*, we can largely leave on one side issues of language. Early signs are that the new English version of the *Missale Romanum*[87] will furnish the Catholic Church with a noble, contemporary, yet distinctly liturgical, vernacular. As regards traditional language, the concession in *Summorum Pontificum* that readings may be in the vernacular, together with a further influx of converts from the Anglican tradition, might be extended so that the Anglo-Catholics' *English Missal* – together with such splendid liturgical books as *Monastic Breviary: Matins according to the Holy Rule of Saint Benedict*[88] and *The Monastic Diurnal*[89] – are authorized (with some directions as to their use)[90] and eventually superseded by new

85 John F. Baldovin, SJ, *Reforming the Liturgy &c.*, p. 134.

86 *Liturgiam Authenticam* (7 May 2001), 'On the Use of Vernacular Languages in the Publication of the Books of the Roman Liturgy Fifth Instruction for the Right Implementation of the Constitution on the Sacred Liturgy of the Second Vatican Council'. This document is available on www.vatican.va. A critique of this document, and a defence of the rationale of its predecessor, *Comme le prévoit*, the 1969 Instruction on the norms for translation of liturgical texts, may be found in Keith Pecklers SJ, *The Genius of the Roman Rite: The Reception and Implementation of the New Missal*, London: Burns & Oates, 2009, pp. 47ff.

87 © 2006, 2008, ICEL Inc. At the time of writing, the English translation of *The Order of Mass I* is available on the ICEL website www.icel/web.org/ but not yet in print.

88 *Monastic Breviary: Matins according to the Holy Rule of Saint Benedict*, Tymawr, Lydart, Monmouth: The Society of the Sacred Cross, 1961, reprinted Glendale: Lancelot Andrewes Press, 2007.

89 *The Monastic Diurnal*, London: Oxford University Press, last printed 1963.

90 Such as dealing with the discrepancy between the similar but divergent Sarum/BCP and pre-conciliar schemes for the collects and readings on Sundays after Pentecost and omitting inappropriate insertions from the BCP Communion Service.

editions on similar principles. The Catholic Church, in whatever way, would do well to keep a rich register of traditional language in good repair: it is not only Catholics coming from the Anglican tradition, but also many of those who use the Byzantine Liturgy in English, who are happiest when the language is archaic. There are presumably many Catholics too who continue to seek out the Douay-Rheims version of the Bible for reading, traditional hymnals for singing, and traditional manuals and primers for personal praying.

We need not delay here over calendrical convergence, which is discussed elsewhere,[91] but from the conservative critics mentioned earlier, there are some good ideas worth exploring. We begin with Francis Mannion, whose template we studied earlier: in looking for a 'recatholicizing of the reform' he is asking for a new attentiveness to aesthetics and, in the best sense of the word, performance. This, we have seen, was also part of the agenda which Pope Benedict XVI initiated. Those who quietly criticized the Pope for bringing old vestments out of mothballs, old furnishings out of the storerooms, and deepening the dignity of ceremonial celebration by reverting to earlier practices, would nonetheless have to admit that things were thereby done more decently and with more attentiveness. Like Mannion, Benedict XVI asked for just this attention to doxological detail in the celebration of the *Novus Ordo* – as he made clear in *The Spirit of the Liturgy*, in the 2005 Christmas address to the Curia, in *Sacramentum Caritatis*, and in the explanatory letter on *Summorum Pontificum*. No one can know any pope's mind intimately, but the signs were that he began with 'recatholicizing the reform' – and then began working towards a significant 'reform of the reform'. The signs too are that, though he has not been concerned with recovering pre-conciliar liturgy for its own sake – 'reform of the reform' is planning the future and not recovering the past – he has seen how desirable it is, amidst the diversity of a pluriform Church, and essential it might be, to bring about reconciliation with the Lefebvrist lobby, to encourage and maintain thriving traditionalist communities, whether parishes, priestly societies or religious houses. All of this is, one might say, the outworking of the hermeneutic of continuity, rather than of the hermeneutic of rupture.

The Australian, Fr Brian Harrison OS, sets out his agenda for a 'reform of the reform':[92] there is an urgent need to recover belief in the

91 See Chapter 3, pp. 82f.

92 B. W. Harrison OS, 'The Postconciliar Eucharistic Liturgy: Planning a Reform of the Reform', an address to the St Thomas Aquinas Society Eucharistic Conference, Colorado Springs, 26 March 1995 and printed in editions of *Adoremus* Bulletin serially from

Real Presence: 'disbelief ... increases in direct proportion to the proportion of their lifetime in which the Eucharist has been celebrated with the post-conciliar Missal'.[93] This, in turn, tends to vindicate what was seen, at the time, as an intemperate outburst, the so-called 'Ottaviani Intervention'. Published in English translation in 1970 as *A Critical Study of the New Order of the Mass (Novus Ordo Missae)*[94] 'by a group of Roman Theologians', the short study – the length of an article – is prefaced by a letter to Pope Paul VI from Cardinal Ottaviani, then Prefect of the Holy Office. The argument is doctrinal: the new Mass is designed to suit Protestants, 'supper' and 'memorial' replace the unbloody renewal of Calvary; no distinction is made between divine and human sacrifice; bread and wine are spiritually, not substantially changed; the Real Presence is not mentioned; Latin is abandoned; the Orthodox Churches will be alienated and all defences of the deposit of Faith are dismantled.

After discounting a wholesale reverting to the pre-conciliar Form, Harrison backs what he calls 'the Gamber proposal', which was endorsed by the commendatory preface by the then Cardinal Ratzinger to the French edition of *The Reform of the Roman Liturgy*.[95] Following Gamber, he looks to a greater faithfulness to *Sacrosanctum Concilium* but by making smaller, mostly ceremonial adjustments to the *usus antiquior*: the 'noble simplicity' called for by *Sacrosanctum Concilium* could be achieved by always carrying out the Liturgy of the Word from the chair and lectern, avoiding the duplication of the *Confiteor*, simplifying the *lavabo* (shortening the accompanying psalmody), simplifying the signing over the elements, and, reducing the number of occasions on which the 'Last Gospel' is read, and reading it in English at the foot of the altar together with the Leonine prayers. More radically, he would seek to strengthen the pneumatology of the Roman Canon by including the phrase *Spiritus Sancti virtute* (by the power of the Holy Spirit) after *quaesumus* in the *Quam oblationem* and say or sing the doxology of the Canon aloud. Harrison would reduce the number of readings, usually jettisoning the Old Testament reading but preserving

---

November 1995 to January 1996. Reprinted in Thomas Kocik, *The Reform of the Reform? &c.*, pp. 151ff.

93 B. W. Harrison OS, 'The Postconciliar Eucharistic Liturgy *&c.*', p. 157. He is working from a 1994 New York Times/CBS poll.

94 © *Lumen Gentium* Foundation, copies available (at least at the time) from the Latin Mass Society.

95 Klaus Gamber, (tr.) Simone Wallon, *La Réforme Liturgique en Question*, Éditions Sainte-Madeleine, 1992. The English edition is Klaus Gamber, *The Reform of the Roman Liturgy &c*. See note 7, above.

the psalm, and making the traditional Epistle-Gospel lectionary Year A of a different three-year cycle. He endorses the need for a homily, for the Prayer of the Faithful (though one might argue that the *diptychs* – the intentions for the living and the departed – are already properly read out in the Roman Canon) and for a Procession of Gifts at the Offertory. With regard to the vernacular, Harrison suggests that whatever is unchanging – the Ordinary – or said in a low voice – the Canon – should be in Latin, whereas whatever would be otherwise unintelligible – the Propers, the readings, the Prayer of the Faithful – should be in the vernacular.

So far, says Harrison, *Sacrosanctum Concilium* could have been implemented without the invention of the *usus recentior* as a distinct liturgical text. He considers its features – the new Offertory Prayers and the new Eucharistic Prayers – and its discarding or alteration of what amounts to 83 per cent of the collects of the *usus antiquior*[96] and the wholesale weakening and even jettisoning of themes of

> human weakness, guilt and repentance on the part of sinners, the wrath of God, hell, the souls in Purgatory, the Church's need for protection from her spiritual and temporal enemies.[97]

The same point was made gently but forcefully by Lauren Pristas in her lecture 'The Post-Vatican II Revision of the Lenten Collects' at the 2005 conference of the Society of St Catherine of Siena in Oxford.[98] Harrison concludes that there had been no need for a wholesale revision of Propers. And, as one might expect, he argues for *ad orientem* celebration and the recovery and safeguarding of the tradition of sacred music, which the Second Vatican Council – and all official pronouncements – have called for.

---

96 In a footnote, see Thomas Kocik, *The Reform of the Reform? &c.*, p. 189, Harrison cites Anthony Cekada, *The Problems with the Prayers of the Modern Mass*, Rockford, Ill: TAN Books, 1991, p. 9, whose calculation this is. There is further information on Cekada's findings on p. 49; of 1,182 orations in the 1962 Missal, 'about 760 were omitted. Of the remaining third, over half were altered before being introduced into the Missal of 1970. Thus only 17% of the traditional orations made it untouched into the 1970 Missal.'

97 B. W. Harrison OS, 'The Postconciliar Eucharistic Liturgy &c.', p. 189.

98 Published in Uwe Michael Lang (ed.), *Ever Directed Towards the Lord: The Love of God in the Liturgy of the Eucharist, Past, Present, and Hoped For*, London: T&T Clark, 2007. Other similar articles by Lauren Pristas are listed in a footnote of Laurence P. Hemming, *Worship as a Revelation*, p. 22. See also Chapter 3, p. 101.

A Programme for Future Reform

Earlier we mentioned Aidan Nichols's vision of the 'convergence of the two rites, the classical and the modern',[99] by incorporating into the *usus antiquior* the fuller cycle of readings, the new Prefaces, the practice of concelebration, where appropriate, and the administration of the chalice to the laity. That does not mean that Nichols would not prefer the post-conciliar Missal which 'contains more features of Oriental provenance than the Roman rite has ever known historically (and notably in the new anaphoras)' to be sidelined. He has proposed that it be used for areas whose culture is very different from the Latin West – mentioning India as an example – and for ecumenical purposes (especially for the reconciliation of those Anglicans and Lutherans not accustomed to 'a high ritual form of worship'). Thirdly, he has recognized, without passing judgement, that there would be 'parishes and religious communities of the Latin church that do not wish to recover the historical and spiritual patrimony of the Latin rite in a fuller form'.[100] Nichols was writing this more than a decade before *Summorum Pontificum*: his position nowadays, one imagines, might be that he would prefer the *forma extraordinaria* to become the *forma ordinaria* and the *forma ordinaria* the *forma extraordinaria*. The *usus antiquior* thus would be the 'ordinary form' for Catholics and the *usus recentior* the 'extraordinary form'.

Equally, setting a more modest goal, we could see the modification of the *usus recentior* – which may be politically the easier task – by a series of small but significant changes. One might be re-introduction of the pre-conciliar *temporale*, slightly modified, restoring Sundays after Epiphany, the '–*gesima*' Sundays, a fully explicit Passiontide, Ascensiontide, the Pentecost octave, and Sundays after Pentecost. The post-conciliar *sanctorale* scheme, however, would be maintained, though feasts, presently superseded by green Sundays, would no longer be superseded. (How else do most people ever encounter the apostles?)[101] Along with this re-arrangement, many, if not most, of the pre-conciliar orations might be introduced, and something like Brian Harrison's lectionary proposal, with the ancient Sunday eucharistic lectionary as the prime scheme[102] and alternative and supplementary schemes, as

---

99 See above, p. 59.

100 Aidan Nichols, *Looking at the Liturgy*, pp. 121f.

101 As Fr Jonathan Robinson observes, 'It is at Sunday Mass that the vast majority of practising Catholics encounter the Church', in *The Mass and Modernity &c.*, p. 53.

102 Klaus Gamber, *The Reform of the Roman Liturgy &c.*, p. 72ff, reminds us of the

approved by local authority, used in appropriate circumstances. The present weekday lectionary would work with that, and the mandate of *Sacrosanctum Concilium* duly fulfilled.[103] Diligent pastors already discern whether a particular midweek congregation is able to enter into the continuous reading of the Scriptures or whether readings appropriate to a memoria or votive, or for a special group, should be chosen instead. They also are encouraged to re-arrange ferial readings within the week to ensure that 'the entire week's plan of readings' is coherent. It was perhaps beyond the scope of the *General Instruction* to suggest that the faithful should be encouraged to maintain the daily reading plan at home when they are unable to be at Mass.[104]

The orientation of the Mass, geographically, would be primarily an architectural and aesthetic decision: fighting the architecture of a church, the liturgy will lose, as it so very often does. The Anglican bishop David Stancliffe, himself Chairman of the Church of England Liturgical Commission which produced Common Worship in the late 1990s, and brother of a distinguished cathedral architect, does a 'Cook's Tour' of church architecture, in engagingly purple prose. He takes us from the cosy interiors of the domestic churches, to the post-Constantinian basilicas, 'where the place of the Procurator and his assessors is taken by the bishop and his clergy', and 'the table with the depositions and the bust of the emperor (before whom a pinch of incense was required as a sign of allegiance) became the altar' to the Northern shrine churches, expressing 'the primeval conflict of light and dark, the twining sea-serpents against the ark of faith'. We move to the 'skeletal rib-vaults of late gothic': in the 'darkened interiors of these spiky and pinnacled exteriors, the distant and vengeful God, apparently seeking his pound of flesh, seemed remote'. Off to the 'jelly-mould churches of the early Italian renaissance with their mathematically perfect forms derived from the Platonic rules of harmony'. Then 'in the Protestant world, sober clarity and severe reason banish not only exuberant excess but all suspicion of emotion in their appeal to the intellect'. Meanwhile

---

ancient lectionaries, including the *Liber comitis*, an Epistolary probably compiled by St Jerome.

103 'The treasures of the bible are to be opened up more lavishly, so that richer fare may be provided for the faithful at the table of God's word. In this way a more representative portion of the holy scriptures will be read by the people in the course of a prescribed number of years' (para. 51).

104 See para. 338 of the 2002 *General Instruction of the Roman Missal* (GIRM), published by the Catholic Bishops' Conference of England and Wales in 2005, London: Catholic Truth Society.

when Palladio begins . . . to link a nave – an auditorium – to a circular form, introducing the proscenium arch and perspective ticks of the opera house, we realize that the liturgy is grand opera, a performance into which – though as spectators – we are skilfully drawn.

There is, of course, quite a bit more to complete the tour – Laud and Wren, the rococo and the neo-gothic – but that is enough to remind us of the variety of contexts and the different social and theological agendas, and more than enough to remind us of the folly of treating every church as if it were England's Liverpool Metropolitan Cathedral, 'the most thoroughgoing of the circular/Body-of-Christ type buildings'. 'For all the warmth of the Body of Christ model', says Stancliffe, 'nothing is so exclusive as the inward look of the closed ring.'[105]

Instead of the closed circle of immanent liturgy, the practice encouraged by Pope Benedict, is to make the crucifix the central focus.[106] Thus, *versus populum*, the priest would need to be standing under a Calvary at a Calvary altar, or in front of what in English usage is called the 'retable',[107] but not obscuring the crucifix – yes, since 2002 it must be a crucifix[108] – and candles.[109] Many, if not most celebrations, would be *ad orientem*, but with the Liturgy of the Word almost always from chair and lectern, a practice cautiously endorsed by Gamber,[110] only half the celebration would be sited at the altar. Uwe Michael Lang considers this proposal and endorses it, mentioning its explicit approval by the Congregation for Divine Worship and the Discipline of the Sacraments who take the view that [though]

---

105 David Stancliffe, 'Creating Sacred Space', in David Brown and Ann Loades (eds), *The Sense of the Sacramental: Movement and Measure in Art and Music, Place and Time*, London: SPCK, 1995, pp. 49ff. For a more detailed survey, see David Stancliffe, *The Lion Companion to Church Architecture*, Oxford: Lion Hudson, 2008.

106 It is not ideal, however, if the priest is facing the crucifix and facing the people too: the people are gathered round the cross but they are, in that circumstance, behind the crucified. Perhaps this arrangement will prove to have been a transitional stage between the priest facing West and everyone facing East.

107 'Retable' in continental usage refers to what the English call a 'reredos', an elaborate carved or painted backdrop to the altar.

108 The 2002 *General Instruction of the Roman Missal* (GIRM), paras. 117, 308, unlike earlier versions, now says that on or close to the altar, there is to be a cross with a figure of Christ crucified.

109 This practice, replacing the use of a free-standing nave altar in front of the high altar, was introduced in Westminster Cathedral, London, for the 2009 installation of Archbishop Vincent Nichols.

110 Gamber (see *The Reform of the Roman Liturgy &c.*, p. 52) points out that, in many churches, the 'chair' already exists within the '*sedilia*'. *Pace* Gamber, the *sedilia* will not always be the best place, strategically, from which to preside over the Liturgy of the Word.

the arrangement of the altar *versus populum* is certainly a desideratum of the current liturgical legislation . . . [t]he principle of there being only one altar [*unicità dell'altare*] is theologically more important than the practice of celebrating facing the people. [111]

Gamber makes the point too that the Prayer of the Faithful (of which he approves) should be said with the priest at the altar, and with priest and people facing East, as on Good Friday.[112] Louis Bouyer had made much the same point.[113] And one would make a similar point about the introduction of the Peace, where that happens at the beginning of the Liturgy of the Eucharist, as it does in the Ambrosian rite, as it does in modern Anglican liturgy, and may well do eventually in the Roman rite.[114] The distribution of Holy Communion is a not an entirely practical question and, clearly, where altar rails exist and kneeling is possible and numbers allow, traditional practice should be restored. There are, of course, circumstances – an international Mass, for example – where queuing and standing to receive is more practicable.

We are very much in the area of aesthetics still, and it has to be said that a return to the baroque is neither possible nor desirable. Gamber says that 'most people in our time cannot relate to the liturgical forms of the baroque'.[115] Nostalgia for the 1950s, for the heyday of popular pre-conciliar Catholicism or for the glories of Anglo-Catholicism, which for a time seemed set to dominate the Church of England at least, if not much of the Anglican Communion, should not mean that liturgy necessarily needs to rediscover a 'retro-' style. There needs to be some ceremonial flexibility, so that appropriate liturgies, for appropriate occasions, are celebrated in ways appropriate to the building, congregation and setting, without compromising an agreed symbology. The Church will not disintegrate if – here – there is a *Missa solem-*

---

111 See *Congregatio de Culto Divino et Disciplina Sacramentorum*, 'Editoriale: Pregare "*ad orientem versus*"', *Notitiae* 29 (1993):245–9. See also Uwe Michael Lang, *Turning Towards the Lord &c.*, pp. 123f.

112 Klaus Gamber, *The Reform of the Roman Liturgy &c.*, p. 53.

113 L. Bouyer, *Liturgy and Architecture*, Indiana: University of Notre Dame Press, 1967, pp. 103f., cited by Uwe Michael Lang, *Turning Towards the Lord &c.*, p. 122.

114 *Sacramentum Caritatis* has this footnote:

150. Taking into account ancient and venerable customs and the wishes expressed by the Synod Fathers, I have asked the competent curial offices to study the possibility of moving the sign of Peace to another place, such as before the presentation of the gifts at the altar. To do so would also serve as a significant reminder of the Lord's insistence that we be reconciled with others before offering our gifts to God (cf. Mt 5:23 ff.); cf. *Propositio* 23.

115 Klaus Gamber, *The Reform of the Roman Liturgy &c.*, pp. 52 and 87.

nis, a 'High Mass' *ad orientem*, with three sacred ministers, a burse, a veil and a maniple, a silent canon said under cover of Renaissance polyphony; whereas – there – we find a concelebrated Mass, with priest fully vested, and concelebrants in matching plain albs and stoles, a free-standing altar with simple accoutrements, and a little communal plain-song, or simple modern setting of the Ordinary.

If ceremonial is largely a matter of aesthetics, it is not entirely so. We must illuminate and enable – and not disguise and disable – the insight of St Thomas Aquinas that it is Christ

> who is the true priest, who offered himself on the altar of the cross, and by whose power his own body is consecrated daily on the altar. And yet, because he was not to remain bodily present to all the faithful, he chose ministers, that through them he might give that same body to the faithful.[116]

The problem with much contemporary liturgy is, of course, its ability to disguise the immensity of what, in more senses than one, is on offer and its sheer banality – a banality which directly undercuts the solemnity it proclaims. To the question 'What happens at Mass?' it is often too easy to say 'Nothing much'. To risk a pun, every celebration needs to be both extraordinary and ordinary. Bishop Peter J. Elliott has been one who has fought hard for decency and dignity, tradition and transcendence in the celebration of the *Missa normativa*.[117]

The Question of Use

As for the question of Use – of rite, as differentiated from ceremony – one might say that, despite the anxieties of Cardinal Ottaviani and his contemporaries, despite Brian Harrison's anxieties around the findings of the 1994 New York Times/CBS poll on declining belief in the Real

---

116 *Summa contra Gentiles* IV, chap. 76. See Peter A. Kwasniewski, 'St Thomas on Eucharistic Ecstasy', in James G. Leachman OSB (ed.), *The Liturgical Subject: Subject, Subjectivity and the Human Person in Contemporary Liturgical Discussion and Critique*, London: SCM Press, 2008, p. 157.

117 Mgr Elliott explains his decision to write *Ceremonies of the Modern Roman Rite*, San Francisco: Ignatius Press 1995; *Ceremonies of the Liturgical Year*, San Francisco: Ignatius Press, 2002; and *Liturgical Question Box*, San Francisco: Ignatius Press, 1998 in 'A Question of Ceremonial', in Thomas Kocik, *The Reform of the Reform? &c.*, pp. 257ff. The Catholic Bishops' Conference of England and Wales produced *Celebrating the Mass: A Pastoral Introduction*, London: Catholic Truth Society, 2005.

Presence,[118] poor catechesis and lumpen ceremonial have probably done more damage than the actual text of the *Missa normativa*. It would be good to lighten the lectionary load a little. It would be easy to re-incorporate the *Veni Sanctificator omnipotens* (Come, almighty Sanctifier) into the Offertory and – less radical than Harrison's suggestion of adding *Spiritus Sancti virtute* (by the power of the Holy Spirit) after *quaesumus* in the Roman Canon.[119] When said aloud, as it would be at celebrations without music, this prayer of invocation would increase people's awareness and understanding of the sovereign action of the Holy Spirit blessing the sacrifice. Similarly the *Suscipe sancta Trinitas* (Receive, Holy Trinity), the climactic prayer of the Gallican Offertory Prayers in the 'extraordinary form' could easily be added, and similarly said aloud. The issue of dramatic displacement – whereby some say that words like 'sacrifice', 'victim', 'unspotted host' should not be used before the Eucharistic Prayer – is quite simply answered: in the 'Great Entrance' in the Byzantine Liturgy at the beginning of the Liturgy of the Faithful, the elements themselves – as yet unconsecrated – are venerated as the eucharistic gifts. Here, in a sense, is the triumphal entry into Jerusalem, 'invisibly escorted by the angelic orders', as the Cherubic hymn in the Divine Liturgy of St John Chrysostom has it. We must proceed not only to the Upper Room but to Calvary, and not only to the Paschal Sacrifice but to the (self)-offering of the High Priest on the Day of Atonement. We must press on towards the welcome of the Risen and Ascended Lord who beckons us, saying 'blessed are those called to the Supper of the Lamb'. As Cardinal Schönborn puts it, 'the whole liturgy is celebrated *obviam Sponso*, facing the Bridegroom'.[120]

One of the ways of defusing the battle between Extraordinary and Ordinary would be to make the Gallican Offertory Prayers an alternative to the *berakoth* prayers, derived from the Jewish *kiddush* – the provision of the *Novus Ordo*. This alternative[121] – perhaps incorporating, as we have suggested, the *Veni Sanctificator omnipotens* (Come, almighty Sanctifier) and the *Suscipe sancta Trinitas* (Receive, Holy Trinity) into the simpler set of prayers – could be managed whatever

---

118 See footnote 93, above.

119 See above, p. 64.

120 Cited in Uwe Michael Lang, *Turning Towards the Lord &c.*, p. 102. Cardinal Schönborn's thought is developed in (tr.) John Saward, *Loving the Church: Spiritual Exercises Preached in the Presence of Pope John Paul II*, San Francisco: Ignatius Press, 1998, pp. 203ff.

121 Alternatives are a feature of the *Novus Ordo*: there is more than one Penitential Rite and a choice of Eucharistic Prayers.

decisions were taken about which should be used when.[122] Either of the sets would work aloud and both would be mandated to be said quietly if the *offertorium* were being sung. There could be similar discretion over the other prayers the priest says quietly during the rite.

Perhaps the largest ritual change might be to try to suggest more insistently – careful reading of the rubrics tells us this already – that neither the Second (because of its doctrinal understatement) nor the Fourth Eucharistic Prayer (because of its invariable Preface) is suitable for Sundays and solemnities,[123] and that the Roman Canon should be used, at least when there is a variable *Communicantes* prescribed, or the name of the saint whose feast is being kept is included in the lists of saints and martyrs. The burden of the longer Canon might be off-set, as mentioned earlier, by omitting the Prayer of the Faithful, except, perhaps, at the principal Mass of the day, when the Canon may be recited silently in Latin, mostly under cover of a beautiful *Sanctus* and a *Benedictus* which functions as what, in French music, is sometimes called an *élevation*, an extended meditation on the eucharistic Presence. In plainer parochial liturgies, the Roman Canon in English would be the usage on 'gold' and 'red' Sundays and the Third Eucharistic Prayer would become – indeed, as it already is – a splendid vehicle for 'green' and 'purple' Sundays, and for midweek feasts.

Conclusions

Some tentative conclusions: the culture wars of contemporary Catholicism teach us that all is not well. The Catholic Church, because it is centripetal, is weathering the battle of post-modern fragmentation and the collapse of a shared meta-narrative better than some – the fissures do not run so deep as in the Anglican Communion, nor are there the ethnic divisions which have imperilled Orthodoxy (divisions which,

---

122 Adding one or both of these prayers would increase awareness that it is a sacrifice that is taking place, and not *Kiddush* before the Sabbath meal, or indeed *Kiddush* after the Sabbath Service.

123 For detailed discussion of the Roman Eucharistic Prayers, and the discussion of the way the shapes of Eucharistic Prayers II and IV were adapted to fit the doctrine that the repetition of the Lord's words at the Last Supper were what effected consecration see Enrico Mazza, *The Eucharistic Prayers of the Roman Rite*, (tr.) Matthew J. O'Connell, New York: Pueblo, 1986; and Cipriani Vagaggini OSB, (tr. and ed.) Peter Coughlan, *The Canon of the Mass and Liturgical Reform*, London: Geoffrey Chapman, 1967, and CCC para. 1353. It was Pope Pius VII in 1822 who finally, in a *sententia catholica*, confirmed that it is the words of Christ which consecrate (Archdale A. King, *Liturgy of the Roman Church*, London: Longmans, 1957, p. 323.) See also Chapter 1, p. 28, note 82.

theologically, Orthodoxy abhors). The progressives' alibis for the Church's decline are weaker than those of the conservatives, but the conservatives' remedies are drastic, even harsh. One is 'extreme traditionalism' – reverting to pre-conciliar Catholicism. Another is 'reform of the reform' – a radical overhaul, achieved perhaps by allowing the 'extraordinary form' to impact on, and win against, the 'ordinary form', thus producing, organically, and within what one might call 'a hermeneutic of reform' a convergent and robust synthesis. The third remedy, meanwhile, 'recatholicizing the reform', rather relies on the full implementation of an aesthetically satisfying, musically sophisticated, and rubrically correct version of the post-conciliar liturgy, and, often though this has been prescribed by Rome as the remedy, it has remained elusive for over thirty years. Tacky vestments and furnishings, mediocre music, and silly stunts – life-size masks, dancing deacons, or processions with focaccia bread held aloft for veneration: there is little sign yet, say the conservatives, that the progressives have got the point. Though it does seem that the energy of priests and musicians is most fruitfully, and least divisively, expended in 'recatholicizing the reform' – building, and remedying, and strengthening what is weak along the way – in the end there will need ultimately to be 'reform of the reform', a fourth edition of the Roman Missal, articulating and synthesizing an authentic organic development of the Roman Rite. Certainly 'recatholicizing' the liturgy has been the papal tactic if not the papal strategy, so those who work at this, at parish level, are in good company.

In the end there will be a place – there must be a place in a house with 'many mansions'[124] – for traditionalists, for reformers and for progressives, and something like the pluriformity of medievalism – before printing, before Trent,[125] before the Reformation, and before Pope Pius V – will emerge again, making the Church of the Counter-Reformation seem to have been unnecessarily and increasingly monolithic, as it lost secular power and aggrandized itself with compensatory spiritual power, as it battled against twentieth-century totalitarianism by strengthening its own centralized structures. The Second Vatican Council, and the essential continuity of the Church, pre-conciliar and post-conciliar, will be absorbed more fully into the bloodstream of a Church which will be leaner and fitter and breathe more easily and naturally, a Church which under Pope Benedict learnt once more its Augustinian theology and

---

124 John 14.2. Both Authorized Version and Douay-Rheims have the phrase 'many mansions'.

125 It was the Council of Trent which entrusted to the Pope the task of supervising the liturgy.

embraced a new, indeed Benedictine spirit. Faithfulness to the liturgy, and openness to the transcendent grace and power of God will lead to the springing up – and not just in new monastic communities but in population centres too (if not always in traditional parishes, whose structure will be increasingly hard to service) – of centres of holiness, of disciplined and radical Christian living, and a glorious offering of worship. Many of these monastic communities – as we have already seen – will be vigorously and winningly traditionalist and groups like the Society of St Catherine of Siena and CIEL (*Centre International d'Etudes Liturgiques*) will continue to point us to the treasure house of the tradition. As the Church learns to cope with new diversity – calendrical, ceremonial, and ritual – and as the culture wars become attentive conversations, the Holy Spirit will continue to till the ground, preparing for the endemic diversity of Orthodoxy and the Oriental Churches, with their chromatic customs, history, languages and tradition, to come once more into full communion, to share the vineyard with the noble simplicity of the Latin rite.

Writing before *Summorum Pontificum*, and therefore at a more uncertain time, but nonetheless reflecting where things still are, the Oratorian, Jonathan Robinson, had this to say:

> the present state of the liturgy reflects the alienation of modern Catholic thought and practice from the tradition of the Church; but now it also contributes to it. Modern liturgical practices are defective, and they are in place, and they reinforce people's understanding both of their faith and of how the faith should relate to the modern world. This means that the 'reform of the reform will be a long, hard business. How the reform will happen is at best opaque.[126]

The last word in this chapter, however, goes to the late Lucien Deiss, exegete, liturgist, missionary, musician and theologian, who, though thoroughly involved in the liturgical reforms of the last generation, and composer of some of the better, and yet ephemeral music which followed, looked to the years ahead and summed up what any combination of what Mannion called 'five different liturgical movements'[127] must take to heart:

---

126 Jonathan Robinson, 'The Mass and Modernity', his paper to the Society of St Catherine of Siena in Oxford in 2005, published in Uwe Michael Lang (ed.), *Ever Directed Towards the Lord &c.*, p. 48. (The title of the paper is the same as the title of the book referred to earlier in the chapter.)

127 See above, p. 48.

For the reform to be successful, there are two essential conditions. The first is a knowledge of the tradition, a tradition that is the wisdom of the past. The second is the peaceful observance of the liturgical laws presented by the Church. We have insisted on both. Tradition and obedience trace the only sure path to an authentic renewal.[128]

---

128 Lucien Deiss, (tr.) Jane M.-A.Burton (ed.), Donald Molloy, *Visions of Liturgy and Music for a New Century*, Collegeville: Liturgical Press, 1996, p. 237.

3

Fast or Feast

Blow the trumpet in Zion; sanctify a fast; call a solemn assembly; gather the people. Sanctify the congregation . . . Between the vestibule and the altar let the priests, the ministers of the LORD, weep and say, 'Spare your people, O LORD'.

Joel 2.15–16a, 17a

Blow up the trumpet in the new moon, in the time appointed, on our solemn feast day.

Psalms 80(81).3 (AV)

The decline of Christian faith and practice in the West is highlighted by the changing patterns of fasting and feasting, and by changes in the way the passage of the year is communally marked. The tossing of pancakes on Shrove Tuesday now relates only distantly to Lenten fasting rules and hot cross buns are on sale in the supermarkets all the year round. Microwaveable luxury foods are marketed as 'ready meals', and special celebrations – birthdays and Christmas – are characterized more by abundance and excess than by eating and drinking special foods. There may be a turkey in the oven at Christmas, but sliced turkey appears all the year round in the lunchbox. How long before goose and figgy pudding cease to be seasonal too? Meanwhile, as the supply of food has grown, and the choice increased, rules on fasting and abstinence have disappeared in the West almost to vanishing point. Perhaps this is an inevitable consequence of abundance. Certainly it is tragic – and ironic – that, when the affluent world becomes obsessed with slimming, the Church ceases to teach fasting, and, when the world is considering how to reduce its dependence on livestock, the Church ceases to teach abstinence from meat. There has been some theological controversy surrounding fasting, of which we shall make passing mention, but it is secularization and economic prosperity, and not religious disagreement, which have brought about what amounts to an entire change in the way we use food and drink, and the decline of families sitting down round a common table to eat a meal together.

Do we invent a new kind of fasting, a new asceticism, as the Russian theologian Paul Evdokimov (1900–70) has suggested? 'Christians of the present era could fast from conspicuous and thoughtless consumption, as well as from addiction to work and entertainment' indeed 'he proposed redistribution of global income as a contemporary form of asceticism, in the spirit of the desert Fathers and Mothers, fully consonant with the radical political criticism of Fathers such as John Chrysostom.'[1] That already sounds dated, redolent of the generation that was urged not to give up something for Lent but take up something for Lent. So, instead of a 'new fasting' do we retrace our steps and seek to recover something of what has been lost?

The Rhythm of Fast and Feast

Journeying back to the late medieval period in England, when food was much less plentiful, one would find fasting and abstinence throughout the forty days of Lent – abstaining from cheese and eggs as well as meat – and individual fast days on the so-called ember days:[2]

> the Wednesdays, Fridays and Saturdays after the feast of St Lucy (13 December), Ash Wednesday, Whit Sunday, and Holy Cross Day (14 September). There was also an obligation to fast on the vigils of the feasts of the twelve apostles (excepting those of SS Philip and James and St John), the vigils of Christmas Day, Whit Sunday, the Assumption of Our Lady (15 August), the Nativity of St John the Baptist (24 June), the feast of St Laurence (10 August), and the feast of All Saints.[3]

We have already quoted an Orthodox theologian and the fasting rules of Orthodoxy, still in force, are a continuing reminder of the rhythm of fast and feast which shaped medieval life in the West. Feast days

---

1 Michael Plekon, 'The Russian Religious Revival and its Theological Legacy', in Mary B. Cunningham and Elizabeth Theokritoff (eds), *The Cambridge Companion to Orthodox Christian Theology*, Cambridge: Cambridge University Press, 2008, p. 210.

2 Originally pagan feasts of sowing and harvesting, ember days have been associated from earliest times with praying for vocations and those to be ordained – labourers in a different harvest.

3 Eamon Duffy, *The Stripping of the Altars: Traditional Religion in England c1400–c1580*, New Haven: Yale University Press, 1992, p. 41.

still pierce the gloom of fasting seasons and the Wednesday and Friday fasts still lend rigour to most of the non-fasting periods. There are four fasting seasons in Orthodoxy,[4] and four non-fasting weeks.[5] The Eve of Epiphany, the Exaltation of the Cross and the Beheading of John the Baptist are also fast days, albeit with wine and oil allowed. Meat, fish, eggs and dairy products are avoided during the fasts and, on Wednesdays and Fridays, and on at least some days of the fasting seasons, wine and olive oil are also forbidden. Cultural influences are evident: it was presumably the livelihood of Greek fishermen that gave rise to the distinction between fish with backbones (which are included in the fast) and shellfish (which are not). Similarly the Slavs drink beer on fast days even when wine is forbidden and some Orthodox use oil from other sources when olive oil is forbidden. The eucharistic fast is maintained from midnight, as it was in the West until the reforms of Pope Pius XII in the 1950s, and there is a marital fast too – broadly speaking, the night before Holy Communion and on fast days and during fasting seasons (or at least during Holy Week). Though the rules are honoured as much in the breach as in the observance, and, in dietary matters there are the expected exceptions for the young, the sick and the old, there is nonetheless a profound sense of rhythm in the life of the Orthodox, maintained most fully in the monastic life. Even those who make little attempt to keep the rules cannot fail to be aware of the underlying rhythm of the Orthodox year, contrasting sharply as it does with the constant partying of secular culture.

Most rigorous of all for the Orthodox is the keeping of Lent, 'Great Lent' as they call it: we describe it here in its full monastic rigour. The week before Lent – 'Cheesefare Week' – is without meat, though eggs and dairy products are permitted, even on Wednesday and Friday. During the first week of Lent only two proper meals are eaten – on Wednesday and Friday evenings after the Liturgy of the Presanctified.[6] Thus the fast from Monday morning until Wednesday evening is the

---

4 For the sake of convenience and comparison we use here, where possible, the equivalent Western names for feasts and seasons: the Advent fast, the Lent fast, the fast (of variable length) between the day after All Saints' Sunday (see below) and the celebration of SS Peter and Paul (29 June), and the fast during the first two weeks of August before the Assumption (15 August).

5 Christmas to the Eve of Epiphany, the week following the Sunday of the Publican and Pharisee (leading up to Lent), Easter Week (called by the Orthodox 'Bright Week') and the week after Pentecost (called by the Orthodox 'Trinity Week'), ending with what in Orthodoxy is All Saints' Sunday. In these weeks there is no Wednesday or Friday fast.

6 The Lenten Liturgies of the Presanctified, with evening communion, require the fast to be maintained throughout the day until after communion, or at least from noon.

longest time without food in the Church year and on the Wednesday and Friday and for all weekdays of Lent, meat, fish, dairy products, wine and oil are forbidden. On Saturdays and Sundays wine and oil are permitted but the fast is not otherwise relaxed. In Holy Week, supper on Thursday should be the last main meal taken until Easter and, in honour of the Last Supper, wine and oil are permitted. The Good Friday Fast is the one fast kept even by those who have otherwise not been observant and a little wine and fruit is recommended for Holy Saturday to maintain momentum throughout the nocturnal celebration of Pascha, the Easter liturgy.

Why is this ancient rhythm still maintained? A deacon of the Greek Orthodox Archdiocese in America, an adviser on environmental issues to the Ecumenical Patriarch, has this to say:

> Orthodox Christians fast from all dairy and meat products for half of the entire year, almost as if in an effort to reconcile one half of the year with the other, secular time with the time of the Kingdom. To fast is not to deny the world, but in fact to affirm the world, together with the body, as well as all of the material creation. It is to recall that humanity is not called to 'live by bread alone' (Matt. 4.4) but rather to acknowledge that all of this world, 'the earth and all the fullness thereof, is the Lord's' (Ps. 23[24]).[7]

The Liturgy of Time

Alongside the rhythm of fast and feast, the state of the larder, the table, and the wine cellar, is the eternal feast – the marriage supper of the Lamb – celebrated and anticipated in the Eucharist. Alexander Schmemann draws our attention to the distinction between the Eucharist – 'all theological theories of the Sacrament agree that its meaning lies in the fact that while it is performed as a repetition in time, it manifests an unrepeatable and supra-temporal reality'[8] – and what he calls 'the liturgy of time'. 'The celebration of the Eucharist is placed within the framework of the liturgy of time, so that being neither bound essentially to time nor determined by it, it is a "correlative" of time.'[9]

---

7 John Chryssavgis, 'The spiritual way', in Mary B. Cunningham and Elizabeth Theokritoff (eds), *The Cambridge Companion to Orthodox Christian Theology*, p. 161.

8 Alexander Schmemann, *Introduction to Liturgical Theology*, Leighton Buzzard: Faith Press, second edition, 1975, p. 35.

9 Alexander Schmemann, *Introduction &c.*, p. 36.

In short, just as there is a tension between the secular rhythm of food and drink and the pattern of fasting and feasting, there is a tension between the secular calendar and the liturgical year, and between the Sacrament of the Eucharist – unrepeatable and supra-temporal – and 'the liturgy of time', a liturgy which holds the daily cycle of the Office within the weekly celebration of creation and redemption and the weekly cycle within the annual cycle of the liturgical year. Indeed, so varied is the Orthodox *Ordo*,[10] with its fixed and moveable celebrations, that one would have to live for over 250 years to find oneself repeating the annual cycle exactly in any one year.

In England it was over 250 years ago, with the introduction of the Gregorian Calendar,[11] that 1 January displaced Lady Day, 25 March, the ancient beginning of the year, as New Year's Day. 5 April, the end of the English tax year, continues to reflect the need to add on extra days to the quarter day of 25 March, days which had been thought to have been lost when people feared that the change from the Julian Calendar was shortening their lives by nearly a fortnight. Who now knows and observes the quarter days and their pivotal religious significance? Who, beyond the core of the Christian community, now knows and lives by the times and seasons of the Christian Year? There is an opportunity here for hand-wringing and lament: better to see how some reform and reconstruction might maintain the tradition more effectively, and even recover some lost ground. Meanwhile, a principle might be ventured: that if less and less is asked of those who practise the faith, fewer and fewer people will practise it, and the faith that they practise will also gradually diminish. That, at any rate, is a premise of this chapter and, as we proceed, it will rank as one at least of the explanations – amidst a great complex of explanations – for the decline of Christian faith and practice in the West.

Catholic, Reformed and Secular

Some of the decline we are charting has been brought about by the Christian community itself. What were understood to be holy days of obligation remain weekday holidays in formerly Catholic countries,

---

10 *Ordo* in the Orthodox Church means the 'definite regulations, according to an order or rite established once for all' (Alexander Schmemann *Introduction &c.*, p. 28). In the West it usually means the ordering of the Calendar for a particular year, including such details as when feasts are superseded by Sundays, when first Vespers is said *&c.*,

11 The Gregorian Calendar, introduced by Gregory XIII in 1582, was finally adopted in England in 1752.

and the attack of the Reformed religion on the cult of saints – and in extreme cases on the observance even of days like Christmas Day – led inevitably to most of the weekday holidays in the British Isles being mere 'bank holidays' and not holy days. In England Cranmer had flattened out the seasons – so that one day's liturgy was very much like another's – and he built his daily Office lectionary on the civil year. Working on the Ten Articles of 1536, the first set of Articles of Religion, Cranmer is reported as seeking to exclude, as a job lot, Purgatory, the observance of Lent and other fasts, the festivals of saints and worship of images.[12] It was about that time that, as Archbishop of Canterbury, he caused a stir by eating meat on the eve of a feast of St Thomas Becket.[13] For the reformers, true fasting was dealing with wickedness and oppression, sharing with the hungry, welcoming the poor and covering the naked (Isa. 58.6–7).

The vigils, fasts and days of abstinence began to find their way back into the Prayer Book in the Latin Prayer Book of 1560, but the table in the Book of Common Prayer (BCP) of 1662, the work of John Cosin, has had very little impact on how Anglicans have lived their lives,[14] except during the Oxford Movement revival of the nineteenth century, with its attempt to recover some continuity with medieval religion. In that secular but deeply religious country, the United States of America, the fourth Thursday in November is kept as Thanksgiving Day. Tracing its roots to a communal expression of thanks to God by the founding fathers, and timed to relate to the completion of the harvest and the onset of winter, the festival has transmuted into a joint secular festival. The same thing has partially happened throughout the West, and is continuing to happen, with Christmas and Easter: and it is notable that in the English language, unlike the Romance languages, neither 'Sunday' nor 'Easter' is a Christian word.

In addition to different theological assumptions, Catholic and Reformed, other factors have added to the complexity of the Calendar in English-speaking countries. One, to which we have already alluded, is the disparity between the Gregorian Calendar, used for both religious and secular purposes in the West, and the Julian Calendar, used in the Orthodox churches for deciding the date of Easter.[15] Though generic-

---

12 See Diarmaid MacCulloch, *Thomas Cranmer: A Life*, New Haven: Yale University Press, 1996, p. 153.

13 Diarmaid MacCulloch, *Thomas Cranmer*, p. 198.

14 The 1662 Table makes no suggestions as to how a Vigil, Fast or Day of Abstinence might be kept.

15 See the Appendix for further details of the different calendars and of the different methods of calculating Easter and of proposals for calculating a common date for Easter.

ally Eastern, the Orthodox now form minorities of significant size in Britain and North America. Not only is Easter usually on a different date, West and East, because of disagreement over what, for Christians, constitutes the Paschal New Moon, there is additional disparity between Orthodox (chiefly the Greeks) who use the Revised Julian Calendar – which, apart from the moveable feasts dependent on the date of Easter, is similar to the Gregorian Calendar – and Orthodox (chiefly the Russians) who retain the Julian Calendar, as used in Pre-Revolutionary Russia.[16] Christmas in Russia is celebrated 13 days later than elsewhere, on 7 January.

Another calendrical complexity is that the Catholic Calendar was revised in 1969. This was far from a purely Roman matter: some Reformed churches proceeded to follow suit, in slightly varying ways, particularly Anglicans whose calendars are versions of the Western Use. In England there is now the National Calendar of the Roman Catholic Church, a version of the 1969 Calendar which was agreed by the Conference of Bishops in 1993 and received *recognitio* from Rome in 2000. There is also the Common Worship (CW) Calendar of the Church of England (2000). Somewhere in the background, for Catholics, is the Extraordinary Form Calendar – that is the 1962 pre-conciliar Calendar – and, for Anglicans, the Calendar of the BCP. Whereas both the Anglican Calendars are fully authorized, there continues to be some doubt as to whether the Extraordinary Form Calendar would be integrated eventually with the 1969 General Calendar, and, if so, how. Other questions would be how and whether the National Calendar of 2000 and General Calendar additions from 1962 onwards might be integrated with the 1962 Calendar. The complexity is not quite Byzantine – a particularly apt word for the calendrical arrangements of the Orthodox world – but it poses some interesting questions.

Diminishment

Just as the rules on fasting and abstinence have gradually diminished, so the reduction of holy days of obligation has arguably contributed to a declining sense and understanding of what obligation entails. 'Obligation' clearly shares a root with 'religion', and the notion of *ligare* – to bind – is relational here and not merely about compulsion. What

---

16 For Russians the Gregorian Calendar is not only a papal imposition but a Bolshevik one.

seems to have happened in the Catholic community is that, once people noticed that other people were not fulfilling the obligation – Sundays or holy days – it became manageable to disregard the obligation. Something similar happened a little bit earlier amongst English Anglican churchgoers. The result is, first, a steep and massive decline in attendance and then, once the voluntary – almost supererogatory – nature of attendance becomes evident, the notion of 'obligation' – being 'bound' to do something – changes into something else. The underlying point, however, is that this process is hindered, not helped, by the reduction of the amount of obligation. There has to be a new, fruitful understanding of 'obligation' as mutual commitment, religious duty, what the Prefaces of the Mass call that which is *vere dignum et iustum* (truly right and just). Celebrating solemnities which fall on Saturday or Monday on the Sunday may be pastorally helpful where this is possible. Moving Ascension Day and Corpus Christi from Thursday to the following Sunday, for example, as the Roman Catholic Bishops' Conference in England and Wales felt necessary, is to risk turning celebrations into themes, and rendering Catholic witness less visible in a pluralist society than the customs of Islam, Judaism and other religions.[17]

Neither bourgeois respectability – which ensured good attendance in Reformed churches – nor the fear of hell fire – which is said to have ensured even better attendance in Catholic churches – still holds sway. The educated in Europe have largely abandoned religion as obsolete or unprovable, and those who seek self-improvement through spirituality of one kind or another see religious belief as a private, bespoke affair, albeit based usually on some residual Christian basis, part ethical and part sentimental narrative. The question of how this residual religion might be transmitted and sustained so that it continues to be ethically and emotionally load-bearing does not seem to be an issue which troubles most parents and teachers. Meanwhile, those who might have been made to fear hell no longer do so and those who once might have wished to inspire fear of hell no longer feel it right, or an accurate account of the workings of Providence, still to do so. None of these general and here unsubstantiated statements are likely to be challenged because the evidence for them is so pervasive.[18] Given the very differ-

---

17 From Advent Sunday 2006 the Holy Days of Obligation in the Roman Catholic Church in England and Wales have been: every Sunday, Christmas (25 December), SS Peter and Paul (29 June), the Assumption of the BVM (15 August) and All Saints (1 November). From that date the celebration of Epiphany, the Ascension and Corpus Christi were transferred to the following Sunday.

18 See Michael Burleigh, *Sacred Causes: Religion and Politics from the European Dictators to Al Qaeda*, London: Harper Collins, 2006; and, more briefly, Ian Linden,

ent picture in the United States of America, where churchgoing, though falling, remains strong, it remains to be seen whether the European experience is explicable in terms of the massive traumas of the twentieth century – the Great War, the rise of National Socialism, the enemy occupation of Europe, Soviet communism of the Stalin era, the death camps and the holocaust – traumas which were more local for Europeans than for most Americans. As Europeans begin to recover from all this, and just as they thought they were finally rid of organized religion (as if that caused any of the traumas we have described), the impact of Islam brings it back into the public square. It is too early to tell whether a full recovery will be marked by a resurgence of religious observance but, in an increasingly atomized society, signs are unpromising. The Enlightenment is not yet dead, though the shrill rhetoric of the secularists suggests that they are engaged in a struggle. They have yet to realize that key public notions, such as equality and liberty, have neither grown nor prospered independently of Christian values, and, though atheist philosophers, such as A. C. Grayling, may find them to be self-evidently desirable social values, there is no evidence that, if Christianity withered on the vine, these values would continue to be upheld by governments and societies. As Dinesh D'Souza puts it:

> [The] idea of the preciousness and equal worth of every human being is largely rooted in Christianity. Christians believe that God places infinite value on every human life. Christian salvation does not attach itself to a person's family or tribe or city. It is an individual matter. And not only are Christians judged at the end of their lives as individuals, but throughout their lives they relate to God on that basis. This aspect of Christianity had momentous consequences.[19]

Other societies have been admired but, D'Souza goes on to say, 'Socrates and the Hebrew prophets came to bad ends. They were anomalies in their societies, and those societies – lacking respect for individual freedom – got rid of them.' Nietzsche warns us, says D'Souza, 'remove Christianity and the ideas fall too'.

Global Catholicism: Diversity and Change since Vatican II, London: Hurst & Co., 2009, especially pp. 261ff.

19 Dinesh D'Souza, 'Created Equal: How Christianity Shaped The West', *Imprimis* 37, no.11, November 2008, pp. 1–5.

Renewal and Re-enchantment

The strategic response to diminishment is, first, a matter for missiology and so-called practical theology, but the renewal and re-enchantment of liturgy and worship are fundamental, whatever else is in the strategy. The liturgy is not only the shop window but the place of serious engagement: here is revealed the authenticity or otherwise of Christian communities, the life and lives they lead, and the worship and prayer they offer. Fasting and abstinence are marks of individual and corporate seriousness: not only that, as Aidan Nichols reminds us, mentioning observations of the social anthropologist, Mary Douglas, 'The Friday abstinence is the only ritual that brings Christian symbols into kitchen and larder', and, even more trenchantly, 'It is as if the liturgical signal boxes were manned by colour blind signalmen.'[20] There was a time when every schoolchild in Britain knew that Catholics did not eat meat on Fridays. They knew this because fish was invariably served up for lunch in school canteens. Few understand that abstaining from meat did not necessarily mean eating fish: it was not necessary to understand the custom, its detail or its meaning. Similarly going to Mass on Sundays and holy days of obligation was a mark of individual and corporate seriousness: many outside the Catholic community knew that to miss Mass deliberately was deemed to be a mortal sin – incurring the risk of hell fire – and they inferred, sometimes correctly and sometimes incorrectly, that the practice of the Catholic religion was therefore based on fear and not on love. As with the use of the confessional, few outsiders and not a few insiders understood that Faith always calls us beyond attrition – fear of God's disfavour – to contrition – sorrow motivated by love.

The question is whether all this cultural distinctiveness is dead and gone or whether anything of it – a new visibility – can be recaptured. Often the problem is not in what is laid down centrally – canons and rubrics continue to lay down requirements for fasting and abstinence[21] – but how these matters are interpreted locally. For instance, in England and America, bishops allow the substitution of some other form of penance for abstinence on all of the Fridays of the year, except Fridays in Lent. The problem is that 'some other form of penance' is

---

20 Aidan Nichols OP, *Looking at the Liturgy: A Critical View of Its Contemporary Form*, San Francisco: Ignatius Press, 1996, p. 72. See Mary Douglas, 'The Contempt of Ritual', *New Blackfriars* 49, nos. 577–8 (1968), pp. 475–82; 528–39. See also Mary Douglas, *Natural Symbols: Explorations in Cosmology*, London: Routledge, 1970, p. 42.

21 See the Appendix to this chapter, p. 102, for the text of the current Catholic canons.

hardly a visible communal act and, though many will conscientiously preserve abstinence on Fridays in Lent, there are not enough Fridays in Lent for this to have much impact. Obvious contrasts are provided by the Orthodox Churches, which preserve comparatively drastic fasting regimes – as we have seen – and, of course, by the observance of Ramadan by Muslim believers. A further problem (and this is in the canons and not in the local rules) is that abstinence rules in Catholic canon law do not apply to those under 14 or over 59 and fasting does not apply to those under 18 and over 59. A growing proportion of churchgoers, therefore, is simply too old to have to bother at all about abstinence and fasting. It is for the proper authority to determine what should be done but others are able at least to make suggestion. There are good reasons to maintain the fasting rule much as it is – after all, as Scripture makes clear, fasting is not a matter to be paraded publicly (Matt. 6.16–18) – but abstinence could be a sign not only of a confident and culturally distinct community but of a religion commending a lifestyle in harmony with creation. Children could remain exempt but adults, of whatever age, in reasonable health, could be invited to abstain from eating meat on Wednesdays and Fridays, except, say, in the Christmas and Easter octaves. That would be 100 meatless days a year, no hardship in the affluent West, and less than half the burden experienced by the Orthodox. Where this regime might provide hardship in the developing world, exceptions could be made, as recommended by local bishops. It would be a powerful Catholic – a powerful Christian – witness.

Diverse Calendars

The search for a more effective apologetic, a more united witness, might be assisted more by unanimity about celebration. Faced with different calendars, therefore, the first instinct is inevitably to try to reconcile them to produce one General Calendar, with local calendars – 'local' in the sense of both national and diocesan – making such adjustments as appropriate: St Piran may be unknown beyond the South West of England but there his feast will fittingly be a solemnity. If the systems East and West are too different, then at least a single Calendar in the East and a single Calendar in the West might still be possible. If the Catholic and Anglican systems are too different, then at least a single Catholic Calendar and a single Anglican one might still be possible. More than that, there might be contradictions and divergences which have occurred accidentally and which are patient of correction. Insights from the Orthodox East have been particularly valuable in this chapter but tackling the Eastern *Ordo* is beyond our competence and our frame of reference. We do note, however, the greatest challenge of calendrical reconciliation, the need for agreement on the date of Easter, and we would do well to privilege one or two features of older Western calendars which remain in the Eastern *Ordo*, most obviously the octave of Pentecost and the ranking of one or two days which are great feasts in the Byzantine tradition but only memorias in the West.[22]

Temporale

In the liturgy of time – the *Temporale* – tidiness is not a governing principle: there is considerable untidiness in the Christmas season which, if it stretches to Candlemas (2 February), has the theophanies of the Baptism of Christ and the Wedding at Cana, as well as other encounters with the adult Jesus, before he is presented as a small child in the temple. An 'Incarnation Cycle', from Advent Sunday to Candlemas, though it enshrines the narrative of the birth of the Messiah, cannot work therefore as a narrative sequence as well as an 'Easter Cycle', from Ash Wednesday to Pentecost. We shall come back to part of this problem – what to do about 'Ordinary Time' – time *per annum* – between Epiphany (6 January) and Lent. Lent in the Western Rite itself begins in a very untidy fashion. Septuagesima (the seventieth [day before Easter]), until it was abolished in 1969, was the beginning of certain Lenten customs (violet vestments, no *Gloria in excelsis* at Mass, no alleluia verses). Sexagesima, despite the name, was not ten days later but the following Sunday. Though Septuagesima and Sexagesima were inexact calculations, Quinquagesima, the Sunday before Lent, was indeed fifty days before Easter and Quadragesima, the first Sunday of Lent, was therefore another misnomer. Accordingly, the beginning of Lent, allowing forty days of fasting, came to be marked by Ash Wednesday. Even so, certain rubrics on Ash Wednesday in the pre-conciliar breviary suggested that the weekdays *post cineres* (literally

---

22 29 August, The Beheading of St John the Baptist, and 21 November, The Presentation of the Blessed Virgin Mary. 8 September, The Nativity of the Blessed Virgin Mary, a feast, is also ranked lower in the West. 2 February, Candlemas, and 6 August, the Transfiguration, are feasts of the Lord, and not solemnities, and are therefore also, arguably, ranked lower than in the East.

'after the ashes') were a pre-Lent period and that Lent itself properly begins on Quadragesima, the Sunday after Ash Wednesday.[23]

The sharpest divergence between the pre-conciliar Roman General Calendar and the 1969 version is the shape of Passiontide, Easter, Ascension and Pentecost. In the pre-conciliar Calendar, Passiontide begins on Passion Sunday, the Sunday before Palm Sunday, and lasts nearly two weeks. In the 1969 Calendar Palm Sunday is re-named 'Passion Sunday' and Passiontide appears to be subsumed under 'Holy Week' and last only one week. This is not quite the case, however: permission is given for crosses and images to be covered and Holy Week office hymns to be sung for what used to be the first week of Passiontide, and 'Preface of the Passion I' is used at the Mass during that week, the week leading up to Passion (Palm) Sunday. A similar piece of re-shaping happens with Ascensiontide: the Paschal Candle is no longer extinguished after the Gospel on Ascension Day, which, in some countries, is observed on the Sixth Sunday of Eastertide and not on Ascension Thursday.[24] The biggest change is that Pentecost Sunday – marking, as the name suggests, the end of fifty days – is now the final day of Eastertide and of the burning of the Paschal candle in the sanctuary, and does not have its own octave. The loss of the Pentecost octave in the West means that Trinity Sunday, the Sunday after Pentecost, comes as a stand-alone feast after a week, Monday to Saturday, of time *per annum*, that is, 'Ordinary Time'. Though the pre-conciliar books suggested that Eastertide finished with None on the Saturday after Pentecost – thus shortening the Pentecost octave somewhat – there is a sense that Trinity Sunday is the celebration of the fellowship of the Holy Spirit and the completing of what is made known to us of the mystery of the triune God and his invitation to share in his life of love and grace (2 Cor. 13.14).[25]

In any reconsideration of the hermeneutic of reform, the post-conciliar refashioning of the liturgical Calendar and year, and particularly of the Easter cycle, will inevitably figure. The case for the reforms of 1969 is made forcefully by Pierre Jounel,[26] who makes the point

---

23 *In hac et aliis feriis usque ad Nonam sabbati sequentis inclusive, omnia dicuntur ut in præcedentibus feriis post Septuagesimam, exceptis iis quæ hic habentur propria.* On this and other weekdays until None on the following Saturday inclusive, everything is said as in the preceding weekdays following Septuagesima, except those things which are given here as proper.

24 Ascension Thursday is the biblical forty days after Easter. The Catholic Church in England and Wales, at the time of writing, keeps Ascension Day on the Sunday.

25 Hence also the appropriateness of the Orthodox keeping the equivalent Sunday as All Saints' Sunday.

26 See A. G. Martimort *et al.* (eds), *The Church at Prayer, Vol. IV: The Liturgy and Time,* London: Geoffrey Chapman, 1986, p. 61.

that 'God willed *paschale sacramentum quinquaginta dierum mysterio contineri* ('that the paschal mystery be contained within the symbolic period of fifty days'), words from the collect for the Vigil Mass of Pentecost in the 1970 Missal, a collect originally in the Leonine Sacramentary. He goes on to quote the General Norms for the Liturgical Year and the Calendar:[27] 'the fifty days from Easter Sunday to Pentecost are celebrated in joyful exultation as one feast day, or better as one "great" Sunday'. That perspective sits slightly strangely with the one which says that 'Each [Sunday] is an Easter, each a feast',[28] a convention which renders invisible to the Sunday worshipper, however regular, most of the feasts of the apostles. There is also the strong possibility, pointed out by John Hunwicke,[29] that the meaning of *paschale sacramentum* here is the Easter sacrament of initiation: that is, that it is God's will that initiation should be confined to the fifty days beginning on Easter Day, with the Day of Pentecost – Whit Sunday – as the last flourish. There are other costs too in limiting Eastertide to fifty days: the destabilization of Ascension Day, the loss of the rogation days, the loss of the Pentecost octave, the loss of the Pentecost ember days, and some diminishment of Trinity Sunday. In short, some loss in fasting and some loss in feasting.

Where there are no Trinity ordinations, the loss of the Pentecost ember days is bearable: the week after Pentecost, in the Orthodox world, is, after all, one of the few non-fasting weeks. Often called 'Trinity Week' by the Orthodox, it is a week of joyful reflection on the mystery of the Godhead, empowered by a new awareness of God the Holy Spirit, celebrated at Pentecost. The joyful reflection which, as we have said, makes the Feast of the Most Holy Trinity apposite for the Sunday after Pentecost,[30] was no quick development: the Preface for the Sunday after Pentecost in the seventh century Gelasian Sacramentary celebrates the mystery of the Triune God, but it is not until 1334 – 700 years later – that the Feast of the Most Holy Trinity is declared a feast of obligation by Pope John XXII.[31] The rogation days – and the designation of

---

27 Paras. 22–6 and 45–6.

28 A. G. Martimort, *The Church at Prayer &c.*, p. 23.

29 http://liturgicalnotes.blogspot.com/ 'Paschaltide?' 1 June 2009.

30 The Orthodox keep the Sunday after Pentecost as All Saints' Sunday (see above p. 88) and that too provides an apposite focus: celebration of God the Holy Spirit leads us to celebrate the mystery of the Communion of Saints, the Spirit-filled community which transcends mortality.

31 The pre-conciliar liturgy continued to commemorate the First Sunday after Pentecost on Trinity Sunday and, until it was abolished, the Last Gospel on Trinity Sunday was accordingly Luke 6.36–42, the Gospel reading that would be used on the weekday ferias following Trinity Sunday.

the Sunday before the Ascension as 'Rogation Sunday' – are more of a loss than the ember days. This short season of rogation usually falls early enough in the year to counterpoint with harvest – rogation asking for a blessing on crops and fields and harvest a time to give thanks. Nor is rogation irrelevant to urban communities: here is a timely reminder for the needy to pray and to pray for the needy.[32] What is perhaps most concerning is the moving of Ascension Day. There may be communities for which Ascension is feasible only on the Sunday but, in the movability, there is a hint too of some of the reductionist theology of a generation ago: 'ascension' as a synonym for glorification, a theme and not an event. Luke–Acts gives us what is clearly an event twice (Luke 24.50–51; Acts 1.6–11) and is specific about the Ascension being after forty days (Acts 1.3). Moving Ascension to Sunday creates a further problem: Ascensiontide in the pre-conciliar liturgy, and the days between Ascension Day and Pentecost in the 1970 liturgy, are the quintessential *novena* of prayer. The liturgy is redolent with invocation of the Holy Spirit. To lose the nine days between Ascension Thursday and Pentecost is to turn a nonet into a sextet and to obscure the first novena when the eleven apostles, 'together with the women and Mary the mother of Jesus, and with his brethren' 'with one accord devoted themselves to prayer' (Acts 1.14).

The tidiness of the present shape – forty days of Lent and fifty days of Easter beginning with Easter Day and ending with the Day of Pentecost – might be an argument for staying with the reformed pattern: forty days reminiscent of Noah's flood (Gen. 7.4), Moses on the mountain (Ex. 24.18), and Jesus in the wilderness (Matt. 4.2 and parallels), and fifty days reminiscent of the year of jubilee (Lev. 25.8–10), the loops and clasps of the tabernacle (Ex. 26), and the length of vestibules in the temple (Ezek. 40). Would it not be enough to bring out Passiontide a little by making some of the Holy Week material obligatory in the week before Palm Sunday,[33] and fix Ascension Day to forty days after Easter? Re-incorporating the Pentecost octave would be less untidy, however, than it may first seem. There is great significance in the notion of 'the eighth day', as Alexander Schmemann reminds us.[34] Up until the time of St Basil the Great, Sunday was 'the eighth day': after six days of

---

32 The annual Christian Aid Week, collecting money for the developing world, happens about this time in Britain. In the modern Catholic Calendar, rogation days are replaced by days of prayer at various points in the year.

33 The distinct titles of *Dominica Prima Passionis* (First Sunday of the Passion) and *Dominica Secunda Passionis seu in palmis* (Second Sunday of the Passion or Palms) could perhaps be restored.

34 Alexander Schmemann, *Introduction &c.*, p. 62. Here he makes reference to J.

creation and a day of rest, the resurrection inaugurates the new and eternal day. There were eight people in the Ark, the First Letter of St Peter tells us, and Baptism too is salvation through water through the resurrection of Christ (1 Peter 3.20–21). The risen Christ appears after eight days (John 20.26) and this makes the liturgical octave fundamental not only to Easter but other feasts too. What is Pentecost but the eighth day after seven times seven weeks? What is the Pentecost octave but the eighth week after seven times seven weeks?[35]

We come now to the question of *tempus per annum*, time through the year – what is now called by Catholics and English Anglicans 'Ordinary Time'. The word 'ordinary' is here slightly misleading: it does not mean what the British call 'common or garden'; rather, it is time 'of the *Ordo*'. There is nothing ordinary about the week by week celebration of the paschal mystery: 'each [Sunday] is an Easter, each a feast', as we said earlier.[36] Here again the 1969 Calendar attempts to do some tidying up. The Christmas season ending with the Baptism of the Lord – the Sunday after Epiphany – and the Easter cycle beginning on Ash Wednesday, and with the complications of Septuagesima, Sexagesima and Quinquagesima swept away, we have a green season lasting for a period of weeks – a minimum of five and a maximum of eight. Beginning on the Monday after the Baptism of the Lord and ending on Shrove Tuesday, this period neither starts nor ends with a complete week. The second green season, beginning – arguably prematurely, as we have seen – on the Monday after Pentecost takes us up to week 34, a week which begins with the solemnity of Christ the King, transferred from its pre-conciliar position of the last Sunday of October to the last Sunday of the Church's Year, the Sunday next before Advent, as it often used to be called. Since there are different numbers of weeks in this second green season, depending on the date of Easter, the 1969 Calendar counts back from 34, with the Monday of Pentecost being anything between week six and week ten. It becomes important to look up what week this is and, if it is six, resume the Daily Office on week two, if it

---

Daniélou, 'La Théologie du dimanche', in *Le Jour du Seigneur*, Paris: R. Laffont, 1948, in which the 'numerous texts on the eighth day have been collected'.

35 Annibale Bugnini discusses the abolition of the octave of Pentecost in a footnote and says, 'The suppression of the octave of Pentecost followed logically from consideration of the inherent structure of the Easter season. Pentecost is the octave Sunday after Easter. An octave of an octave is illogical.' He adduces impressive support for the abolition of the Pentecost octave, from scholars, from Pope Pius XII's liturgical commission, and from historical debates as far back as the eleventh century, but his own judgement, as we have just quoted it, reads somewhat strangely. See Annibale Bugnini CM, (tr.) Matthew J. O'Connell, *The Reform of the Liturgy 1948–1975*, Collegeville: Liturgical Press, 1990, pp. 319f., n. 38.

36 A. G. Martimort, *The Church at Prayer &c.*, p. 23. See above, p. 89.

is seven, on week three, if it is eight, week four, if it is nine, week three, and if it is ten, week two, the only nerdish interest in calendrical intricacy required from the consumer.

English Anglicans have stopped short of entirely adoping this new system. Instead of the 34 sets of Mass Propers, as in the Roman Missal, and the rubric permitting any of them to be used on any feria, they have remained faithful to something like the 'after Epiphany' cycle and 'after Pentecost' (ASB) or 'after Trinity' (CW) cycle of the pre-conciliar Calendar. Anglicans have dissented from the Catholic Calendar in two respects here: first, they have sought to preserve a sense of Epiphany between 6 January (the Epiphany) and 2 February (Candlemas), CW deeming the latter to be a 'principal feast' (what Catholics would call a 'solemnity');[37] second, they have sought to count forwards from Trinity rather than backwards from week 34 as regards the Sunday orations, thus preserving many of the collects traditionally associated with particular Sundays in the BCP and the pre-conciliar Catholic liturgy. This has created additional complexities. For one thing, there is the period between Candlemas and Ash Wednesday – anything between one and five Sundays and, because there are sometimes less than three, the old sequence of Septuagesima, Sexagesima and Quinquagesima would not work often enough to be useable. Second, the Revised Common Lectionary, which, broadly speaking, CW adopts,[38] provides for the needs of a number of calendars and denominations and, though it follows the 34 week principle of the Roman Lectionary of 1969, 'users should follow one of the two numbering systems provided for the propers'.[39] In short, one needs to know which Sunday after Trinity it is and then, depending on the year and the date, which proper readings from the Revised Common Lectionary to select.

We have done some describing here of the problems of 'Ordinary Time' but, so far, not very much suggesting. It would be good to synthesize extraordinary and ordinary forms of the Catholic Calendar to the extent that Sundays and solemnities happen at the same time and are described in the same way. Preserving the old October date for Christ the King, for example, would be to lose the new insight that Christ, whom we worship as Alpha and Omega at the beginning of the Christian Year, is worshipped as Omega and Alpha on the last Sunday

---

37 Sundays are called 'of Epiphany' in CW, analogous with 'of Lent' and 'of Easter' in both the Catholic Calendar and CW.

38 It is a further complication that the Church of England's lectionary follows closely, but not entirely, the provision of the Revised Common Lectionary.

39 *The Revised Common Lectionary: The Consultation on Common Texts*, Norwich: Canterbury Press, 1992, p. 12.

of the year: the Kingship of Christ, instituted by Pope Pius XI in 1925, and celebrated in the old Calendar on the last Sunday of October, is not just a bulwark against bolshevism and fascism. Conversely the loss of the '-gesima' Sundays before Lent and the Pentecost octave seems a pity. Sundays *after* Epiphany and Sundays *after* Pentecost would preserve the notion that what we celebrate is in the light of God's self-revelation and in the might of the Spirit. Whatever the synthesis, there needs to be interchangeability, for Catholics – as CW already provides for Anglicans – between pre-conciliar and post-conciliar lectionaries, old and new, so that either system can be used with 'extraordinary' and 'ordinary' forms of the Mass. Then, as time goes on, the ingenious device of adjusting the middle of the lectionary cycle to accommodate a moveable Easter – with material for weeks six to nine expendable in any one year – may have created too much complexity. The older system of tailing off Sundays after Epiphany wherever you have got to by the Sunday before Septuagesima and tailing off Sundays after Pentecost wherever you have got to before the last Sunday after Pentecost, nowadays Christ the King (and borrowing the end of the Sundays after Epiphany cycle if there is insufficient Sundays after Pentecost material), will surely commend itself again, for calendrical purposes, though it may be combined, as in the pre-conciliar Breviary, with a system of readings for the weeks of the month from August to November, allowing, pre-eminently, the scheduling of the eschatological readings in November in the period between All Saints' Day and Advent Sunday.

Sanctorale

Less needs to be said about the reform of the *Sanctorale* – the saints' days of the Calendar. There were two major reforms in the twentieth century: first, the breviary of Pope Pius X (1911) radically changed the relationship of the Tridentine Calendar (1568) with the Liturgy of the Hours. The problem of the 1568 breviary, as Robert Taft puts it, quoting Joseph Jungmann, was that the *Sanctorale*

> was predominant, with the inevitable result that the small number of psalms in the common of the saints was repeated *ad nauseam*. Pius X attempted to integrate the sanctoral and temporal cycles instead of having the former replace the latter on most days.[40]

---

40 Robert Taft SJ, *The Liturgy of the Hours in East and West*, second revised edition, Collegeville: Liturgical Press, 1993, p. 312.

The Calendar of Pius V had contained less than 200 feasts. To that 145 were added before 1960,[41] most of them before the reign of Pius X. The Roman Martyrology contains many more saints than the General Calendar and the late twentieth century saw, under Pope John Paul II, the canonization of a galaxy of new saints and martyrs. The number of saints is not the issue: the issue is how they are celebrated and what impact those celebrations have on the rhythm of fast and feast. The Catholic hearing Mass on a weekday before the Second Vatican Council would usually be attending a celebration of this saint or that, with the Sunday Epistle and Gospel replaced by other readings, but those who used the breviary – mainly clerics and religious admittedly – would find that the weekly *cursus* of *psalmody*, decimated before 1911 by the frequency of feasts, ran smoothly after 1911. Lesser feasts would be celebrated by antiphons, collects, and commemorations, but the whole balance of *Temporale* and *Sanctorale* was adjusted and restored. As Laurence Hemming says, 'The effect on the actual printed book may have been minor, but what the faithful experienced week by week, what they heard, and what was actually prayed and when was dramatic.'[42]

The revisions of 1911 were just a start. The second major reform was the Calendar of 1969. The reforms of Pius XII[43] and John XXIII[44] had simplified the system of classification considerably. The obscure term 'doubles' – together with the phrases 'greater doubles', 'doubles of the second class' and 'doubles of the first class' – disappeared and the post-conciliar terminology appeared. 'Solemnities', 'feasts' and 'memorias' – with many of this last category optional – and a much simplified system of commemoration,[45] became the new pattern and, as with the breviary reforms a half a century earlier, the *Temporale* resumed its ancient importance and daily eucharistic celebration was much enriched by a weekday lectionary, with the Gospels read in a one-year cycle and the other books of the Bible in a two-year cycle. Here moreover was a new daily Bible reading scheme which was immediately accessible and relevant to the needs of lay people, whether they were at home or at Mass. No less significant was the revision of names and dates: names

---

41 A. G. Martimort, *The Church at Prayer, Vol. IV: The Liturgy and Time*, p. 125. Pierre Jounel (or his translator) makes a mathematical error here or perhaps there is a misprint. He says that, between 1568 and 1900 there were '145 more', but the breakdown by centuries suggests that there were 119 more before 1900 and a further 26 between 1900 and 1960.

42 Laurence P. Hemming, *Worship as a Revelation: The Past, Present and Future of Catholic Liturgy*, London: Burns & Oates, 2008, p. 126.

43 General Calendar of 1954.

44 General Calendar of 1962.

45 These are virtually confined to weekdays of Advent and Lent, where the collect of the saint replaces the collect of the day at Mass.

without historical foundation were excised and, because many dates
had been chosen for arbitrary or insubstantial reasons (whether by Ado
of Vienne in the ninth century or during the canonizations since 1568)[46]
there was a radical reordering which took the opportunity to conform
some dates in the Western Calendar to the dates of feasts in the East.
Some of the changes arose from the thinning out of the Lenten period,
so that feast would not occlude fast. Whereas earlier generations had
sought to fill up the months of Spring to alleviate the monotony of Lent,
the Calendar of 1969 sought to keep Lent as clear of other celebrations
as possible.

As in other liturgical matters, Anglican revision has followed in the
wake of – and sometimes anticipated – Roman revision. Thus the Church
of England's 1928 Prayer Book, though not authorized by Parliament,
introduced a scheme of additional 'black letter' saints, less important
than 'red letter days',[47] but attempting to meet the Anglo-Catholic need
for calendrical richness and to forestall the Anglo-Catholic tendency to
use the Roman Catholic Calendar. We have described further developments of this elsewhere,[48] in particular the piece of work done in
1957 in England in preparation for the 1958 Lambeth Conference.[49]
The Calendar of the ASB 1980 accordingly incorporated 20 famous
names as 'lesser festivals and commemorations', most of whom lived
their lives in eucharistic communities separated from the Holy See, and
one or two of whom were from pre-Reformation times but either had
not been (the Lady Julian of Norwich) or would not be (John Wyc-
lif) canonized by the Catholic Church. In other respects, the Alternative Service Book 1980 was content to follow the revised dates of
the Catholic Calendar of 1969[50] but the list is interesting too for its
omissions: as the Church of England's CW 2000 continued to increasingly shadow the General Catholic Calendar of 1969, other dates were
added.[51] Most startling was the incorporation of 15 August as the feast
of the Blessed Virgin Mary. Nothing of 'dormition' or 'assumption'
was said: the logic was that this was the traditional date for the end of

---

46 See A. G. Martimort, *The Church at Prayer, Vol. IV: The Liturgy and Time*, p. 126.

47 'Red letter days' in the BCP 1662 were called thus because they were often printed in
red and were thus readily distinguishable from 'black letter days'.

48 See Chapter 1, pp. 24–5.

49 See *The Commemoration of Saints and Heroes of the Faith in the Anglican
Communion; the Report of a Commission appointed by the Archbishop of Canterbury*,
London: SPCK, 1957. The 1958 Lambeth Conference (Resolution 79) allowed Anglican
Calendars to include such heroes of the Christian Church as Josephine Butler, Edward
King, and C. S. Lewis.

50 See the Appendix, p. 104.

51 See the Appendix, p. 104.

her earthly life and this brought the celebration into conformity with
the normal way of celebrating a saint's anniversary. What we notice
is that, as well as John and Charles Wesley and John Bunyan – who
were included in the ASB Calendar – quite a few Catholic saints are
included, notably from the post-Reformation period. To show a certain
independence of spirit, there are also one or two legendary saints from
the pre-conciliar martyrology in the CW Calendar, not included in the
General Calendar of 1969: Valentine (14 February), Crispin and Crispinian (25 October). The first shows deference to English folk religion,
the others to medieval religion: the legendary shoemaker Crispin, omitted by Cranmer, was restored in the BCP, and his brother, Crispinian,
was added in 1928.

It is at first sight extraordinary that CW should concern itself with
legendary figures from the Diocletian persecution, people who are
celebrated no longer in the General Calendar of the Catholic Church.
Then we look at some of the other names – January has Seraphim,
Vedamayagam Samuel Azariah, William Laud, Mary Slessor, Aelred,
Benedict Biscop, Kentigern, George Fox, Charles Gore, Wulfstan,
Richard Rolle, King Charles the Martyr – and a pattern emerges. Some
are national figures commemorated by the Catholic Church: Aelred
and Wulfstan are both in the Catholic National Calendar for England,
Kentigern in the Catholic National Calendar for Scotland. Others are
overseas saints or heroes of other denominations or provinces: Seraphim, Vedamayagam Samuel Azariah. Some are figures in English religious history: William Laud, Mary Slessor, Benedict Biscop, George
Fox, Charles Gore, Richard Rolle, Charles Stuart. Here is a sustained
attempt at building a Calendar of truly representative character with,
as further examination shows, some balancing of denomination ethnic-
ity and gender.[52]

There is the whole question of national and diocesan calendars: CW
2000 is not a General Anglican Calendar but a national, English version of the General Calendar. The CW Calendar includes, therefore, the
equivalent of the Italian saints of the past 500 years, St Vincent Palotti,
St John Bosco, St Catherine dei Ricci, St Lucy Filippini, St Leonard
Murialdo (to pick a few names from *Butler's Lives* for the first three
months of the year, most of whom are in the Italian National Calendar

---

52 The following names from the first half of the year give a fuller perspective: Janani
Luwum (17 February), Oscar Romero (24 March), Harriet Monsell (26 March), Christina
Rossetti (27 April), Pandita Mary Ramabai (30 April), Caroline Chisholm (16 May), John
Calvin (26 May), Joan of Arc (30 May), Apolo Kivebulaya (30 May), Ini Kopuria (6 June),
Richard Baxter (14 June), Evelyn Underhill (15 June).

rather than the General Roman Calendar).[53] In its 'Rules to Order the Christian Year', CW allows for 'diocesan and other local provision' to 'be made to supplement the national Calendar'.[54] There is no space here to compare Anglican and Catholic versions of the National Calendar for England: given the Reformed religion which has prevailed for half of the last millennium, there is an inevitable preponderance of early and late medieval English saints as against canonized saints from after the Reformation period. Broadly speaking, the Anglican Calendar deals with this by admitting its uncanonized heroes and the Catholic National Calendar by restricting severely the number of pre-Reformation saints: formal canonization was anyway unknown in the first millennium of Christian history.

The question remains as to how those who inspire contemporary Christians by their example – but have not been subject to rigorous scrutiny as to the holiness of their interior life – should be honoured in the Church. As we have said elsewhere,[55] commemorating such figures remains controversial amongst Anglo-Catholics because there has been no formal canonization process. But, as we also said, none of the collects for uncanonized saints invokes their intercession. CW, in any case, makes an advance on the ASB 1980 by distinguishing between 'lesser festivals' (printed in Roman type) and 'commemorations' (printed in italics). One might have wished[56] that 'lesser festivals' (what Catholics call 'memorias') had been restricted to those formally acknowledged – by acclaim or canonization – as saints. As it is, the celebration of George Herbert (27 February), Edward King (8 March), Thomas Cranmer (21 March), William Law (10 April), John and Charles Wesley (24 May), Josephine Butler (30 May), Thomas Ken (8 June), John Keble (14 July), William Wilberforce (30 July), Mary Sumner (9 August), Jeremy Taylor (13 August), John Bunyan (30 August), Lancelot Andrewes (25 September), William Tyndale (6 October), Henry Martyn (19 October), Richard Hooker (3 November) and Charles Simeon (13 November) remains controversial. All are 'lesser festivals', entitled to their own orations and liturgical colours. Amongst the 'commemorations' are many canonized saints, less immediately relevant, perhaps, to the

---

53 Michael Walsh (ed.), *Butler's Lives of the Saints*, Tunbridge: Burns & Oates, and North Blackburn, Victoria: Collins Dove, revised edition, 1991. A more recent resource is Michael Walsh, *A New Dictionary of Saints: East and West*, Collegeville: Liturgical Press, 2007.

54 See *CW: Services and Prayers &c.*, p. 530.

55 See Chapter 1, p. 19.

56 Indeed the author argued this point in the late 1990s on the Revision Committee of the General Synod of the Church of England considering the CW Calendar proposals.

English context. This ranking is not controversial since 'a commemoration may be observed as a Lesser Festival, with liturgical provision from the common material for holy men and women. . . . where there is an established celebration in the wider church or where the day has a special local significance'.[57]

Does any of this matter?

Apart from the issue of rank – 'lesser festival' or 'commemoration' – the CW Calendar has two further implications of interest and significance to the discussion of feast and fast. One is the method of commemoration 'made by a mention in prayers of intercession and thanksgiving'[58] and by using such collections as Robert Atwell's *Celebrating the Saints*[59] for the homily at Mass or in the recitation of the Office. This kind of commemoration enriches the cycle of feast and fast without necessarily making any claims about the sanctity of the subject or even the orthodoxy of his or her spirituality and theology. For example, Martin Luther King Jnr (who is not in the CW Calendar), a Baptist minister and pioneer of civil rights assassinated in 1968, remains an inspiring figure, despite his alleged sexual adventurism. To reflect on his example, on the third Monday of January, a federal holiday in the United States of America, is a godly thing to do. Like Origen from the third century, disqualified by self-mutilation, and Peter Abelard from the twelfth, disqualified by his tragic affair with Heloïse, Martin Luther King reminds us that 'all have sinned and fall short of the glory of God' (Rom. 3.23). If there were to be unanimity, Catholic and Reformed, about matters of celebration, fasting and feasting, Catholic and Orthodox would do well to insist on the rigour of canonization; the rigour of Orthodoxy is such that canonizations are rare – once or twice a century.[60] Equally, the Reformed tradition would want to commend ways of being enriched daily by the life, thought and writings of and about those who have not been – and are unlikely to be – canonized.

---

57 See CW: *Services and Prayers &c.*, p. 531.

58 See CW: *Services and Prayers &c.*, p. 531.

59 Robert Atwell (compiler), *Celebrating the Saints: Daily Spiritual Readings to accompany the Calendars of the Church of England, the Church of Ireland, the Scottish Episcopal church and the Church in Wales*, Norwich: SCM Press, enlarged edition 2004. Robert Atwell (compiler), *Celebrating the Seasons: Daily Spiritual Readings for the Christian Year*. Norwich: Canterbury Press, 1999, is a companion volume.

60 Seraphin of Sarov was canonized by the Russians in 1907 and Lydia (see Acts 16.6–11) by the ecumenical patriarchate in 1972. See A. G. Martimort, *The Church at Prayer, Vol. IV: The Liturgy and Time*, p. 123.

The other issue raised by CW concerns what it calls 'days of discipline and self denial'.[61] One might have wished for something more explicit about fasting and abstinence, especially in connection with Ash Wednesday and Good Friday, whose significance was highlighted better in the ASB 1980[62] and is more prominent in the Catholic canons.[63] The designation of 'the weekdays of Lent and every Friday in the year', and the excepting of feast days on Fridays outside Lent and during Eastertide seems to be about right, though the Catholic rule is that only on solemnities – including Easter Friday[64] – is the Friday abstinence rule lifted. The issue, however, is not what is said – though one might have hoped for unanimity on this to try to create a distinct culture of Christian living and lifestyle – but how it can be brought to pass. As we saw earlier, new Catholic flexibility in disciplines of abstinence and fasting has been ineffective in encouraging participation in these disciplines and there is little evidence that the conventions and rules of English Anglicanism over days of discipline have ever leapt off the pages of the liturgical books into people's lives.

Any programme of re-enchantment must recognize that the cycle of fast and feast, the daily living of the Christian life, will be like concentric ripples in a pool. At the centre – the smallest circle – will be the religious communities, living a well-ordered liturgical life of daily Eucharist and Office, fast and feast. Beyond that will be the parish circle: the parish priest and devoted laity living something like the community life in the parish, with daily Eucharist, Lauds and Vespers, fast and feast. Within this relatively small parish circle will be those whose lives are enriched and supported by being oblates, or similar, of religious communities. This circle should be inherently small – without being in any sense a clique – because, necessarily, the larger the proportion of fully committed, the smaller the proportion of less committed: 50 committed people in a congregation of 100 might do well to wonder why it is that the congregation has not grown to 300 with such a significant number of already committed.

Beyond the small parish circle will be the general congregation whose committed members participate in the liturgy on Sundays and solemnities and take some part in the daily life of prayer. It is this concentric ripple – the 'middle ripple' – where renewal is most urgently needed.

---

61 See CW: *Services and Prayers &c.*, p. 531.

62 See *ASB 1980*, p. 22.

63 See the Appendix, p. 102.

64 The Friday after Easter: the way that Good Friday is increasingly known in Britain as 'Easter Friday' and Holy Saturday as 'Easter Saturday' shows diminishing Christian influence and understanding, not that 'Easter' itself has a religious etymology.

The strength of this ripple affects the further ripples of occasional and very occasional attendance and participation – out beyond the ripple of Christmas, of baptisms, weddings and funerals,[65] to the ripple of those who have barely heard the story. It is here in the 'middle ripple' where the task of catechetics is most urgent, the need to develop effective and shared ways of participating in the life of prayer most necessary, and the challenge to model an attractive and alternative lifestyle, in harmony with creation, most challenging.

What we are seeking for the 'middle ripple' is not help with running the parish but rather what was at the theoretical heart of the 'Parish and People' movement in the Church of England of the 1950s[66] and what is so graphically described in Pope Paul VI's 1975 Apostolic Exhortation *Evangelii nuntiandi*:[67]

70. Lay people, whose particular vocation places them in the midst of the world and in charge of the most varied temporal tasks, must for this very reason exercise a very special form of evangelization.

Their primary and immediate task is not to establish and develop the ecclesial community – this is the specific role of the pastors – but to put to use every Christian and evangelical possibility latent but already present and active in the affairs of the world. Their own field of evangelizing activity is the vast and complicated world of politics, society and economics, but also the world of culture, of the sciences and the arts, of international life, of the Mass media. It also includes other realities which are open to evangelization, such as human love, the family, the education of children and adolescents, professional work, suffering. The more Gospel-inspired lay people there are engaged in these realities, clearly involved in them, competent to promote them and conscious that they must exercise to the full their Christian powers which are often buried and suffocated, the more these realities will be at the service of the kingdom of God and therefore of salvation in Jesus Christ, without in any way losing or sacrificing their human content but rather pointing to a transcendent dimension which is often disregarded.

---

65 Baptisms, marriages, funerals.

66 'Parish and People' was founded in 1949 in response to the Liturgical Movement in Europe. Prominent were Fr Gabriel Hebert SSM and Henry de Candole, later Bishop of Knaresborough. The aim was 'The Lord's Service for the Lord's People on the Lord's Day' as the main act of worship in each parish, to empower the Monday to Friday life and work of individual lay people in the world. Canon Eric James was Parish and People's best-known Director.

67 The encyclical is available (2009) at www.vatican.va

Therefore it is here, in this 'middle ripple', that the rhythm of fast and feast must be developed. A worked example of how much ground has been lost was made forcefully by Lauren Pristas in her lecture 'The Post-Vatican II Revision of the Lenten Collects' at the 2005 conference of the Society of St Catherine of Siena in Oxford.[68] Her conclusion was that

> hidden in the revisers' supposition that modern persons do not fast and their evident disinclination to urge fasting in the collects of Lent is a conviction that modern persons are somehow different from those of earlier generations – that is, their human nature itself is somehow different – so that the means which God gave earlier generations for obtaining great spiritual graces are not available to the modern person. This is patently absurd.[69]

To achieve again a purposeful rhythm of fast and feast means careful attention to and, following Pristas, some re-consideration of how Lent is celebrated and proclaimed, as well as the celebration of the Sunday liturgy week-by-week and the liturgy on solemnities – performance, practice and preaching – but, most of all, it means attention to the daily round, nurturing the life of prayer in the home and in the life of the individual baptized Christian. The cycle of fast and feast, the practice of daily prayer and spiritual reading, the inspiration offered by the life of the saints and the stories, and writings about those who have hero-ically lived the Christian life: this is the stuff of renewal. It may even be that it is what is on the family table – the shared meal, simple and meatless or festal and full-fat – and the giving of thanks beforehand that gives order to lives of prayer and service and links together those who, on fast and feast, gather round the table of the Lord, throughout the world and throughout the ages, until the end of time and the endless banquet in heaven, the Marriage Supper of the Lamb.

---

68 Published in Uwe Michael Lang (ed.), *Ever Directed Towards the Lord: The Love of God in the Liturgy of the Eucharist, Past, Present, and Hoped For*, London: T&T Clark, 2007.

69 Uwe Michael Lang (ed.), *Ever Directed Towards the Lord*, p. 89.

Appendix

I Fasting and Abstinence

The rules for fasting and abstinence in the Catholic Church are set out in *The Code of Canon Law. The Code of Canons of Oriental Churches* (for the Eastern Catholic churches) requires (Canon 882) that on days of penance the faithful observe fast or abstinence in the manner established by the particular law of their Church *sui iuris. The Code of Canon Law* prescribes (Canons 1250–53):[70]

- Can. 1250: The days and times of penance for the universal Church are each Friday of the whole year and the season of Lent.
- Can. 1251: Abstinence from meat, or from some other food as determined by the Episcopal Conference, is to be observed on all Fridays, unless a solemnity should fall on a Friday. Abstinence and fasting are to be observed on Ash Wednesday and Good Friday.
- Can. 1252: The law of abstinence binds those who have completed their fourteenth year. The law of fasting binds those who have attained their majority, until the beginning of their sixtieth year. Pastors of souls and parents are to ensure that even those who by reason of their age are not bound by the law of fasting and abstinence, are taught the true meaning of penance.
- Can. 1253: The Episcopal Conference can determine more particular ways in which fasting and abstinence are to be observed. In place of abstinence or fasting it can substitute, in whole or in part, other forms of penance, especially works of charity and exercises of piety.

Fasting generally means one full meal and some food (less than a full meal) at breakfast and either midday or in the evening, depending on when the full meal is eaten. Abstinence forbids the use of meat, but not of eggs, milk products or animal fat ingredients.

II Different Calendars

Most Greek Orthodox, since 1923, use the Revised Julian Calendar – which preserves the Julian Calendar version of calculating Easter, and moveable feasts dependent on Easter, but, for the sanctorale, adopts the secular (Gregorian) Calendar dates. This makes one unusual fea-

---

70 *The Code of Canon Law in English Translation*, London: Collins, 1983, p. 218.

ture of the Julian Calendar – the possible co-incidence of the Annunciation and Easter Day (the liturgy of *Kyrio-Pascha*) – no longer possible. There are Greek Orthodox ('Old Calendarists'), inspired by communities on Mount Athos, who regard the Revised Julian Calendar as a compromise with the West and the papacy, and form jurisdictions not in communion with the main body of Greek Orthodox.

Beyond Greece the churches of Constantinople, Alexandria, Antioch, Cyprus, Romania, Poland and Bulgaria are all 'New Calendarists'. Some Orthodox churches – notably the Russian Orthodox Church, the Orthodox Church of Jerusalem, the Serbian Orthodox Church and the Georgian Orthodox Church – remain in full communion with the Greeks and yet continue to use the unrevised Julian Calendar. Some 'Old Calendarist' bodies have permitted some of their dioceses or parishes, for practical reasons, to embrace the revised Calendar. Syria is notably a place where the smallness of Christian minorities has led to all the churches effectively adopting the Gregorian Calendar for the sake of Christian solidarity. The Finnish Orthodox Church follows the Gregorian Calendar.

III A Common Date for Easter

A consultation, meeting in Aleppo, Syria, 5–10 March 1997, and sponsored by the World Council of Churches and by the Middle East Council of Churches, recommended that all churches seek to achieve a common date for Easter, maintaining 'the Nicene norms (that Easter should fall on the Sunday following the first vernal full moon)', and calculating 'the astronomical data (the vernal equinox and the full moon) by the most accurate possible scientific means . . . using as the basis for reckoning the meridian of Jerusalem, the place of Christ's death and resurrection'. 'Nicene norms' refers to the decision of the Council of Nicaea in the year 325. Since the Council did not fix the methods to be used to calculate the timing of the full moon or the vernal equinox (21 March in the Gregorian Calendar and 21 March in the Julian Calendar usually relating to different full moons), the Orthodox Easter is as much as five weeks later than the Catholic and Protestant one.

Hosted by the Syrian Orthodox Archdiocese of Aleppo, the consultation recommended that the churches use the co-incidence of the astronomical, Gregorian and Julian dates for Easter in 2001 as a spur to seek agreement. This recommendation was endorsed on 15 May 2009 by an international ecumenical seminar organized by the Institute of Ecumenical Studies at the Ukrainian Catholic University in Lviv. Available online (2009) at www.oikoumene.org.

IV 1969 Feasts in the Calendar of the Alternative Service Book 1980

For these feasts the ASB 1980 was content to follow the revised dates of the Catholic Calendar of 1969: Hilary (13 January),[71] Timothy and Titus (26 January),[72] Thomas Aquinas (28 January),[73] Polycarp (23 February),[74] Perpetua and her Companions, (7 March),[75] Catherine of Siena (29 April),[76] Matthias (14 May),[77] Bede (25 May),[78] the Visit of the Blessed Virgin to Elizabeth (31 May),[79] Thomas (3 July),[80] Benedict (11 July),[81] Clare (11 August),[82] Gregory the Great (3 September),[83] Ignatius of Antioch (17 October).[84]

V 1969 Feasts in the Common Worship Calendar 2000

Feasts from the Catholic Calendar of 1969 added by CW to the ASB 1980 Calendar included: Basil the Great and Gregory of Nazianzus (2 January),[85] Anskar (3 February),[86] Martyrs of Japan (6 February),[87] Scholastica (10 February),[88] Cyril and Methodius (14 February),[89]

---

71 Instead of 14 January in the General Calendar (1962).

72 Instead of 24 January and 6 February respectively in the General Calendar (1962).

73 Instead of 7 March in the General Calendar (1962).

74 Instead of 26 January in the General Calendar (1962).

75 Instead of 6 March in the General Calendar (1962).

76 Instead of 30 April in the General Calendar (1962).

77 Instead of 24 February in the General Calendar (1962).

78 Instead of 27 May in the General Calendar (1962).

79 Instead of 2 July in the General Calendar (1962).

80 Instead of 21 December in the General Calendar (1962).

81 Instead of 21 March in the General Calendar (1962).

82 Instead of 12 August in the General Calendar (1962).

83 Instead of 12 March in the General Calendar (1962).

84 Instead of 1 February in the General Calendar (1962).

85 We use here for this list the nomenclature of the CW Calendar. St Basil the Great is 14 June, St Gregory Nazianzen (as he is called) is 9 May in the General Calendar (1962).

86 Not in the Roman General Calendar (1962).

87 Not in the Roman General Calendar (1962) and called St Paul Miki and Companions in the General Calendar (1969).

88 The same date as in 1962 and 1969.

89 Instead of 7 July in the General Calendar (1962).

Cyril of Jerusalem (18 March), Peter Chanel (28 April),[90] Philip Neri (26 May),[91] Ephrem (9 June),[92] Bonaventure (15 July),[93] Ignatius of Loyola (31 July),[94] John Vianney (4 August),[95] Dominic (8 August),[96] Maximilian Kolbe (14 August),[97] Monica (27 August),[98] the Beheading of St John the Baptist (29 August),[99] Jerome (30 September),[100] Denys (9 October),[101] Leo (10 November),[102] Clement (23 November),[103] the Conception of the Blessed Virgin Mary (8 December),[104] and Lucy (13 December).[105]

---

90 Canonized in 1954, Peter Chanel was incorporated into the General Calendar in 1969.

91 The same date as in 1962 and 1969.

92 Not in the Roman General Calendar (1962).

93 Instead of 14 July in the General Calendar (1962).

94 The same date as in 1962 and 1969.

95 Instead of 8 August in the General Calendar (1962).

96 Instead of 4 August in the General Calendar (1962).

97 Not in the Roman General Calendar (1962).

98 Instead of 4 May in the General Calendar (1962).

99 The same date as in 1962 and 1969.

100 The same date as in 1962 and 1969.

101 The same date as in 1962 and 1969.

102 Instead of 11 April in the General Calendar (1962).

103 The same date as in 1962 and 1969.

104 'Immaculate Conception' in the Roman Calendars: the Conception was in the BCP 1662 Calendar but omitted from the Calendar of the ASB 1980.

105 The same date as in 1962 and 1969.

4

Said or Sung

When the burnt offering began, the song to the LORD began also
. . . The whole assembly worshipped, and the singers sang, and the
trumpeters sounded; all this continued until the burnt offering was
finished.

2 Chronicles 29.27–28

The offering of sacrifice and the singing of psalms were interwoven in
the worship of the Old Covenant. This is the inescapable conclusion,
says the American musicologist and liturgist, Robin A. Leaver, not only
from such verses as Psalm 26(27).6 and Psalm 42(43).4 but from the
Dead Sea Scrolls, where, amidst a vast collection in the Psalms Scroll
(Qumrân Cave 11), 82 psalms are prescribed 'for the fasts and festivals of the year', and 364 as 'songs to sing before the altar over the
whole-burnt *tamid* offering every day, for all the days of the year'.[1] It is
not least because of a sense of cultic continuity that the Orthodox Liturgy is always sung and celebrated with ceremony. It sees itself as 'the
regeneration of the Hebrew cult within Christianity' where 'only by the
"transposition" of its basic categories – Temple, priesthood and sacrifice – was it possible to express and reveal the newness of the Church
as the revelation of what had been promised'.[2] It is in the West where
we see a spoken eucharistic liturgy eventually emerge and, inevitably,
with the growth of a spoken liturgy, the decline – and in modern times,
sadly, the decadence – of singing as the medium of worship. As we seek
the re-enchantment of liturgy, we take the view that music is not incidental to the Mass and that, with regard to both the Ordinary and the
Proper of the Mass – terms which we shall define as we go along – there
are traditions which are in urgent need of recovery and refurbishment.

---

1 Robin A. Leaver, 'Liturgical Music as Anamnesis', in Robin A. Leaver and Joyce A.
Zimmerman (eds), *Liturgy and Music*, Collegeville: Liturgical Press, 1998, p. 400.

2 Alexander Schmemann, *Introduction to Liturgical Theology*, Leighton Buzzard: The
Faith Press, 1966, second edition 1975, p. 80.

The Decline of the 'Missa Solemnis'

In the medieval period, the practice of priests each saying their own Mass daily meant that, beyond the cathedrals and monasteries where said and sung existed alongside each other, the *Missa Solemnis*, the sung 'High Mass', became the exception and the *Missa Privata*, the said 'Low Mass', the rule. There were many reasons for this development, unparalleled in the East as we have seen, and disowned by the Reformers, for whom private masses were anathema. Some reasons for the development of Low Mass (the daily spirituality of priests, pastoral urgency in the face of battle and plague, a form of eucharistic celebration which is neither complex nor prolix) are better than others (the multiplication of masses, the aggregating of stipends, an excessive fear of death and judgement). The *Missa Solemnis* – and its smaller parish cousin the *Missa Cantata*, the Sung Mass with simpler ceremonial – were not only eclipsed by the Low Mass but further diminished by political events. The dissolution of the monasteries in England in the sixteenth century was also, in the three or four dozen institutions with choral foundations,[3] the dissolution of much of the distinctive splendour of the English choral and musical tradition, its lofty filigree creating an ethereal timelessness so different from the linear, sparser, more contrapuntal continental style. Briefly resurrected under Queen Mary, what emerged under the benign ægis of Queen Elizabeth and the Stuart Kings, with many of the pre-reformation choral foundations re-fashioned for the purpose, was a Reformed tradition of cathedral music, of full anthems, verse anthems and Evensong canticles. It was enough to upset the Puritans but it was not the music of the Mass nor indeed of the masses, who for music, relied on the metrical psalms, as did the sixteenth-century *literati*.[4] Meanwhile, the spread of Protestantism made inevitable inroads on the Catholic musical tradition on the continent. In eighteenth century Germany the musical centre of gravity was Lutheran, sublimely captured in the cantatas and passions of J. S. Bach. Though France remained mainly Catholic, the French choral tradition suffered irrecoverably from the French Revolution and its impact

---

3 This figure represents approximately 25% of the monastic institutions. Of the remaining three-quarters, those which received incomes of less than £300 per year, we know little.

4 No publication in sixteenth-century England fared better than the Elizabethan *Whole Booke of Psalms* (1562). In the seventeenth century, metrical psalms were increasingly treated as a Puritan aberration by High Church polemic: see Beth Quitslund, *The Reformation in Rhyme: Sternhold, Hopkins and the Metrical Psalter, 1547–1603* (St Andrews Studies in Reformation History), Aldershot: Ashgate Publishing, 2008.

on Catholic faith and practice. Even in such Catholic countries as Spain and Italy, where there was more continuity, the *Missa Solemnis* hardly can be said to have flourished. Partly, it has to be said, the requirement that a Catholic should hear Mass on Sundays and holy days of obligation rendered the shorter Low Mass, available at several times in the forenoon, more convenient than the High Mass, particularly in the days when there was no general communion, except for the elderly, at the High Mass.

The 'Novus Ordo' Mass

Following the liturgical reforms initiated by the Second Vatican Council in the 1960s, the distinction between High Mass and Low Mass in the Roman Catholic Church began to disappear. For one thing, the new rubrics blurred the distinction by encouraging the use of music and incense at any Mass. For another, the practice of concelebration tended to replace the traditional hierarchy of three sacred ministers. The pre-conciliar reforms of Pius XII had introduced evening masses and abolished fasting before communion from the previous midnight, and the Mass without general communion largely disappeared. Also disappearing was the carefully prepared act of communion – with individual attendance at the confessional and the use of prayer manuals – an aspect of disenchantment which lies beyond our immediate remit here.

With the *Novus Ordo* – the 'new Order' – new settings of the Ordinary of the Mass, with vernacular texts, began to appear and there were, to begin with, some rather approximate paraphrases, set to little ethnic dance tunes – the 'Israeli folk Mass', for example[5] – and even, for longer pieces such as *Gloria* and Creed, worship songs and four-square hymn tunes, vehicles of a barely recognizable paraphrase.[6] Most of the clergy seemed never to have learned to sing the chants in the Sacramentary[7] and, increasingly, a Mass with music became a said

5 *Celebration Hymnal for Everyone* no. 313, *Celebration Hymnal for Everyone*, Great Wakering, Essex: McCrimmon, 1995.

6 Examples are Graham Kendrick's 'We believe in God the Father' (1986), see *Celebration Hymnal for Everyone* no. 771, the ubiquitous Peruvian Gloria, see *Celebration Hymnal for Everyone* no. 198 and John Ainslie's 'Glory be to God in heaven' (1996) which *Laudate*, (Mildenhall, Suffolk: Decani Music, 1999) sets to 'St Helen' (87 87 47) but which seems to be sung often to 'Cwm Rhondda' (87 87 47 extended).

7 The word '*Sacramentary*' is used here because the pre-conciliar *Missale Romanum* incorporated readings in the propers whereas the post-conciliar Roman Missal (called by North Americans *The Sacramentary*) does not. The post-conciliar lectionary is published in discrete volumes.

Mass with hymns, or more usually worship songs, and, sometimes, a sung responsorial psalm and alleluia verse. Much polemic seems to have focused on the appearance of the guitar as the main instrument of accompaniment – an unamplified guitar ill-suits all but the smallest and most intimate and attentive of auditoria and an electric guitar represents an alien musical genre – but what this focus on the guitar symbolized was not reaction to a particular musical instrument but the discovery of a supposedly popular music style, a musical vernacular, so to speak. Often, where the style was definable, it was the popular style of a previous generation and elderly folk were bemused by singing the kind of music to which they used to dance.

Congregations sang along with the music group such ditties as:

Sons of God, hear his holy Word,
Gather round the table of the Lord.[8]

In the 1970s 'Sons of God' and 'fellow man' were not problematic expressions and the concluding words of the song, 'so we make a holiday, so we'll live for ever' seemed as fresh then as they seem banal now. Without doubt, the *Missa Solemnis* had all but disappeared and the *Missa Cantata* replaced by a Mass with varying amounts of congregational song-singing.

Catholics, in the English-speaking world, were learning from the Anglican Parish Eucharist with hymns, and we shall be looking presently at the development of hymnody in Anglicanism. A difficulty of the Liturgical Movement is that, though different denominations came to share more and more – the shape of the Eucharist, ceremonial practice, lectionary material, prayers and music – there remained singular cultural differences. An obvious one was the congregation's expectation of participation – and this requires some further examination of the assumptions of *actuosa participatio*, 'active participation' not being quite reducible to 'joining in'.[9] Thomas Day's famous book *Why Catholics can't sing*[10] lampoons popular aesthetics – the subtitle, indeed, is 'the culture of Catholicism and the triumph of bad taste'

---

8 Words and music by James Thein (1966), *Celebration Hymnal for Everyone* no. 662

9 Laurence Hemming discusses and provides references for Aidan Nichols' suggestion that *actuosa* means 'actual' rather than 'active'. He concludes that, when Pius X referred in 1903 to *partecipazione attiva* in the *motu proprio* on Church music *Tra le sollecitudini*, he meant 'something much closer to what "actual" means now – in this sense Nichols' emphasis is not wrong'. See Laurence P. Hemming, *Worship as a Revelation*, London: Burns & Oates, 2008, pp. 31ff.

10 Thomas Day, *Why Catholics can't sing*, New York: Crossroad, 1990.

– but, if he is right in saying of the Catholic Irish that 'after centuries of associating liturgy with suffering and silence, they now encountered new and strange music added to their silent Mass'.[11] It is small wonder that they never learned the art of congregational singing, an essentially Anglican and Protestant phenomenon. From an Anglican point of view, Catholics were poor singers just as, from a Methodist point of view, Anglicans were diffident singers.

The Ordinary of the Mass

The music for the Mass divides into the Ordinary – what is more or less unchangeable – and the Proper – the ever-changing cycle of prayers, readings and texts. First we must consider the Ordinary. These texts are privileged. As the *General Instruction of the Roman Missal* says, 'It is not permitted to substitute other chants for those found in the Order of Mass, such as at the *Agnus Dei*.'[12] Music for the Ordinary of the Mass traditionally includes the *Kyrie eleison, Gloria, Credo, Sanctus* and *Benedictus qui venit*, and *Agnus Dei*.[13] Musical settings fall into three convenient categories: plainsong,[14] polyphony, and modern congregational settings. Polyphony – music for several voices – includes choral settings from the Baroque, Classical, Romantic and contemporary periods as well as from the heyday of the Renaissance.[15]

---

11 Thomas Day, *Why Catholics can't sing*, p. 21.

12 *General Instruction of the Roman Missal*, London: Catholic Truth Society, 2005, (hereafter GIRM in the footnotes), para. 366. This English translation of the most recent version of *Institutio Generalis Missalis Romani* was prepared by the International Committee on English in the Liturgy (hereafter ICEL) in 2002 in preparation for the new translation of the *Missale Romanum* into English.

13 As well as such items as the acclamation during the Eucharistic Prayer, the *Pater Noster*, and the *Ite missa est* (the formal dismissal).

14 The best introductions to plainsong currently seem to be David Hiley, *Western Plainchant: A Handbook*, Oxford: Oxford University Press, 1993; Richard L. Crocker, *An Introduction to Gregorian Chant*, New Haven: Yale University Press, 2000; and Daniel Saulnier OSB, (tr.) Mary Berry, *Gregorian Chant for Musicians: A Complete Guide to the History and Liturgy*, Brewster, Mass.: Paraclete Press, 2007. Bennett Zon, *The English Plainchant Revival*, Oxford: Oxford University Press, 1999, is a valuable guide to the plainchant revival amongst eighteenth- and nineteenth-century Catholics in England and in the nineteenth century Anglo-Catholic movement.

15 There are also one or two examples of medieval masses extant, such as Machaut, *Messe de Nostre Dame* (c. 1365), linked to the Saturday Lady Mass in Reims Cathedral. One of the first surviving settings of Mass movements, this is the first setting of the Mass Ordinary to be conceived as a unit, both liturgically and stylistically. There are earlier surviving polyphonic settings of individual movements of the Ordinary (and Proper), but not an entire Mass. The cyclic Mass form does not begin to appear widely in manuscript tradition until the fifteenth century.

Modern congregational settings have proliferated since the rise of the Liturgical Movement, and especially since 1970. As we shall see in a moment, these categories are not of similar value. Two of the categories are almost exclusively for the Latin Mass (though the words of the *Kyrie*, in Greek, were an early mark of the universality of the Church). Modern settings, the third category, are almost entirely settings in the vernacular. There is no space here – nor need – to survey the riches of the vast polyphonic – that is, choral – repertoire,[16] nor to make arbitrary value judgements on which of the settings of English words are meretricious and which are serviceable. As regards the classical corpus of music for the Mass, it is worth making the point that the argument that good music is a hindrance to church growth, though common, is untested and unlikely. Robin A. Leaver, from an American context but with experience of working in Britain too, suggests imaginatively that 'liturgical music stresses the vertical relationship between us and God; evangelistic music stresses the horizontal relationship between us and others'.[17] This fits well with St Thomas Aquinas' definition of a hymn: *Hymnus est laus Dei cum cantico; canticum autem exultatio mentis de aeternis habita, prorumpens in vocem* (A hymn is the praise of God with song; a song is the exultation of the mind dwelling on eternal things, bursting forth in the voice).[18]

As regards vernacular settings of the Mass, it might be worth noting, that very little of the music setting ICEL English texts from the 1970s will adapt well to the English texts of the Ordinary appearing forty years later. It follows that much of the liturgical music of the period 1970 to the present day, even that which is not by its nature ephemeral, is obsolescent. Also, a lesson for musicians and parish priests alike, some of the settings which appeared at first to be most serviceable were not designed to withstand constant use. To quote an obvious example, Paul Inwood's *Gathering Mass*,[19] a fine and justifiably popular

---

16 GIRM para. 41 gives pride of place to Gregorian chant and commends 'other types of sacred music, in particular polyphony'. There is a discussion of the use of choral music in Chapter 2, p. 53.

17 Robin A. Leaver and Joyce A. Zimmerman (eds), *Liturgy and Music*, p. 403. See also Alcuin Reid, *The Organic Development of the Liturgy*, Farnborough: St Michael's Abbey Press, 2004, pp. 19ff. for a discussion of Pius XII's encyclical *Musicæ Sacræ*.

18 Thomas Aquinas, *St Thomas's Introduction to his Exposition of the Psalms of David*, (tr.) Hugh McDonald, Latin Text according to the Venice Edition MDCCLXXV available (2009) The Aquinas Translation Project http://www4.desales.edu/~philtheo/loughlin/ATP/index.html)

19 Published by OCP Publications, 5536 NE Hassalo, Portland, Oregon 97213 and available in such collections as *Celebration Hymnal for Everyone*, Great Wakering: McCrimmons, 1995.

congregational setting for special occasions from a very able musician, became, with punishingly frequent repetition, a work much less helpful to devotion – in much the same way as a diet of doughnuts would soon pall. Every parish, where vernacular congregational settings are used, surely needs a minimum of three – one for 'Ordinary Time', one for penitential seasons, and one for special occasions (made familiar, perhaps, through use throughout the Christmas and Easter seasons). Some would argue that these congregational settings should all – or mostly – be from our first category, plainsong. A fuller discussion of the *Kyriale*, the plainsong resource for the Ordinary of the Mass, of less interest to the general reader, appears in an appendix to this chapter.[20] Meanwhile it is sufficient to note that in *Sacrosanctum Concilium*, the Liturgical Constitution of 1963 (para. 116) the Fathers of the Second Vatican Council said:

> The Church acknowledges Gregorian chant as specially suited to the Roman liturgy: therefore, other things being equal, it should be given pride of place in liturgical services.

They went on to say:

> other kinds of sacred music, especially polyphony, are by no means excluded from liturgical celebrations, so long as they accord with the spirit of the liturgical action . . . (para. 116)

and more specifically:

> In certain parts of the world, especially mission lands, there are peoples who have their own musical traditions, and these play a great part in their religious and social life. For this reason due importance is to be attached to their music, and a suitable place is to be given to it, not only in forming their attitude toward religion, but also in adapting worship to their native genius . . . (para. 119).

Here, then, is a hierarchy of importance: plainsong has 'pride of place'; amongst 'other kinds of sacred music' polyphony is given special status and then, for 'peoples who have their own musical traditions', 'due importance' 'and a suitable place' is 'attached to their music'. It seems unlikely, therefore, that the Council had determined to promote either the pop music culture of the West – although it cannot be excluded

---

20 See below, p. 133.

categorically – or indeed any burgeoning of vernacular congregational settings of the Ordinary of the Mass.

English Plainsong

There is equally a hierarchy of importance in *Sacrosanctum Concilium* in respect of liturgical language:

> the use of the Latin language is to be preserved in the Latin rites. But since the use of the mother tongue, whether in the Mass, the administration of the sacraments, or other parts of the liturgy, frequently may be of great advantage to the people, the limits of its employment may be extended. This will apply in the first place to the readings and directives, and to some of the prayers and chants . . . (para. 36)

As Anglo-Catholic congregations used to know – and some still know – plainsong settings have long been available in English. There are settings of prayer-book words[21] and, more recently, of the ecumenical texts used by ICEL since 1970.[22] In these resources there has been regard to the chants of the Sarum Use as well as to the Vatican Edition of the Solesmes Benedictines.[23] Very recently, settings of plainsong to the newest ICEL texts[24] have gradually appeared, first of all on the internet.[25] Introducing this material was a document on the ICEL site, *Music for the English Language Roman Missal: An Introduction*.[26] This not only explained the approach, methodology, and scope of the work undertaken, but assumed an encouraging, if not entirely convincing, expectation that priests and people would sing the Mass to plainchant, using both Latin and English. Perhaps of the three settings with which we suggested even the most modest congregation should aim to be familiar, two at least should be plainsong, of which one at least might be in Latin and the

---

21 Such as *The Ordinary of the Mass*, published by the Plainsong and Medieval Music Society in 1896 and revised in 1937, and, more familiarly, *The English Gradual: Part I The Plainchant of the Ordinary*, London, 1871, which ran to seven editions, the seventh revised by Francis Burgess in 1961 and published by the Plainchant Publications Committee. The Royal School of Church Music, Sarum College, Salisbury, nowadays has custody of this and other historic English plainsong resources.

22 Peter Allan CR, *et al.* (eds), *An English Kyriale*, Mirfield: Community of the Resurrection, and London: HarperCollins Religious, 1991.

23 See p. 133.

24 Translating the *Missale Romanum editio typica tertia*.

25 Facilitated by the Church Music Association of America (founded in 1874), Richmond VA.

26 www.icelweb.org/ICELMusicIntroduction.pdf – hereafter *Music for the English*.

other in English.[27] One complaint about ICEL's approach in *Music for the English* – certainly pertinent when we are talking about the setting of translated texts and not about ecclesiology – is that there is no mention of the extensive and scholarly work of Anglicans in this field. In contrast with this, homage is paid to 'vernacular chant adaptations such as Spanish, French, and German' (the last being particularly valuable not only because of its similarity to English but also because work on setting plainsong to German goes back to the 1920s).

Though the chants for the priest in the 1970 Sacramentary had a Cistercian simplicity, they have been much less well used than was envisaged. Time will tell what use will be made of the musical settings in the new English version of the *Missale Romanum* but the English settings are essentially the Latin ones minimally adapted. The singing of the preface, with its introductory dialogue, leads very fittingly into the *Sanctus* and the singing of the final doxology of the Eucharistic Prayer into the singing of *Amen* and *Pater Noster* by the whole assembly. A priest with modest musical ability might limit his solo chanting to these parts, though the singing of the orations is not taxing. If the punctuation (as in *Graduale Romanum*[28] tones A and B) proves too difficult, a self-selected monotone would surely suffice. The priest with more ability might well sing the orations, the preface and the doxology most Sundays and, on certain Sundays and solemnities, sing the whole Mass – including the whole of the Canon. As is increasingly the case once more, it is intended that the deacon or priest should sing the Gospel – whether in Latin or in English – to the pointing available in the *Graduale Romanum* and the new English language Missal. (Tone A shows how to punctuate full stops and questions whereas Tone B shows punctuation for commas as well.) Meanwhile, *Music for the English* has shown considerable ambition by demonstrating the use of the Epistle tone in English, a tone which few congregations, Anglican or Roman Catholic, have heard for a generation. Nothing emphasizes more the enchantment and mystery of the liturgy than the extensive use of music, especially at just the points where, in the prosaic secular culture which surrounds us, one might expect speaking rather than singing.

Music in Latin and the vernacular can co-exist well: the Benedictine monks at Saint-Benoît-sur-Loire, for example, sing the Ordinary and Propers of the Mass in Latin. Though the Mass itself is in French, as is the psalmody of the Office, what is particularly arresting is the

---

27 There is further reflection on this in the Appendix, p. 183.

28 *Graduale Romanum*, 1974, the Roman Gradual: chants for the Ordinary and the Proper of the Mass of 1970.

concelebrants' singing of the institution narrative in French, the most solemn moment of the eucharistic prayer.[29] Here surely is an instance of 'the scribe . . . trained for the kingdom' being 'like a householder who brings out of his treasure what is new and what is old' (Matt. 13.52).

The Emergence of the Hymn at Mass

One of the constant characteristics of modern eucharistic worship is the hymn or worship song. As we saw earlier, Aquinas defines the hymn 'as the praise of God with song'. Early examples of hymns include the *Gloria in excelsis*, used at Mass, and the *Te Deum laudamus*, used in the Office. The phrase *psalmi idiotici*, found in the fourth century Council of Laodiceæ, means psalms written 'by private individuals', (as opposed to from Scripture).[30] Gradually 'hymn' began to describe Christian verse, composed to be sung alongside, and in the spirit of, the psalter during the Office, and for many of these St Ambrose (c. 339–97), was given the credit.[31] As recently as the pre-conciliar Breviary (1961) the *Te Deum* was referred to as *Hymnus Ambrosianus*. Musically, we can say that hymns in the West – and here we now mean settings of verse (Latin verse and not Hebrew poetry) – were usually written strophically, meaning that the music could be repeated, over and over again. This made hymns essentially accessible and corporately useable by clerics and monastics without special musical skills. Liturgically, we can say that hymns – like prayers – were original compositions, often centonizing (that is, creating a patchwork) of allusions and quotations from Scripture and creeds. They were often doctrinally freight-bearing in ways which could be seen as developments, rather than paraphrases, of Scripture and creeds. It is this loose relationship with Scripture which, at the Reformation, was to lead Bucer and Calvin, on the principle of *sola scripura* (Scripture alone as authoritative) to restrict hymnody to metrical psalms – the Hebrew psalms of the Bible recast into verse paraphrases. Zwingli, an accomplished musician himself, famously went

---

29 Such was the tradition as experienced on a visit to Saint-Benoît-sur-Loire in Spring 2009.

30 See Joseph A. Jungmann SJ, (tr.) Francis A. Brunner CSSR, *The Mass of the Roman Rite: Its Origins and Development*, vol. I, pp. 346f., New York: Benziger Bros, 1955, replica edition, Dublin: Four Courts Press, 1986.

31 See for example David Hiley, *Western Plainchant: A Handbook*, pp. 140ff. For a discussion of music from the early Christian period (New Testament to c. AD 450) see James W. McKinnon, *Music in Early Christian Literature* (Cambridge Readings in the Literature of Music), Cambridge: Cambridge University Press, 1987.

further, and distrusting emotionalism and sensuality, forbade music in worship altogether. Thomas Cranmer, ever the moderate, gave succour to the principle of metrical psalms, which exactly matched his criterion of 'for every syllable a note',[32] but omitted all mention of hymns in his Book of Common Prayer. He nonetheless included a version of the *Veni Sancte Spiritus* (Come Holy Ghost) in the 1550 Ordinal.

It is easy to forget how recent hymn-singing is within the Mass. The medieval Mass, since the days of Notker Balbulus (ob. 912) and later of Adam of St-Victor (twelfth century), developed a whole repertoire of sequences but the development of the sequence is complex and controverted.[33] It used to be thought that the sequence – as its name might suggest – 'followed on' from the alleluia before the Gospel in the sense of its words and music deriving from the concluding, long, ecstatic phrase set to the final '-ia' of the alleluia before the Gospel. The early sequence, however, showed other influences and the melismatic tail of the alleluia, often known as the *jubilus*,[34] is but one example of melismatic writing ('melismatic' being the singing of many notes to one syllable, the very thing Cranmer sought to banish). Hence the 'sequence', though some may indeed have been composed that way, was not inevitably born out of the alleluia in quite the way once thought. Furthermore, though the rhymed sequences of the later period have characteristics in common with the hymn, musically the relationship between hymn and sequence is no more than that of cousins. They are different forms, sharing certain characteristics, more literary and theological than musical. And there is not always even literary and theological common ground: the sequence was sometimes performed without words, vocalizing the joy of heavenly worship, that which was ineffable, beyond words, a glory that can be glimpsed only as 'through a glass, darkly' (1 Cor. 13.12 [AV]).[35] The words of rhymed sequences, like those of hymns, were

---

32 Cranmer's instruction to John Merbecke when he commissioned *The Book of Common Prayer Noted* (1550), 'containing so much of the Order of Common Prayer as is to be sung in Churches' was to have 'for every syllable a note'. See John Caldwell, *The Oxford History of Music*, Oxford: Oxford University Press, second edition 1999, vol. 1, p. 269.

33 See for example David Hiley, *Western Plainchant: A Handbook*, Oxford: Oxford University Press, 1993, pp. 172ff.

34 The *jubilus*, as the name implies, is a joyful and often extensive phrase of music. *Jubilus*, we now think, was a word that had developed in meaning by the fourteenth century to describe any piece of highly melismatic chant, and not just the alleluia.

35 See Lori Kruckenberg, 'Neumatizing the Sequence: Special Performances of Sequences in the Central Middle Ages', *Journal of the American Musicological Society*, Summer 2006, vol. 59, no. 2, pp. 243–317. See also Margot Fassler, *Gothic Song: Victorine Sequences and Augustinian Reform in Twelfth-Century Paris*, (Cambridge Studies in Medieval and Renaissance Music), Cambridge: Cambridge University Press, 1993.

strophic – though it is quite usual for a sequence to change melody for some of the strophes[36] – but are usually too complex for congregational participation. Nonetheless, for our purposes, we can see that the sequence as it developed – a piece of sung verse, which was neither Scripture nor usually constructed in the format of a prayer – was the antecedent of the hymn at mass.

There has been an ambivalence about the role of sequences: the Council of Trent reduced the number of sequences to four (later becoming five) and, a century later, Pope Alexander VII pronounced that 'nothing be said at Mass but the words prescribed by the Roman Missal'.[37] That did not prevent the lively development of hymns for extra-liturgical worship but, after 1970, only four of the medieval sequences remain amidst the Propers of the Mass, *Victimæ Paschali* (Easter week), *Lauda Sion* (Corpus Christi), *Veni, Sancte Spiritus* (Pentecost) and *Stabat Mater* (Our Lady of Sorrows).[38] Nowadays the sequence precedes rather than follows the alleluia, out of whose *jubilus* it was once thought to have grown. The instinct of many Anglican congregations to sing a hymn before the Gospel, originally the 'gradual hymn' between Epistle and Gospel, often seems like a shade of the sequence, particularly when an alleluia verse is also sung. As for the Reformed Communion Service, though hymns, as we have seen, were rejected by the Swiss Reformation as unscriptural, Lutherans, by contrast, discovered the usefulness of hymns – chorales – at the Sunday liturgy. Later, though not in direct descent from the Lutherans, the role of hymns as doctrinal vehicle, and, above all things, the means of arousing spiritual fervour, was discovered by the Methodists at the end of the eighteenth century, Charles Wesley (1707–88), younger brother of John Wesley (1703–91), the founder of Methodism, being undoubtedly one of the greatest hymn writers in the English language.

---

36 Ralph Vaughan Williams imitates this feature in his fine setting of *Salva Festa Dies* (*English Hymnal* nos. 624 [Easter], 628 [Ascension] 630 [Whit-Sunday] and 634 [Dedication]) (*English Hymnal*, London: Oxford University Press, 196, new edition 1933) where, ancillary to the refrain, two tunes, one for even-numbered verses and one for odd-numbered, are to be sung by the 'clerks only'.

37 Quoted by Michael J. Molloy, 'Liturgical Music as Corporate Song 3', in Robin A. Leaver and Joyce A. Zimmerman (eds), *Liturgy and Music*, p. 328.

38 *Liber Usualis* (1961, 1963) has, in addition, *Dies iræ* (masses for the dead). There are also several other sequences – *Salus æterna* (Advent), *Lætabundus* (Christmas), *Ierusalem et Sion Filiæ* (Dedication), *Sponsa Christi* (All Saints) in *New English Hymnal*, Norwich: Canterbury Press, 1986 – though they seem to be rarely used.

The Oxford Movement

One of the gifts of the Oxford Movement as it developed in the second half of the nineteenth century was to popularize the use of hymn singing by incorporating hymns as well as chanting into the celebration of the Eucharist. This resort to the hymn, though found in almost every revivalist movement in modern times, was in this instance essentially a Catholic idea. First, the hymn was not only a cousin of the sequence, as we have seen, but of the Office hymn, one of the features of the medieval Office that had not survived Cranmer's reforms. Second, and most importantly, the hymn allowed the importing of 'Catholic' teaching, particularly eucharistic teaching, through devotional texts. This was the aim of parish priests, whether their inclination was for the pre-reformation Sarum Use or they were of ultramontane disposition. Most striking of these eucharistic hymns was 'Wherefore, O Father'[39] bringing before God the 'all-perfect offering, sacrifice immortal, spotless oblation', sung at the end of the Cranmer's Prayer of Consecration, whilst the priest muttered Cranmer's Prayer of Oblation, brought forward from its Post-communion position in the 1662 rite, or completed the Canon of the Roman Mass *sotto voce*. Anglo-Catholic congregations learnt their eucharistic theology not from Archbishop Cranmer but from their hymn singing.

Whereas Lutherans had replaced the Ordinary of the Mass with hymn paraphrases, the high-church movement encouraged the musical setting of the *Kyrie, Gloria, Credo, Sanctus* and *Agnus Dei*.[40] Ironically it was the music of that ardent and early Protestant John Merbecke whose congregational setting of the Prayer Book Ordinary in the *Booke of Common Praier Noted* (1550) was most often pressed into service. Those who went to the Eucharist in the Catholic tradition more or less anywhere in the Church of England until the mid-1960s (and in many places until the present day) would encounter a sung Ordinary, with often more than half a dozen supplementary hymns. With the liturgical revisions beginning in the 1960s, portions of psalmody began also to be used, as in the Roman Catholic *Novus Ordo*, where the psalm became one of the Scripture readings. Perhaps psalmody at the Eucharist was in compensation for the loss of Evensong as, increasingly, the

---

39 Text by W. H. H. Jervois, see for example *English Hymnal*, new edition, London: Oxford University Press and Mowbray, 1933, no. 335.

40 Sometimes the Lutherans retained the *Kyrie* in Greek and the *Gloria* in Latin: J. S. Bach set the Lutheran Mass (*Kyrie* and *Gloria*) in the late 1730s, probably for his Leipzig churches.

Parish Communion became the only Sunday service attended by most of the parish congregation and hence their only opportunity regularly to encounter the psalms.[41]

After a generation of evolving liturgical reform, the Common Worship (CW) Order for the Eucharist 2000, unlike Holy Communion in the Book of Common Prayer (BCP), indicates places where hymns may be sung: at the Gathering, at the Preparation of the Table, during the Distribution and at the beginning of the Dismissal. By now one senses both a certain reining back of the excessive hymnody of the Parish Communion and, building on the Alternative Service Book (ASB) 1980, a moment of formal recognition of the hymn by the Anglican liturgical tradition, hitherto an ingredient closely identifiable with the tradition but virtually unknown in and unmentioned by official liturgies. One other development in England – small but not insignificant – has been the adopting, in the liturgical reforms which crystallized in the ASB 1980, and the discarding in CW 2000, of the Introductory Sentence and the Post-communion Sentence. Before examining the complexity of the Catholic Propers, therefore, it is worth noticing in passing that English Anglicans did attempt for a time, it seems unsuccessfully, to incorporate a catena of short scriptural texts into the Proper.

The Proper of the Mass

If one did not know otherwise, one might have presumed that the traditional treasury of Catholic polyphonic music contained a whole repertoire of Catholic Propers. It could easily have been the case that composers other than Palestrina and Byrd, giants of the Renaissance, had systematically set the Propers. As it is, there are myriads of masses and motets (a motet being a sacred text set to music which can be performed at any time) but very few polyphonic sets of Propers. That does not mean that plainsong Propers were invariably used. The fifteenth-century Milanese *motetti missales* tradition, of Josquin des Pres (1450–1521) and his contemporaries, shows otherwise,[42] as does the later

---

41 It would have been possible to incorporate into this chapter a discussion of the singing of the Office, noting such encouragements as the new Solesmes editions of the *Antiphonale Monasticum* and *Antiphonale Romanum*. It remains pre-eminently the case, however, that, where the sung Office flourishes outside the monasteries, what is striking is the persistence of traditional forms, though Anglicans increasingly use pared-down psalmody and pillar lectionaries (that is, lectionaries where readings do not rely for their sense on having heard the readings the day before or the day after).

42 See for example Paul A. Merkley and Lora L. M. Merkley, *Music and Patronage in the Sforza Court*, Turhout, Belgium: Brepols, 1999.

use of Baroque trio sonatas in place of Propers. There is every reason to suppose, too, that resourceful musicians were happy to replace a plainsong proper with a motet at the height of the Renaissance just as, later, they were content in seventeenth-century French organ masses to interpolate organ interludes in place of portions of the liturgical text.[43] François 'le grand' Couperin (1668–1733), who succeeded his father as organist of Saint Gervais, Paris, would be astonished to return there now and hear the same organ – and extracts from his two organ masses, the *Messe pour les paroisses* and the *Messe pour les couvents*, still played, albeit in brief *éclats*. The context has changed dramatically: now Saint Gervais is home to the mission of the Monastic Communities of Jerusalem, founded in 1975, monks and nuns, in various European cities, who sing the *Novus Ordo* in the vernacular, with *a cappella* psalms and acclamations in four-part harmony.

The Second Vatican Council's Liturgical Constitution of 1963, *Sacrosanctum Concilium*, encouraged composers 'to cultivate sacred music and increase its store of treasures', and provide not only for large choirs, but 'also for the needs of small choirs and for the active participation of the entire assembly of the faithful'. There is encouragement here not only for anthems and motets – 'the texts intended to be sung . . . should be drawn chiefly from holy Scripture' – but also, in the mention of 'liturgical sources',[44] not only settings of the Ordinary of the Mass but also of the Proper. Appearing here is the phrase *actuosa participatio*, 'active participation', which we considered earlier[45] and will shortly consider again, giving rise, in the modern Roman Catholic tradition also, to the ubiquity of the hymn and worship song, the staple diet of Protestant liturgy. *Sacrosanctum Concilium*, itself a prospectus rather than a programme, led to the 1967 Instruction *Musicam Sacram* and, as László Dobszay, the Hungarian professor of music and liturgist, points out, somewhat too colourfully, 'the "anthrax in the envelope" was paragraph 32'.[46] Paragraph 32 permits substitution of other songs for the Introit (Entrance chant), Gradual, Offertory and Communion chants in the *Graduale Romanum*.[47] This concession, referred

---

43 An analogy can also be found in the *alternatim* performance of the psalms in the Offices of the medieval Church. The organ played polyphonic settings of the psalm tone in place of a verse that would have been sung by a polyphonic choir otherwise absent.

44 Para. 121.

45 See above, p. 54.

46 László Dobszay, *The Bugnini-Liturgy and the Reform of the Reform*, Front Royal, VA: Church Music Association of America, 2003, p. 86. See also his *The Restoration and Organic Development of the Roman Rite*, London: T&T Clark, 2009.

47 For a fuller discussion of the *Graduale Romanum*, see Johannes Berchmans Göschl,

to in the rubrics as *alius cantus aptus* ('another suitable song'), became the norm for several reasons.[48] First, there were problems surrounding the *Graduale Romanum*. The edition to accompany the *Novus Ordo*, though it received its *imprimatur* in 1973, did not emerge until 1979, by which time many of the local musical decisions about the new liturgy had been made. Second, the *Graduale Romanum* was in Latin and, no doubt to the astonishment of those who had drafted *Sacrosanctum Concilium*, Latin was swiftly and almost universally replaced by the vernacular. Third, though the earlier plainsongs in the collection are somewhat simpler than later additions, the *Graduale Romanum* consists mainly of the kind of arcane plainsong which demands performance by a skilled *Schola Cantorum* (the choir of singers in the monastery, cathedral or major church).[49] Compounding these circumstances, as we saw a moment ago, has been the inclination of church musicians to devise and perform choral and instrumental alternatives to the plainsong repertoire.

We must now look further at *actuosa participatio*.[50] This phrase of Pius X's, repeated over half a century later in *Sacrosanctum Concilium*, – and normally and uncritically translated as 'active participation', 'joining in' – gives rise to the assumption that participation is active in the sense of being corporately vocal. In historical context, *actuosa participatio* surely suggests a move from the kind of participation in the Mass where members of the congregation might privately pray the Rosary in attendance on a liturgical action done on their behalf to a fundamentally different kind of participation. Following the Liturgi-

---

'One Hundred Years of the *Graduale Romanum*', *Sacred Music*, Summer 2008, vol. 135, no. 2, pp. 8ff., Richmond VA: Church Music Association of America.

48 http://authenticupdate.blogspot.com/2008/12/alius-cantus-aptus-transitional.html available (2009), argues, interestingly, that the reference is not to alternative texts but to alternative musical settings of the texts of the propers, as given in the Lectionary or in one of the two *Graduale* collections.

49 See also Kurt Poterack, 'The Strange Rejection of the *Roman Gradual*', in *Sacred Music*, Summer 2008, vol. 135, no. 2, pp. 91f., Richmond VA: Church Music Association of America.

Also of interest is Nicholas Sandon (ed.), *The Use of Salisbury*, Newton Abbot, 1984 onwards, a project to retrieve and republish the treasury of Sarum chant, that is, the chant of the Use of Salisbury which was prevalent in England before the Reformation. The volumes so far are:

1. The Ordinary of the Mass 2. The Proper of the Mass in Advent 3. The Proper of the Mass from Septuagesima to Palm Sunday 4. The Masses and Ceremonies of Holy Week 5. The Proper of the Mass from Easter to Trinity 6. The Proper of the Mass from Trinity to Advent.

50 See above, p. 109.

cal Movement, they were to listen attentively to readings in their own tongue, pray the prayers, and be caught up in the drama of the action. That kind of participation does not require everyone to sing all the musical bits any more than it requires everyone to read the readings, ring the bells, stand at the altar or, indeed, water the flowers.[51]

We have seen some of the drawbacks of the post-conciliar *Graduale Romanum* – it was late, it was in Latin, and it was labyrinthine. There was a further problem with the *Graduale Romanum*, moreover, in that its music and texts, though hallowed by time, and arguably as integral to the tradition as any other part of the liturgy, were not, in the *Novus Ordo*, the texts given in Sacramentary and Lectionary.[52] The Sacramentary provides a distinct set of Propers (that is, different from those in the *Graduale*) and the Lectionary a set of psalms and alleluia verses, which, at first sight, have more authority and weight than the texts of the *Graduale Romanum*, that is, when people realize that the texts of the *Graduale Romanum* even exist.

Of comparable authority are the chants of the *Graduale Simplex*, the first edition of which was printed in 1967. These chants, are not, as one might suppose, the same texts as the *Graduale Romanum*, nor yet of Sacramentary and Lectionary. Part of the simplicity is achieved by setting a restricted number of texts – eight for the *per annum* ('Ordinary Time') Sundays – and part by using less elaborate music than the *Graduale Romanum*. Here then is a set of musical resources for choirs and parishes insufficiently equipped to tackle the *Graduale Romanum*. The comparative simplicity of the chants and the opportunity for repetition[53] are not the only features that make the *Graduale Simplex* accessible. Extensive use is made of psalm chanting, a method more normally associated with the monastic Office, where the psalms are the responsibility not of the *Schola Cantorum* but of the community. One can imagine that, at the beginning of the *Novus Ordo* stage of the Liturgical Movement, many would have hoped, and some would have imagined, that the Solemn Mass in abbeys and cathedrals and major churches would have been sung routinely to the Propers of the

---

51 'Joseph Ratzinger (Pope Benedict)', in *The Spirit of the Liturgy*, (tr.) John Saward, San Francisco: Ignatius Press, 2000, pp. 171ff., has a section on 'Active Participation'. See also Chapter 2, p. 54.

52 One reason for the musical problems and unresolved musical issues of *Novus Ordo* might be that Annibale Bugnini, who piloted the reforms, was entirely uninterested in music, as his autobiography shows. This inevitably impacts more on the Propers than on the Ordinary.

53 The eight settings of Propers for Ordinary Time, rather like the eight Sunday prefaces in the Missal, suggest a cycle repeated four times in the year.

Graduale Romanum – as indeed sometimes happens.[54] They would have hoped and imagined that most other churches would have made use of the *Graduale Simplex* at the Sung Mass on Sundays and holy days, which seems seldom to happen.

Given that the texts of neither the *Graduale Romanum* nor the *Graduale Simplex* are those provided in Sacramentary and Lectionary, it is scarcely surprising that these books are hardly known and barely used. With no ready access to musical settings of the texts that are provided in Sacramentary and Lectionary, and with an emphasis on popular participation, it is no wonder too that *alius cantus aptus* ('another suitable song') became the norm for the Entrance chant, the Offertory chant and the Communion chant. Unfortunately, hymns and worship songs not only ground the liturgy in certain cultures – whether nineteenth-century hymnody or the 1970s' folk Mass – but also carry their own doctrinal and devotional content, often all too loosely connected to the ritual texts. The General Instruction stresses the importance of singing (para. 39) and 'due consideration for the culture of the people and abilities of each liturgical assembly' (para. 40) and gives the Conferences of Bishops, 'with the prior *recognitio* of the Apostolic See' responsibility for such matters as 'the texts of the chants at the Entrance, at the Presentation of the Gifts, and at Communion' (para. 390). Appropriate directions may be included in the Missal and, therefore, in the General Instruction.[55] Just as the Council of Trent had confronted the necessity for missionary work, so, for the Fathers of the Second Vatican Council, even Europe had become a mission field.

The flight from the use of liturgical Latin in the *Novus Ordo* has been so markedly noticeable that nowadays the media and the general public regard any reference to 'the Latin Mass' as indicating the pre-conciliar Mass. The early expectation that Latin would remain the customary language of the *Novus Ordo* Solemn Mass in large centres proved not to be the case. Similarly, the expectation that the Sung Mass in smaller centres would be a mix of Latin and the vernacular proved equally unfounded. More than that, the ever changing nature of the Propers and their scriptural content meant that, even where there is a mix of Latin and the vernacular, it is likely that it will be the Ordinary that is sung in Latin and what does service for the Propers – in practice *alius cantus aptus* – that will be sung in the vernacular. In short, the modest

---

54 This has been the regular pattern at the capitular mass in Westminster Cathedral, for example.

55 See for example GIRM, London: Catholic Truth Society, 2005, paras. 48, 74, 87 for the directions of the Bishops' Conference of England and Wales.

use of the *Graduale Romanum* and the *Graduale Simplex* reflects a poor process of induction. If that is so, campaigns to increase the use of either Gradual in its Latin form will have limited success, almost none at all in an Anglican context (for language reasons) and very little in a Roman Catholic context.

Propers in English

It could be argued that losing a collection of Latin texts, scripturally based and with long associations with particular feasts and seasons, is not too much of a misfortune if the language and therefore the meaning of those texts remains elusive to most worshippers. If we take seriously, however, the intrinsic link between psalms and sacrifice in the worship of both temple and church,[56] we cannot rest content at the loss of psalmody, or its reinvention as one of the passages of Scripture set in the lectionary more often read than sung. The early history of the Propers suggests that the sentences which remain are, anyway, the truncated remnant of whole psalms sung at the various points of the liturgical action in the earliest centuries.[57] Perhaps we can find compensation in the complementariness of Office and Mass, the one focusing on psalmody, the other on sacrifice. And yet psalmody is a sacrifice of praise and the cultic sacrifice is a time for singing psalms – and, in the West at least, blowing trumpets![58] Laurence Hemming makes the point that

> it becomes clear why Psalm 109 (110) is by long tradition the Vesper psalm in the Roman rite. Because it extended (with its mention of Melchisedech) the priestly, sacrificial meaning of the Eucharist into the most important of the liturgical offices . . . it indicates the fundamental connection between the sacrificial character of the Mass and the liturgy of the hours.[59]

---

56 See the references to 2 Chronicles 29.27–28, Psalm 26(27).6 and Psalm 42(43).4 at the beginning of the chapter.

57 For an account of this, see Joseph A. Jungmann SJ, *The Mass of the Roman Rite: Its Origins and Development*, vol. I, pp. 320ff., 421ff., vol. II, pp. 26ff., pp. 391ff.

58 In the East musical instruments, other than the human voice, are not permitted in the Divine Liturgy: though a very different explanation would be offered, this may accidentally derive from the Jewish convention that, following the destruction of the Temple, instruments are no longer used in worship, a sign of mourning.

59 Laurence Hemming, *Worship as a Revelation*, London: Burns & Oates, 2008, pp. 74f. Hemming explains in the section omitted here from this paragraph the association between Vespers and the baptistery on Easter Day.

Besides the loss of psalmodic texts, the musical loss remains considerable and it may be that the growing corpus of vernacular material available, published in books and online, which makes the singing and understanding of the texts of the *Graduale Romanum* possible, is the best way forward for many parishes.

A fuller discussion of resources, past and present, for singing the Propers will be of less interest to the general reader and appears in the appendix to this chapter.[60]

Priest and layperson alike, looking in a Sunday missal, sees neither the texts of the *Graduale Romanum* nor those of the *Graduale Simplex* and, as we have suggested, may not realize that the texts of either Gradual are an integral part of the Roman Rite. A pertinent question might be what resources exist for the singing of the texts of Entrance chant, Psalm, Acclamation and Communion chant which are apparently integral to the celebration, that is, the texts in Sacramentary and Lectionary. Usually it is assumed that, at these points, the texts, if not read out, are replaced by a hymn or song – *alius cantus aptus*. In the United States, in particular, there have been anyway copyright issues with liturgical texts. Since 2009, English chant Propers composed by Fr Columba Kelly OSB, monk of St Meinrad Archabbey, have been published online. This 'Sacred Music Project', as it is called, has been permitted by ICEL to use its copyright texts for the purpose. No doubt settings of the newly translated Propers of the *Missale Romanum editio typica tertia* will increasingly be sourced on line by choir directors and by those who compile orders of service for printing or projecting on to screens. Meanwhile there has always been much more industry on the setting of the responsorial psalms in the Lectionary. Quite a number of non-plainsong versions already exist of these, some of considerable beauty, some workaday, some unworthy. What is to be hoped is that a significant plainsong version of the Lectionary psalmody appears, using the version of the psalter incorporated in the new version of the lectionary.[61]

In the first decades of the twenty-first century, some closely related questions remain. Can one make use of the present liturgical ferment to discourage the temptation of clergy and musicians to do what is easiest and most obvious? Can one break free from the anarchy of *alius cantus aptus* (where 'anything goes', musically and textually) and recover the

---

60 See below, p. 137.

61 The English liturgical psalter is expected to be the Revised Grail Psalter. At the time of writing it is uncertain when a new version of the Lectionary in English will be published and when a new lectionary – that is, cycle of readings – will appear. There is further discussion of lectionary issues in Chapter 5, pp. 162ff.

plainsong and polyphonic tradition? Can one see an opportunity – now that congregational vocal participation is normal – for the establishing of, what would be for the first time in most places, an authentic and vigorous congregational use of plainsong? The new-found passion for the Extraordinary Form of the Roman Rite provides one opportunity – for there is no provision there for *alius cantus aptus*. Indeed those who love the Latin liturgy, solemnly celebrated, in Extraordinary or Ordinary Form, profess to love plainsong.[62] Nevertheless, what some would call the acquired experience and others the prejudice of the Anglican tradition – the older vernacular tradition – is that the singing of hymns and songs is not necessarily some second best, for lack of adequate vernacular versions of the Propers. Rather, intelligently planned, it can be a very particular and wise understanding of *actuosa participatio*, a recognition of the need to involve folk in the offering of the liturgy more appropriately and directly. Undoubtedly some Catholics too, in embracing *alius cantus aptus*, were deftly and devoutly appropriating a vigorous popular tradition, pioneered by Lutherans and developed by Anglicans. Catholics would notice how integral to Methodism, and its setting out of its theological position, was the choice of hymns and, indeed, the ecumenical sharing of the finest hymns of the different traditions has been a fruit of the Liturgical Movement. In short, *alius cantus aptus* has its place but not the default position it acquired in Catholic circles. A Mass with singing is no substitute for a sung Mass.

What the Roman Rite and *Sacrosanctum Concilium* seem to envisage is a layering of liturgical celebration in which abbeys and cathedrals might well make use of the *Graduale Romanum* for the Propers of the Mass and some alternation of psalmody between the verses set in *Graduale Romanum* and the psalms set in *Graduale Simplex*.[63] Major parishes should manage something similar, though here the *Graduale Romanum* might well be in one of its English recensions. There would be space too for a hymn or two: perhaps during procession and recession, with the Entrance chant reserved for the censing of the altar; perhaps during the Offertory or distribution of Communion. Let us call this the 'first division' of musical solemnity.

A 'second division' of musical solemnity would be characterized by more systematic use of *Graduale Simplex*, with occasional resort to the

---

62 One of the best online resources for keeping up to date with the renaissance of the Extraordinary Form and of Sacred Music is www.newliturgicalmovement.org (*New Liturgical Movement*).

63 According to Jeffrey Tucker, 'Music at St Peter's: The Transformation', *New Liturgical Movement*, 10 August 2009, this alternation is in place at St Peter's, Rome, under Fr Pierre Paul, director of music from 2008.

Graduale Romanum, and more generally the singing of a simple Introit, Offertory or Communion as provided in the *Graduale Simplex*. Again there are Latin and English options, as we shall see. In this 'second division' there would be no less a space for hymns. A 'third division' – not necessarily less musically demanding than the 'second division' – would be the principled and invariable use of the Propers as they appear in Sacramentary and Lectionary. Here resources such as the 'Sacred Music Project' mentioned earlier could be brought into play, again balanced by hymnody. From time to time the psalm settings of the *Graduale Simplex* (Latin or English), many of them responsorial, might be sung – where texts match – but there would be no good reason why one of the many responsorial psalm settings based on the Joseph Gélineau or Dom Gregory Murray methods might not be part of the overall scheme. Here we should note that what happens between the readings – which will often, and perhaps usually, be in the vernacular, even in a Mass otherwise celebrated in Latin – is different from what happens at the Introit, Offertory or Communion. The General Instruction seems to suggest priority of the Responsorial Psalm of the Lectionary over the texts of the Graduals which 'may be sung in place of the Psalm assigned in the Lectionary'. It also says that 'it is preferable that the responsorial psalm be sung, at least as far as the people's response is concerned' (para. 61). The Instruction similarly seems also to privilege the Lectionary provision for the Acclamation before the Gospel (para. 62).

Some of the decisions, and some of the anxieties, are about musical skill and discernment. The modern vernacular collections tend to avoid plainsong notation, not because it is intrinsically difficult but because it is perceived to be so.[64] Round or square, staves of five lines or four, notation is no more than a means to an end and the exact means usually remains invisible to the beneficiary, the listener. That would suggest the need for pragmatism to triumph over musical purism. There can be an assumption too that plainsong is inherently dull, primitive and lacking good tunes. That this is not necessarily so is evident from the music charts – where plainsong remains immensely popular – and from the number of melodies which have survived and become part of the hymn repertoire. Who does not know *Veni, veni Emmanuel* (O come, O come, Emmanuel)[65] or the *Veni Creator*, at least in its simplified Mechlin ver-

---

64 Arlene Oost-Zinner and Jeffrey Tucker, 'An Idiot's Guide to Square Notes', *Crisis*, May 2006, gives a very simple introduction to plainsong notation. A fuller guide is Mary Berry, *Plainchant for Everyone*, RSCM Handbook, third edition, 1996.

65 *Adoremus Hymnal*, no. 301, San Francisco: Ignatius Press, 1997; *Catholic Hymn Book*, no. 8, Leominster: Gracewing, 1998; *English Hymnal*, no. 8.

sion?[66] Most of the best plainchant grows slowly within one. The very opposite of being catchy or ephemeral, it gradually implants itself, and slowly reveals its fruitfulness and mystery. Many churches have discovered the haunting beauty and simplicity of the Advent Prose (*Rorate Cæli*)[67] and Lent Prose (*Attende Domine*)[68] whether sung in Latin or English. Nor need the performance decisions be daunting. The chants in the *Graduale Romanum* require a *Schola Cantorum* (or at least one or two skilled cantors) but much of the material in the *Graduale Simplex* – or its vernacular version – can be performed by less-skilled singers and congregations, perhaps led by one or two cantors who have learnt their part. None of this requires the kind of resources which polyphonic singing requires, and yet there will be churches where choirs of very limited ability – whose singing demands much of the congregation's patience and generosity – will attempt four-part music which cannot be made to sound effective and worthy but who would regard even the simplest monodies of the timeless repertoire of chant as somehow too demanding or dull.

The Task of Re-enchantment

A programme of rediscovering the liturgical musical tradition is beyond the formation, skills and training of the parish clergy, just as, say, the intricacies of pharmacology are beyond the expertise of most general medical practitioners. As we have seen in the scramble for new settings and songs for the vernacular Mass since 1970 – less so in the Anglican context, where, however new the vernacular texts, the concept of the vernacular at least was not new – there has been the discarding of the old and its replacement by a particular genre. This genre has been, in the main, the tried and trusty products of a small, talented group of Catholic musicians, at the height of their productivity in the 1970s and 1980s. Inevitably the best of the music – Dom Gregory Murray's *New People's Mass*,[69] Peter Jones's *Coventry Gloria*, and Christopher

---

66 *English Hymnal*, no. 154, usually sung to the words of no. 153, Come Holy Ghost, not least because they are the words of the hymn in the Prayer Book Ordinal.

67 *Adoremus Hymnal*, no. 307, *Catholic Hymn Book*, no. 305, *English Hymnal*, no. 735.

68 *Adoremus Hymnal*, no. 366, *Catholic Hymn Book*, no. 292, *English Hymnal*, no. 736

69 © 1975, 1987 McCrimmon Publishing Co. Ltd and available, for example, in *Celebration Hymnal for Everyone*, Great Wakering: McCrimmons, 1995.

Walker and Fintan P. O'Carroll's *Celtic Alleluia*[70] – has been grossly over-exposed. Musically, it is simple, none too eventful – even plaintive – melodies which bear constant repetition. 'Big tunes' do not. Meanwhile one of the real opportunities of the new music – the singing of a cantor, echoed by the congregational singing of the same phrase – has been used much less adventurously than it might have been. We have learnt to sing the chants of Lourdes and Taizé without learning the secret and versatility of the technique upon which they rely: the ability to communicate new and imaginative musical material quickly and simply, to large, freshly convened, and not especially musically skilful congregations.

All of this – over-use and under-use of what is possible in the new liturgical music – is eclipsed by the much graver problem of disenchantment, the loss, as we have seen, of the Latin Ordinary and of the Propers, whose texts (in whichever language) are integral to the *lex orandi*, that is, what is learnt from what we are asked to pray. The task of re-enchantment is a rediscovery of all that can be sung, and how this can be achieved. It is both possible and necessary at once to judge that attempts at reviving the fortunes of the Gradual collections might not succeed widely and yet vigorously promote them so that some progress is made. It is unsurprising that parish musicians, unaware of the treasure-store of the tradition of liturgical music, seek opportunities for choirs and groups to perform pieces of various kinds – anthems, canticles, even masses and motets from the classical repertoire – without understanding that the musical layers must be built one upon another, beginning not with these larger-scale pieces but with the demands and opportunities of the Ordinary and the Proper. The musicologist, Thurston Dart (1921–71), often in conversation used often to describe music as 'the bicycle of the liturgy'.[71] Nowhere is this more apparent than in the flourishing Anglican tradition of choral Evensong, in cathedrals and college chapels. Nowhere is this less apparent than in the 'said Mass' with hymns.

When that milestone of hymnody, the *English Hymnal*, first appeared in 1906, the number of hymns in circulation was already vast, more than twenty times more than the number in that book, and Percy Dearmer and Ralph Vaughan Williams were nonetheless finding new words and tunes and matching words and tunes in a new way. Something like that

---

70 Published by OCP Publications, Portland, Oregon, and available in such collections as *Celebration Hymnal for Everyone*.

71 This is a personal recollection but it was retold, for instance, by Simon Lindley in an address to the Church Music Society, 'Muse and the Mass', 6 October 1990, in Salisbury Cathedral.

kind of shakedown is happening again in the wake of the worship song explosion and such collections as the London Oratory's *Catholic Hymn Book* and, from America, the *Adoremus Hymnal*, have shown that, from a conservative vantage point, this process of filtering out what is not of enduring value can be done well. Anglicans are much more experienced in this field and it is encouraging that *Common Praise*[72] has served the *Hymns Ancient and Modern* tradition better than *New English Hymnal*[73] served the English Hymnal tradition. To be fair, *New English Praise*[74] has put some of the mistakes right and, in the wake of a proper *rassourcement*, the number of hymns any parish needs to have in currency for the celebration of the Eucharist is small: only about 150 are needed to provide for the liturgical year; any more and either some of the tunes will remain inaccessible and unfamiliar or we shall see once more the ousting of the Propers by a burgeoning number of indifferent hymns. Very few of the worship songs are likely to survive to be 'classics': those prematurely judged to be so now seem very jaded. And yet, every generation has produced its enduring contribution, and, amongst the hymn tunes of the last century, it seems certain that John Barnard's 'Guiting Power',[75] Kenneth Nicholson Naylor's 'Coe Fen'[76] and Maurice Bevan's 'Corvedale',[77] will survive every test, not least because they are set to hymn texts which themselves are well wrought and likely to be enduring .

Effective liturgy is achieved by contrast: silence or sound, said or sung, choral or congregational, plainsong or polyphony, accompanied or unaccompanied, vocal or instrumental, soothing flutes or sounding brass. These choices are routinely available in the parish of modest musical means: taking the contrasts very literally, even the smallest community usually has someone learning the flute who could manage a meditative melody, or a trumpeter who could be recruited to play a descant or two on Easter Day. Not every parish can manage choral singing or polyphony regularly but there can be few who have no experience of listening to a group of musicians singing and playing. Again, some communities have never dared to experience and explore silence, whether the silence during a Passiontide procession and recession, an occasional event, or silence regularly observed at the end of readings and homilies. Musicians know that the most significant moments in any

---

72 Norwich: Canterbury Press, 1986.
73 Norwich: Canterbury Press, 2000.
74 Norwich: Canterbury Press, 2006.
75 *New English Praise*, no. 613.
76 *New English Praise*, no. 699.
77 *New English Praise*, no. 700.

piece of music are the rests, the most significant moment in any musical performance the two or three seconds' silence after the final chord. Silence or sound is the basic and most necessary liturgical contrast.

Does all this mean that good taste is everything and that there is no place for the folk Mass, the youth Mass, and the explosions and experiments of popular culture? As we saw in Chapter 2, Pope Benedict, writing as Cardinal Ratzinger, issued some stern warnings about the nature of 'pop' and 'rock' music.[78] Certainly what the Church has often presented as popular culture has been no more than a relaxed and often cheesy style of its own. Inculturation demands boldness and ingenuity and there will always be contexts where certain styles may make particular evangelistic impact and have particular relevance to social circumstance. Anyone who has witnessed the impressive musical ministry of Mike Stanley and Joanne Boyce of CJM Music in the Catholic Archdiocese of Birmingham, England, or at the Youth Pilgrimage sponsored by the Anglican Shrine of Our Lady of Walsingham, will want to find a place for that approach in the somewhat specialized area of outreach to young people. The same is true of vibrant African American gospel music groups in such places as the St Alphonsus Liguori Rock Church, St Louis, Missouri, where authentic liturgical inculturation has borne fruit in a remarkable ministry of outreach and community health care in the neighbourhood. Though good music is intrinsically engaging, worship in itself is neither meant to be an entertainment nor to be more than incidentally entertaining.[79] The twin tests of any liturgical celebration are whether it has integrity – including æsthetic integrity – and whether it is truly sacramental – evoking the numinous and deepening discipleship. The common perception – the sense of disenchantment – is that most modern worship presently fails these tests and neither evokes the numinous nor deepens discipleship. Those who witnessed the liturgies marking the passing of Pope John Paul II and the inauguration of the papacy of Pope Benedict XVI in the Spring of 2005 glimpsed something of what all liturgy is meant to achieve, as, in a very different way, did viewers of the dramatic public funeral rites of Princess Diana in September 1997.[80] Most 'actual

---

78 See p. 53.

79 '[t]he rapt evocation of the wonder of music in the fourth Discourse is promptly followed by a warning against its temptation, "rather to use Religion than to minister to it"', Ian Ker, *John Henry Newman*, Oxford: Oxford University Press, 1988, reissued 2009, p. 385. The Newman quotation is from *The Idea of a University*, p. 80.

80 The funeral rites, liturgically speaking, probably took place at the graveside, beyond the public gaze. The public ceremonies were, more properly speaking, a form of memorial service in the presence of the coffin.

participants' in these rites at St Peter's, Rome, and Westminster Abbey, were, in one sense, not even present at them, but were watching by television at home. Those who designed, executed, and presented the rites had the task, in which they succeeded brilliantly, of combining authentic celebration and proclamation and an appropriate, but necessarily passive, popular participation. Without the one, these ceremonies would have been unconvincing pageants, whimsies of nostalgia and sentimentality. Without the other, the viewers would have switched channels or gone shopping. The tragedy of much liturgical celebration at a parish level is that we may avoid the pageantry and the whimsy, we may even manage the nostalgia and the sentimentality. Too often, however, most of those whom we should like to be there have long ago switched channels or gone shopping.

The most serious problem of all in church music, as in other areas of church life, is the collapse of work with the young. Beyond the centres of choral excellence – which themselves are not without their recruiting difficulties – the youngsters on the front row of the church choir – where church choirs persist – have given way to adults, often very senior adults, whose musical contribution is less surefooted than perhaps it once was. For the most part parish choirs have disappeared entirely, sometimes suppressed in the interests of 'congregational participation', and their passing is often unlamented. How often, one wonders, is it realized that there is a link in the decline of church choirs and the disappearance of young people from church?

Vocal apprenticeship, especially amongst boys, is not only the finest of educations, it is essential to the emergence of confident and skilful part-singing. The work of reconstruction does not begin with press-ganging not very able people into rôles for which they are untrained: after all, our standards are set nowadays not by the local town music festival or the singing of Handel's *Messiah* to organ accompaniment in nonconformist chapels but by the élan of the broadcasting media. Reconstruction begins by recruiting the talented musician who, with a mellifluous cantor or two, can set a standard. Such cantors must manage at least to make a good sound: the ability to read music, sight sing, and cope with melismata increase the quantity, but not necessarily the quality, of what cantors contribute. Much the same is true of children's choirs: in most urban contexts a children's choir ought to be possible, and, in many parishes, a quartet, quintet or octet of adults who, from time to time, perform the *a cappella* repertoire, perhaps, to begin with, at midweek solemnities. The greatest prize of all, a very great prize indeed, is recovering something of the *mysterium tremens et fascinans*,

Rudolf Otto's notion of the sacred.[81] When it comes to the refurbishing of the music of the Mass there could not be a more apt word than re-enchantment.

Appendix

I *The Plainsong Mass*

The music for the Ordinary of the Mass is contained in the *Kyriale*, which itself exists in several forms. Three resources are of particular interest here: one is the Solesmes edition, found not only in the *Liber Usualis*,[82] the plainsong compendium from the Benedictines of Solesmes, but also in the *Graduale Romanum* 1974, referred to earlier with regard to its collection of music for the Propers.[83] The second is the *Kyriale Simplex*, found in the *Graduale Simplex* 1988, also mentioned earlier. The third is a small but significant batch of vernacular settings of plainsong. Various hymnals and other musical collections also have music from one or more of these resources, Latin and vernacular. The *Kyriale* in the *Graduale Romanum* provides 18 settings of *Kyrie*, *Gloria*, and *Sanctus*, and six settings of the *Credo*, together with a few extra pieces – half a dozen *Kyries*, three or four *Glorias*, three settings of the *Sanctus* and two of the *Agnus Dei*, under the heading '*Cantus ad libitum*'. Here, then, is a whole plainsong repertoire for the *Schola Cantorum* (the choir of singers). Many of the settings are assigned to particular occasions – Eastertide, feasts of apostles, solemnities, feasts and memorias of the Blessed Virgin Mary, Sundays throughout the year, Sundays in Advent and Lent, weekdays. Not only is the array of material bewildering but much of it would not be useable congregationally – because of its complexity, because of its variety, because of its occasional nature, all of which conspire against congregations gaining a successful familiarity.

Some of the sorting out of what might become more current is done for us by the *Graduale Simplex*. The *Kyriale Simplex* has five settings of *Kyrie*, *Gloria*, and *Sanctus* and four of the *Credo*. They are not assigned to particular seasons and feasts and are simple enough for congregations who have become familiar with them to perform confidently and

---

81 Rudolf Otto, *The Idea of the Holy*, Oxford: Oxford University Press, 1923 (English translation of German original).

82 *Liber Usualis* (1961), published by Tournai-New York: Desclée Co., 1963, is also available (2009) online.

83 See above, p. 121.

well, perhaps supported by an able cantor or two. Leaving aside the question of choral performance, we need to suggest which of these settings might be part of a congregation's repertoire. Having made such a selection, we are not then faced with the daunting prospect of 18 settings in the *Graduale Romanum*, nor even with all five in *Graduale Simplex*, but with a manageable two or three. A similar exercise was carried out in April 1974 when Pope Paul VI sent to all the bishops a booklet, *Jubilate Deo*,[84] containing a 'minimum repertoire of Gregorian chant'. In his covering letter, *Voluntati obsequens*, Paul VI gave permission for the chants to be reprinted and, though an enlarged edition was issued by the Congregation for Divine Worship in 1987, this reinforcement of the primacy of plainsong seems to have made little or no impact. Pope Benedict gave fresh impetus to the need to make use of Gregorian chant in the Apostolic Exhortation *Sacramentum Caritatis*, issued in the wake of the October 2005 Synod on the Eucharist. The consistent message has been that what is needed for national and international gatherings of Catholics should surely be regularly used and well known in Catholic parishes. [85]

Jubilate Deo contains not only settings of the traditional Latin Ordinary: there are also useful settings of the *Magnificat*, the *Salve Regina* and one or two Latin hymns, as well as acclamations and other responses, but it is its choice of chants for the Ordinary which interests us here. These are: *Kyrie* XVI (in *Graduale Romanum* set for weekdays *per annum* ['Ordinary Time']), *Gloria* VIII (often associated with the popular *Kyrie* VIII, *de angelis*), *Credo* III, *Sanctus* XVIII and *Agnus* XVIII (in *Graduale Romanum* set for weekdays in Advent and Lent). The inclusion of the *Pater Noster* (setting 'A' in the *Graduale Romanum*)[86] should also be noticed. Though its neglect for nearly forty years suggests that even this collection is too adventurous for most, here is a slightly timid choice overall and there is little to lose, therefore, by making our own supplementary suggestions, perhaps along the lines that three plainsong settings might be selected for a modest parish. Musical fashion and cultural diversity preclude specific recommendations of modern settings but the timelessness of plainsong makes such

---

84 *Adoremus*: www.adoremus.org provides downloadable files of music from *Jubilate Deo* (in plainsong and modern notation) and MP3 files of the music, as it appears in the *Adoremus Hymnal*, and from the CD recordings of the *Adoremus Hymnal*. The hierarchy of England and Wales put *Jubilate Deo* on-line in 2009: see www.liturgyoffice.org.uk/resources.

85 This point is made too by GIRM para. 41 which makes particular mention of 'the Creed and the Lord's Prayer, set to the simpler melodies'.

86 *Graduale Romanum*, p. 812.

recommendations possible. Recommendations are set out conveniently in the form of a table and with an explanation following on.

For the purposes of comparison, we give first a record of what was used in St Peter's, Rome, in 2009. Given that congregations in the basilica are vast and varying, and that the daily rhythm and definitive repertoire of, say, the Abbaye Saint-Pierre de Solesmes is not therefore possible, it is heartening to discover that, as well as Mass XI (with *Kyrie Orbis Factor*) being used on Sundays *per annum*, Mass XVII is used in Advent and Lent, Mass I in Eastertide, and Mass IV for feasts of Apostles. *Credo* IV is used as well as *Credo* I and *Credo* III, and Mass IX is used from time to time. The so-called *Missa de Angelis*, well known and well loved, comes into its own for large international masses.[87] Our own suggestions are perforce more modest.

Advent and Lent	Christmas and Eastertide	Sundays and Feasts *per annum*	Requiem Mass
Kyrie XVIII B or *Kyrie* XVI	*Kyrie* VIII *de Angelis*	*Kyrie* XI *Orbis factor*	*Kyrie* XVIIIB
No *Gloria*	*Gloria* VIII	*Gloria* VIII	No *Gloria*
Apostles' Creed or Nicene Creed (in English)	*Credo* III	*Credo* I in English or *Credo* III (Latin)	No Creed
Sanctus XVIII	*Sanctus* VIII	*Sanctus* XI	*Sanctus* XVIII
Agnus XVIII	*Agnus* VIII	*Agnus* XI	*Agnus* XVIII
Lord's Prayer in English	Festal *Pater Noster* (Latin or English)	**Sundays:** Merbecke (English) **Feasts:** Festal *Pater Noster* (Latin or English)	Lord's Prayer in English

---

87 Jeffrey Tucker, 'Music at St Peter's: The Transformation', *New Liturgical Movement*, 10 August 2009.

Of these suggestions, detailed in the table, *Kyrie* VIII *de Angelis*, is undoubtedly the best known, despite the intricacies of its melismas. It is ideal for Christmastide and, when the Rite of Blessing and Sprinkling Holy Water is not used, Eastertide. *Sanctus* VIII and *Agnus Dei* VIII are part of the same set, if they can be managed. *Kyrie* XI, *Orbis factor*, is anyway intended for Sundays *per annum*. Again, *Sanctus* XI and *Agnus* XI complement naturally and would work well even in places of modest performance, if the main text is allocated to a cantor and the congregation sings only the phrases *Hosanna in excelsis, miserere nobis* and *dona nobis pacem*. For Advent and Lent, *Kyrie* XVIII B – also suitable for Mass for the dead – is ideal (perhaps better for general use than *Kyrie* XVI as recommended by *Jubilate Deo*), and *Sanctus* XVIII and *Agnus* XVIII are part of the set. Less variety is necessary for *Gloria* and *Credo*: for most parishes, and, given that it is omitted in penitential seasons, *Gloria* VIII would suffice.

Light and shade in the reciting of the Creed might be achieved by singing *Credo* I in English (as suggested by *Music for the English*) or *Credo* III in Latin for most of the year but saying the Creed in English during penitential seasons – when the focus may be more catechetical than doxological and, for baptisands and confirmands at least, the Apostles' Creed the more appropriate parochial text. As for the Lord's Prayer, we have already mentioned setting 'A' in the *Graduale Romanum*, a 'festal tone' well known in English to Anglo-Catholics,[88] and appearing also in the English language version of the *Missale Romanum* 2002. Also frequently sung by Anglo-Catholics is the Merbecke Lord's Prayer which, not least because of its date of publication,[89] and its free metre and unison character, is related to the genre of plainsong. A church which used the 'festal tone' – whether in Latin or English – on high days and in high seasons, the Merbecke on 'green Sundays' and a spoken Lord's Prayer on other occasions would experience simple and effective variety.

In making these recommendations one is conscious of patiently recovering and refreshing a lost tradition rather than seeking to discover a new one. In the heyday of English Catholicism – the increasingly confident 1950s when, however, things were surely not as rosy as nostalgia suggests – most parish musicians would have known what was meant by '*de Angelis*' and '*Orbis factor*' even if successful per-

---

88 Francis Burgess, *The English Gradual: Part I The Plainchant of the Ordinary*, seventh edition, London: Plainchant Publications Committee, 1961, p. 136.

89 *The Booke of Common Praier Noted* was published in 1550, the year after the first BCP. Though the second BCP was significantly different, no adaptations were made to Merbecke's book.

formance remained elusive. If re-enchantment is to work (and in this particular there could not be a more apt word etymologically than 're-enchantment'), there are pitfalls to avoid and good strategies to avoid them. One is the modification of musical complexity in the interests of successful musical outcomes: a wise musical director might, initially at least, ensure that the final (sixth) line of the *Kyrie* whether *de Angelis*, *Orbis factor* or XVIIIB is not an extended version or new music, but a repeat of the fifth line – at least until the settings become embedded. As a general rule, when the congregational line is a repeat of the cantor's line, success is assured; when the congregational line is different, success is less predictable. The least successful – and, one might wager, the least used – of the congregational plainsong responses in the *Graduale Romanum* is the response to the Gospel,[90] where the congregation is asked to sing something intricate and melodically unrelated to what has just been sung.

II Resources for the Propers

The relative size of the North American market and the very different cultural history of English Church Music mean that, for the narrower brief discussed here, the Royal School of Church Music (RSCM)[91] is less helpful than the Church Music Association of America[92] for finding resources for the Propers of the Mass. Sharing the RSCM's address, however, is the Plainsong and Medieval Music Society[93] – albeit mainly of academic and historic interest – and the Gregorian Chant Association Site has useful lists of resources.[94] Though the RSCM took over the catalogue of the Plainchant Publications Committee, and continues to be custodian of that tradition, it may be that after the RSCM's downsizing, first from Addington Palace to Dorking, and move thence to Sarum College, Salisbury, that much will be out of print.

The Plainchant Publications Committee resources are far from new: the Revd G. H. Palmer's *Plainchant Gradual* revised by Francis Burgess[95]

---

90 *Graduale Romanum*, pp. 806ff.

91 The Royal School of Church Music, Sarum College, Salisbury, Wiltshire, UK, www.rscm.com

92 Church Music Association of America, Richmond, Virginia, USA, www.musicasacra.com

93 admin@plainsong.org.uk

94 www.beaufort.demon.co.uk

95 G. H. Palmer and Francis Burgess (eds), *The Plainchant Gradual*, Wantage: St Mary's Press, revised edition, 1962. The Royal School of Church Music, Sarum College, Salisbury, nowadays has custody of this and other historic English plainsong resources.

and Francis Burgess's own *English Gradual* long provided resources for the singing of the Propers of the pre-conciliar Missal in English. A certain amount of caution is necessary here. With Francis Burgess's collection, for instance, we have music for the texts published as numbers 657–733 in the *English Hymnal* and designed to fit the lectionary of the BCP 1662 as adapted by Anglo-Catholics, that is, broadly, the lectionary of the pre-conciliar Missal. Burgess gives us greatly simplified and stylized chants – so that the Introit, for example, sounds similar from Sunday to Sunday, though the words change.

More recently, C. David Burt's *Anglican Use Gradual*[96] and Bruce E. Ford's *American Gradual*[97] have provided resources for the 1970 Missal. With Burt we have a collection for the Anglican Use, that is, for Roman Catholics of the Anglican Use, who have used the Book of Divine Worship. (To be fair, Burt intends and commends his collection for a much wider English-speaking audience, Anglican and Roman Catholic, but his use of traditional language limits its appeal for some.) Bruce Ford's collection, by contrast, makes use of the (copyright free) modern language psalter of the American BCP 1979, together with the Revised Standard Version (RSV) and, though he follows the lectionary of the Episcopal Church of the USA, he provides material for those occasions where the Roman lectionary differs from that of the Episcopalians. It is not unfair to say that, though the *American Gradual* is underpinned by signs of much scholarship, its workings show something of the problems of setting English words to plainchant. The rhythms of English and the rhythms of Latin are very different.

As for the *Graduale Simplex*, there is also available an English-language version. Paul F. Ford – a different Ford – is a liturgist and musicologist who has secured the approval of the US Bishops' Committee on the Liturgy for his collection, *By Flowing Waters*.[98] There is no doubt that here would be a very good place to start, if it were thought desirable that the chant should be used, and that the chant for the Propers ought to be in the vernacular, because of the constant subtle and thematic comment of the texts on the meaning of solemnities, Sundays and seasons. Whereas the *American Gradual* (a version of the *Graduale Romanum*) looks to the RSV, *By Flowing Waters* (a

---

96 C. David Burt (adaptor and ed.), *The Anglican Use Gradual*, Mansfield, Mass.: Partridge Hill Press, 2007. The *Anglican Use Gradual* is available online (2009) as an Adobe Acrobat file.

97 Bruce E. Ford (adaptor and ed.), *The American Gradual*, second edition, Hopkinsville, KY, 2008. *The American Gradual* is also available (2009) online: www.musicasacra.com/books/americangradual1.pdf

98 Paul F. Ford (arranger), *By Flowing Waters*, Collegeville: Liturgical Press, 1999.

version of the *Graduale Simplex*) looks to the New Revised Standard Version, which almost certainly will be the basis – with adaptation – of the next version of the Lectionary for the English-speaking world. Until then, the best plainsong psalm resource for parishes is undoubtedly the *Graduale Simplex* – and the best vernacular option of that *By Flowing Waters*. But, of course, unison singing is only one form of singing and attention should be drawn to such settings as those of Richard Rice's *Simple Choral Gradual*,[99] which provide choir and congregations with an alternative to the hymn sandwich, and which are a salutary reminder that choral chanting, integral to the Orthodox Liturgy and to the Anglican church music tradition, is a suitable medium also for the Catholic Propers.

This is a time of immense change and, as we have noticed, most of what is available in English will be superseded when use of the English language Roman Missal translating *Missale Romanum, editio typica tertia* (2002) has become firmly established everywhere. The internet has already shown some of its potential, even in a specialized cultural area not known for innovation. Most of the weblinks in this chapter, indicating something of what was online in 2009, will provide information and material that is constantly up-to-date, a facility that has never been possible in printed bibliographies. Not only that, but as information and material becomes more widely available, so too we can expect and work for the transformation of the musical resourcing of the Mass. Hence we shall recover not only the interweaving of psalms and sacrifice, integral to the liturgy, but also the understanding, never lost in the East, that music is an essential part of the eucharistic cultus.

---

99 www.musicasacra.com/books/simplechoralgradual.pdf

5

Town or Country

My eyes are awake before the watches of the night that I may medi-
tate upon your promise . . . Seven times a day I praise you for your
righteous ordinances.

Psalms 118(119).148, 164

The history of the Divine Office,[1] the Prayer of the Church, can be
told as a series of struggles, with different patterns and different interest groups gaining prominence at different times. In the fourth century there was the emerging pattern of public prayer, where praise was
offered with the ceremonial of candles, incense and processions, and
the singing of familiar canticles and psalms – and this is often referred
to as the 'cathedral Office'. Meanwhile there was the pattern of monastic prayer, the 'monastic Office', ultimately ascendant, where – at first
daily, then weekly, then monthly – recitation of the whole psalter lay
at the heart of what St Benedict called the *Opus Dei*, the work of God,
the monk's daily prayer. A further contrast can be drawn between the
requirements of the individual priest or friar (and, later, sister) for what
is needed outside the monastic choir to sustain an essentially solitary
life of prayer – the rise of the breviary, with what was needed from the
choir books collected into a volume or two – as against the needs of
the baptized corporately playing their part. The laity, no less than the
secular clergy, are outside the monastic choir and, if they are to play
their part in the daily offering of prayer and praise, they must gather
in the naves of the churches, or say their prayers in the quiet corners of
their own homes, confident in their use of some shared forms of praying, such as those in the medieval books of hours and primers. The
story has never been told better than by Archimandrite Robert Taft,

---

1 The terms 'Divine Office' and 'Liturgy of the Hours' are collective terms. They are
also names of liturgical books. When used in that latter sense they are here italicized. The
'Office' (upper case) refers to a whole genre. Any one 'hour' is referred to as an 'office'
(lower case), except for the Office of Readings.

in *The Liturgy of the Hours of East and West*,[2] nor more enjoyably than by George Guiver CR in *Company of Voices*.[3] For those unfamiliar with the story, and for those amused by broad generalizations, one might summarize the outcomes by saying that, particularly in the West, 'monastic' won out against 'cathedral', the needs of the cleric won out against the needs of the laity, and, beyond the walls of the convents and monasteries, the needs of the individual praying alone won out against the needs of the community praying corporately. We shall stay with these contrasts, not least because they are a useful way of making some progress, but we shall gradually see that they have their limitations.

Town

It is particularly interesting to see where the less successful side of a struggle nonetheless gains something of a foothold: Solemn Vespers – that is, Evening Prayer sung with 'cathedral' ceremonial – can still be found occasionally in Catholic churches and, in the Church of England, cathedral Evensong nowadays arguably fares better than the common discipline of any one form of the daily Office amongst Anglican clergy.[4] Less obvious 'cathedral' elements – the frequent use of certain psalms and canticles – remain, and there is a growing interest in the revival of such ceremonies as the evening lighting of lamps (the *lucernarium*, known at least in principle in the second century by Tertullian)[5] and the use of incense at Lauds and Vespers, not least because of the relationship of these two offices to the twice daily offering of temple sacrifices. Though daily provision for the laity has never been very successful, there have been many informal Office books produced for the lay market, offshoots of the Divine Office, which have at least demonstrated that there continues to be a lively market for a privatized lay participation in the Office.[6] What is undoubtedly still underdeveloped, beyond

---

2 Robert Taft SJ, *The Liturgy of the Hours in East and West*, second revised edition, Collegeville: Liturgical Press (LP), 1993.

3 George Guiver CR, *Company of Voices*, revised edition, Norwich: Canterbury Press, 2001.

4 There are interesting signs of the revival of choir schools in France – public choral celebration of the Office was common before the French Revolution – and we may yet see a significant revival of sung Vespers in some centres.

5 Robert Taft, *The Liturgy of the Hours &c.*, p. 18.

6 The most successful of these in English was *A Short Breviary for Religious and Laity*, Collegeville: LP, 1941, which in later editions had a four-week psalter and a daily long scriptural reading. Examples since the 1971 reforms have included Maxwell E. Johnson *et al.* (comp.), *Benedictine Daily Prayer*, Dublin: Columba, 2005; and (the pre-conciliar

the choirs of convents and monasteries, is the communal celebration of the Office. Yet there is renewed interest in this too: we have noted the persistence of solemn Vespers and the continuing popularity of choral Evensong. One marks the re-emergence of what might almost be called a 'High Church Catholicism', evinced, for instance, by Vespers congregations at the churches of Oratorians. The other shows the need of many to remain in touch with – without necessarily believing in or belonging to – some rooted memory of prayer, vicariously offered. More locally, at the back of church many parishes have a few copies of *Morning and Evening Prayer*[7] from the Divine Office, or of the Church of England's *Daily Prayer*,[8] suggesting that it is more common than it once was for small, committed groups to join the parish priest for Lauds and Vespers, or, indeed, join lay-led groups to maintain the Office.

We have labelled one side of the struggle 'town', because what is more usually known as the 'cathedral Office' was essentially a town affair, what went on in town parishes as well as in cathedral churches. More than that, 'town' suggests the participation of ordinary townsfolk, lay people living nearby and coming together to pray. We have called the other side 'country' because the 'monastic Office' encompasses the prayer of communities in remote places – Benedictine abbeys are usually in less accessible rural areas – and the prayer of those in isolation, whether living alone as hermits, or praying alone at home, quiet havens separate from the bustle and noise of the town.

Twentieth-century Disruptions

All of this is part of the background necessary for understanding something of the revision of the Office which, as yet, has incompletely evolved. That, at least is the contention here, but it is being argued from the perspective of admiration for, and extensive experience of, the 1971 Liturgy of the Hours, though with considerable reservations about the dislocations and unnecessary innovations of the twentieth

form) *The Monastic Diurnal*, Farnborough: St Michael's Abbey Press, 2004, a sixth edition of a 1948 Collegeville publication intended for Benedictine sisters 'engaged in apostolic work away from their convents'. Anglican contributions are included in Andrew Burnham (comp.), *A Manual of Anglo-Catholic Devotion*, second edition, Norwich: Canterbury Press, 2001; also Andrew Burnham, *A Pocket Manual of Anglo-Catholic Devotion*, Norwich: Canterbury Press, 2004; and John Pitchford, *Discovering Prayer with the Church*, Norwich: Tufton Books, 2006.

7 London: Collins, 1974.
8 London: Church House Publishing, 2005.

century. The Office in the West suffered from two major disruptions in this period: the reforms of Pius X in 1911, resulting in a new edition of *Breviarium Romanum* in 1914, and the post-conciliar reforms of Paul VI in 1971. Both sets of reforms attempted to tackle major structural difficulties, not without success, yet both, as we shall see, failed to solve two of the most serious problems. In a different way, as we shall see, the revision of the Church of England Office in the period 1980–2005 tackled similar problems and fared better in some ways and less well in others. The Church of England represents only two provinces in a Communion in which there are as many liturgical traditions as there are provinces but, as elsewhere in this book, despite the arbitrariness of looking at only one Anglican liturgical tradition, it remains a useful comparison: the laboratory is small, the field work restricted, and the results of the experiments come in quickly. One of the unresolved problems is the question of how continuity is assured, so that those praying the Office know themselves to be engaged in a time-honoured cycle of prayer, united throughout the ages and across the world. The other is how provision is made, within the uniform structure of the Office, for the very different needs of individuals and groups, clergy and laity, monastics and seculars.

There has been considerable enthusiasm, particularly during the papacy of Benedict XVI, for reverting to the pre-conciliar breviary, the 1961 breviary[9] (albeit with the Gallican Vulgate psalter rather than the Pian psalter, the recension of the psalter authorized by Pius XII).[10] Such enthusiasm for what the Pope has referred to as 'the hermeneutic of reform',[11] as opposed to 'the hermeneutic of discontinuity and rupture', seems to have rather ignored the 'discontinuity and rupture' of 1911, which, in its way, was almost as great a revolution as the 'discontinuity and rupture' of 1971. It was in 1911, after all, that the pattern of psalms in the breviary of Pius V (1568) was disrupted by a new allocation of the psalms. Whatever the merits of the new *cursus* – and the

---

9 There had been a revision of the rubrics of the breviary in 1955, one of the liturgical reforms of Pius XII, but it was in the pontificate of John XXIII that these rubrics were published as *Codex Rubricarum* (1960) and a new typical edition of the breviary published (1961). In J. B. O'Connell's words, 'No reform will be more heartily welcomed than the simplification of the rubrics of the Roman breviary and missal – a reform long overdue', see Alcuin Reid, *The Organic Development of the Liturgy*, Farnborough: St Michael's Abbey Press, 2004, p. 197.

10 See Appendix I, p. 165 for a brief discussion of the Latin psalter.

11 In an address to the Roman Curia on 22 December, Pope Benedict spoke of the Second Vatican Council and difficulties in its interpretation and implantation as a problem of hermeneutics. On the one hand, he said, there is 'a hermeneutic of discontinuity and rupture' and, on the other hand, 'a hermeneutic of reform'. See also p. 55, above.

principle of dividing longer psalms up into manageable portions was new, and sensibly was retained in 1971 – the *cursus* it replaced, though modified by Pius V, was essentially that which St Benedict had inherited from antiquity and modified for his Rule a millennium and a half earlier.[12] (There had been a similar disruption in 1535, when Cardinal Quiñonez's reformed breviary, with its distinctive *schema* of psalms had held sway briefly, but it was its very discontinuity which led to its suppression, despite its popularity. For similar reasons, neo-Gallican versions of the breviary, common in French dioceses of the seventeenth and eighteenth century, failed to gain a permanent foothold.[13]) Whatever the merits of the *cursus* of the 1971 psalter, it was even more intrinsically disruptive of continuity than that of 1911.[14] History suggests that, like that of Quiñonez and the diocesan breviaries of pre-revolutionary France, the 1971 *cursus* itself might not be lasting. An observable feature of liturgy, because of the strong pull of tradition, is the more recent and radical the innovation, the less likely it is to endure. Given how similar the 1971 reforms are, structurally, to the Quiñonez Office – and indeed welcome – one dares to hope that the *cursus* will be reviewed but that the 1971 framework will evolve and endure.

As for providing for the very different needs of individuals and groups, clergy and laity, monastics and seculars, it is not unfair to say that 1911 somewhat ignored their distinctive needs. That is to say, whilst considerably assisting the whole Church by shortening and simplifying what was required to be said, and by freeing the weekly cycle from undue disruption from the celebration of saints' days (and the consequent over-use of some psalms and neglect of others),[15] the breviary of Pius X nonetheless did little to provide for the distinctive needs of the laity or for the corporate praying of the Office in parishes. More

---

12 Laurence Hemming makes the point that the order 'in at least some of the offices appears to have been taken over from the Jerusalem Temple and predates Christianity itself'. See Laurence P. Hemming, *Worship as a Revelation*, London: Burns & Oates, 2008, p. 159.

13 There was a further edition of *Breviarium Romanum* in 1623 but that was substantially the 1568 (Tridentine) breviary. The 1568 breviary itself had simplified and shortened the traditional *cursus* somewhat. For a discussion of the neo-Gallican reforms, including Dom Guéranger's sharp critique, see Alcuin Reid, *The Organic Development &c.*, pp. 40ff. See also note 46, below.

14 Only about 3% of the time do the psalms set in the Benedictine *Schema* A coincide with their use in the 1971 Liturgy of the Hours. See note 33 below and Appendix II.

15 It might be said that the 1911 *cursus*, revolutionary though it was, would not have felt like the main change introduced by the Pius X breviary. The calendrical balance – from celebrating a round of feasts to celebrating weekdays often with commemoration of saints merely appended (by means of antiphon and collect) – would have felt to be the greatest change.

than that, though it continued to focus on secular clergy praying alone, the breviary remained essentially monastic in content and shape. The notion of diocesan clergy being dispersed monastics, mostly praying alone, may suit the spirituality or temperament of the priest reciting the Office alone but accords neither with the rhythm of parish life nor with the responsibility of the parish priest to lead the public celebration of the prayer of the Church.[16]

The *Liturgia Horarum* (Liturgy of the Hours) of 1971[17] tried to improve on 1911 by acknowledging the distinctive needs of the different groups.[18] Recognizing the needs of those praying alone and leading busy lives, the night office of Matins or Vigils was recast as the Office of Readings, a pattern of longer, historical psalms, and readings from the Bible, the Fathers and the Lives of Saints, to be used at whatever time of day best suited – a brilliant idea, if as yet imperfectly executed. It was recognized that many religious would use the Roman Office (for not every order would have its own Office) and, amidst its reforms, the Paul VI breviary made provision for them too. Thus the innovation of a single minor office during the day (*'ad horam mediam'*) – to be used at whatever time suited – was complemented by sets of psalmody which permitted the continuing pattern of Terce, Sext and None where the Office is said in community. Again, recognizing that people have different temperaments, there were concessions in the rubrics, allowing such things as the omission of responsories by those reciting the Office alone, the use of a longer reading at the public celebration of Lauds or Vespers, and the repetition of the Sunday Compline psalms, so that those who wished to pray Compline walking the dog at night or in the darkness of the bedroom could do so. The English version of the Liturgy of the Hours offers popular hymns and, at the back of the book, some fine poems to be used in lieu of the office hymn. These hymns and

---

16 There have been various attempts to lessen the rigour of the breviary: the requirement that the lips as well as the eye move during private recitation, and the requirement that all three nocturnes are used at Matins (whenever there still are three nocturnes), and all three of the little hours during the day, were relaxed after the Second Vatican Council – exact references unavailable. How to maintain the *cursus*, using only one nocturne and only one minor office during the day, remains unclear.

17 Published as *The Divine Office* in Great Britain and *The Liturgy of the Hours* in the USA: for a timeline of the emergence of the different liturgical books and resources for the office, official and unofficial, see www.kellerbook.com/timeline.htm and the Bibliography. When the reference to 'Liturgia Horarum', 'Liturgy of the Hours', or 'Divine Office' is to the publications of that name, italics are used. Otherwise, for 1971 provisions generally, italics are not used.

18 Close accounts of the reforms of the office are provided in Annibale Bugnini CM, *The Reform of the Liturgy 1948–1975*, Collegeville: LP, 1990; and Stanislaus Campbell, FSC, *From Breviary to Liturgy of the Hours*, Collegeville: LP, 1995.

poems show indebtedness to the Anglican tradition, an indebtedness which reflects something of the ecumenical optimism of the 1970s and, in the poetry, the burgeoning of middle-class Catholicism. There are suggestions in the General Instruction on the Liturgy of the Hours too about the use of ceremonial and singing. Those for whom the daily recitation of the Divine Office in full is 'of obligation' will surely appreciate that the psalter spread over four weeks is much more manageable than the psalter recited every week. Those who celebrate the Divine Office communally will surely appreciate that three portions of psalmody at Lauds and Vespers – two psalms and a canticle – is more manageable than Pius X's five.

Some of this is surely along the right lines. Robert Taft hails the structural reforms of 1971 as 'a courageous break with the past' but suggests that 'many believe that the unwillingness to make a more radical break with not just the forms, but with the mentality of this past, has marred the recent reform of the Roman Office'.[19] This perspective is itself open to challenge: certainly the 1971 Liturgy of the Hours remains monastic in feel, not easily adaptable for parish celebration, but there are problems of discontinuity and rupture too and the discontinuity, not so much of form as of content, is also a disengagement, somewhat, with positive aspects of the mentality of the past.[20]

Reform of the Reform?

If there were to be a 'Reform of the reform' with regard to the Divine Office – a new look at what was done in 1971 in the light of the Office as previously celebrated – it would be necessary to go back further than 1911 and see that reform as itself at once too radical and too cautious. As we have seen, the breviary of Pius X, the 1911 revision, was much too radical with regard to the *cursus* of psalmody and yet much too cautious with regard to the needs of groups and of the laity. It was realized at the time that the reform of Matins was very inadequate and that further work would need to be done on that,[21] and the 1971 reform,

---

19 Robert Taft, *The Liturgy of the Hours &c.*, p. 314.

20 To gain some idea of the degree of discontinuity and rupture, it might be helpful to note that on some 70 of approximately 250 occasions each week the breviaries of Pius V and Pius X prescribe the same psalm or portion of Psalm 118(119), that is, only just over a quarter of the time. See Appendix II for further details.

21 This further work was promised by Pius X in the *motu proprio, Abhinc duos annos,* October 1913. For the text see AAS 5 (1913), pp. 449–551.

The breviary changes were authorized by the *motu proprio Divino afflatu,* 1911.

the scheme of readings, scriptural and non-scriptural, in the Office of Readings, as we have suggested, marks significant progress. It was a pity that the optional two-year cycle of biblical readings did not emerge into the daylight in the United Kingdom until *The CTS New Catholic Bible* appended it as a table,[22] a quarter of a century after the rubric in the General Instruction described it in the present tense (GIRM para. 145). Equally, at the time of writing (2009), the optional lectionary of readings from the Fathers and Church writers, similarly described and promised (para. 161) is imminent but has yet to appear. In that sense at least, but also in the persistent rumours that a new English version of the authorized Liturgy of the Hours will not be authorized until some further, possibly major, revision of Liturgy of the Hours has taken place, the work is far from complete. Before examining what reforms might be beneficial, the development of the monastic Office a few years' later than the 1971 reform is worth a brief look.

Country

The reform of the Benedictine Office, after the Second Vatican Council, followed in the wake of Paul VI's reform of the Liturgy of the Hours. Though many religious availed themselves of the 1971 reforms, it was inevitable that Benedictines, amongst others, would undertake their own reform. The *Thesaurus Liturgiae Horarum Monasticae* (Thesaurus of the Monastic Liturgy of the Hours) was approved in 1977 by a decree of the Sacred Congregation of Sacraments and Divine Worship[23] and, as 'thesaurus' implies, is a directory – a treasury – rather than a set order. There is no space here for examining in detail a resource which is, anyway, not generally available. The emerging culture of choice is evident: the shape of the day is flexible, with the office of Prime (suppressed in the 1971 reforms) retained as an option for Benedictines, and discretion given to the abbot over the ordering – the shape and the detail – of the minor hours during the day. There are opportunities to follow the Roman Liturgy of the Hours (for instance, using a New Testament Canticle as one of the pieces of psalmody at Vespers[24] and the *Nunc Dimittis* at Compline).[25] What interests us most amongst these

---

22 Published by the Catholic Truth Society, London, 2007.

23 *Operi Dei*, 10 February 1977.

24 In addition to the *Magnificat*.

25 Though the *Nunc Dimittis* is intrinsic to Compline in the Roman Office it was not traditionally part of the Benedictine Office of Compline.

choices are the *schemas* of psalmody – A, B, C and D.[26] St Benedict was less prescriptive in his Rule than is sometimes supposed: Dom Patrick Barry OSB, in his translation of *A Rule of Saint Benedict*,[27] relegates chapters 8–18 to an appendix, on the grounds that Benedict's 'order of psalms is no longer normally observed in the monastic Office nor in the Roman Divine Office'. More than that, he reminds us that St Benedict 'himself, in a typically modest and far-seeing comment, strongly recommends that any who think of a better disposition of psalms should make the change as they think best'.[28] There is, however, one principle which seems important to St Benedict:

> Any monastic community which chants less than the full psalter with the usual canticles each week shows clearly that it is too indolent in the devotion of the service of God. After all, we read that our holy Fathers had the energy to fulfil on one single day what we in our lukewarm devotion only aspire to complete in a whole week.[29]

Since the approval of the *Thesaurus*, new books resourcing the Benedictine Office have been steadily appearing: a monastic psalter,[30] a hymn book with a supplement of monastic propers,[31] and, for the day hours, a monastic antiphonal in three volumes published in 2005, 2006 and 2007.[32] Unlike Abbot Barry's edition of *The Rule*, the *Psalterium monasticum* privileges Benedict's scheme – *schema* A[33] – and merely provides references for the other *schemas*. The psalter within volume II of *Antiphonale monasticum* similarly privileges Benedict's *schema*, indeed without referring specifically to other *schemas*, but helpfully gives the psalms for all the minor hours – including those for Prime – to

---

26 The four schemas are available (2009) online: www.kellerbook.com/SCHA.HTM; www.kellerbook.com/SCHB.HTM; www.kellerbook.com/SCHC.HTM; www.kellerbook. com/SCHD.HTM

27 Patrick Barry OSB (ed. and tr.), *A Rule of Saint Benedict*, Leominster: Gracewing, 1997.

28 Patrick Barry, *A Rule of Saint Benedict*, p. 27.

29 Patrick Barry, *A Rule of Saint Benedict*, p. 103, from Chapter 19 of the Rule.

30 *Psalterium monasticum* (Monastic psalter), Solesmes, 1981, including psalms for Vigils.

31 *Liber hymnarius*, Solesmes, 1983.

32 *Antiphonale monasticum*, Solesmes (five vols, one for internal use), 2005, 2006, 2007, 2009, replacing the *Antiphonale monasticum* (1934).

33 'Schema A' throughout this chapter refers to the Benedictine schema and not to the 1965 proposal for a two-week cycle, considered by the Consilium in April 1965 (see Stanislaus Campbell, *From Breviary &c.*, pp. 145ff.).

be arranged and used as the abbot directs.[34] Despite occasional reports of communities seeking permission to use the pre-conciliar monastic liturgy, there is more continuity between the post-conciliar monastic liturgy and what preceded it than there is in the Roman Divine Office. More than that, with no equivalent of the 1911 rupture, the monastic liturgy preserves a recognizable continuity with the whole Benedictine tradition. There are varieties of forms (pre-conciliar and post-conciliar), different psalm *schemas* (A, B, C or D), different languages (Latin and the vernacular), and even different English translations (communities having more autonomy in this matter than secular clergy).

A Culture of Choice

If the Benedictine Liturgy of the Hours seems to be altogether in better shape than the Roman Liturgy of the Hours, it may be partly because, as the Office has developed, the needs of 'country' have won over those of 'town', the notion of struggle with which we began. It may be partly because the reforms have been achieved by adding options to – rather than by making changes to – what has gone before. In one way it is sensible to give options. How else does one accommodate a whole series of different needs? Yet the bewildering bazaar of choices on offer, for instance in the Church of England's Common Worship (CW), the liturgies produced at the turn of the third millennium, makes the very word 'common' problematic. To be fair, Anglicanism has always had different and divergent traditions, and the days are long gone – and never quite existed – when the services of the 1662 BCP were acceptable as the sole and unifying liturgy of Anglicanism.[35] And yet the explosion of choice since 1970 is not just the Church – any church – discovering the range of its needs and ways of catering for those needs, it is also a beguiling feature of post-modernism, that deeply disturbing philosophy which encourages tolerance in a liberal democracy but ultimately offers meaninglessness by undermining any prospect of a shared

---

34 See volume III, pp. 183ff. This privileging of *Schema* A in the Solesmes publications does not indicate the success or otherwise of the other schemas: an American survey in 1993 suggested that B (produced by Dom Notker Feuglister OSB, ob. 1996) was the most popular of all (*American Benedictine Review*, December 1993). Anecdotal evidence suggests that *Schema* C, produced in Scheyern Abbey, Bavaria, is also very popular, especially in Europe, but that less is heard of the Waddel cycle, *Schema* D.

35 Note the impact of the abortive Scottish Episcopalian Prayer Book of 1637 on the 1789 Prayer Book of American Episcopalians. Here, especially in the eucharistic rite, is a distinct Anglican tradition with continuing influence thereafter.

truth, a common meta-narrative, a common liturgy. Briefly, should the Church be as seduced as manifestly as it has been here by the culture of choice?

The Reform of the Church of England Office

The BCP Office has been the glory of the Church of England and for-mative (and, in most places until surprisingly recently, normative) for the Anglican Communion. Cranmer's fairly successful telescoping of Matins and Lauds to form Morning Prayer, and ingenious combination of Vespers and Compline to form Evening Prayer,[36] were consciously a continuation of the Quiñonez project and, like that reform, the prior-ity was allowing the Bible to be read consecutively. Of course Cranmer went well beyond Quiñonez: only two offices, the vernacular, a full programme of education for the laity as well as the clergy, for public prayer as well as for private devotion. Attempts to modify Cranmer's Prayer Book in 1927/1928 failed legally, though most of what had been suggested for the Office then re-emerged experimentally in the 1960s Alternative Services Series 1 and Series 2.[37] What appeared in the *Alternative Service Book 1980*[38] were revised offices, characterized by choice of canticle and available in full and shortened forms. That these forms were thought to be ill-judged for public worship and private prayer was apparent from the number of churches which, though adopting a modern eucharistic rite, persevered with Prayer Book Evensong, or abandoned the public celebration of the Office altogether. To be fair, this was when the Parish Eucharist movement was at its height and, for complex sociological reasons, Sunday evening attendance in a vast number of churches collapsed, along with any sense of the necessity to attend church more than once on a Sunday.

---

36 The core sequence of BCP Morning Prayer – psalms, Old Testament lesson, *Te Deum*, New Testament lesson, *Benedictus* – works less well chronologically and thematically than the core sequence of BCP Evening Prayer – psalms, Old Testament lesson, *Magnificat*, New Testament lesson, *Nunc Dimittis*. Morning Prayer would work better if the *Benedicite omnia opera* (Dan. 3.57–88, 56, [Three Ch. 35–68, 34]) or *Benedictus es Domine* (Dan. 3:52–57, [Three Ch. 29–34]) always displaced the *Te Deum*, which, on appropriate Sundays and feasts, might come after the third collect.

37 The proposals to the Convocations and the Church Assembly were published by the Society for Promoting Christian Knowledge (SPCK), London, and issued in booklet form on various dates in the later part of the 1960s.

38 Published jointly by Oxford: Mowbray and Oxford University Press, and Cambridge: Cambridge University Press, Colchester: William Clowes, and London: SPCK, 1980.

Another attack on the 1980 offices came from the radically different, though unofficial, provision of *Celebrating Common Prayer*,[39] drawn up by the Society of Saint Francis only a decade later, with the active support of the Church of England Liturgical Commission, one of whose members was the late Br Tristam SSF. This volume, with its minor offices, and its recasting of Morning and Evening Prayer in a shape similar to that of Lauds and Vespers in *Liturgia Horarum* (that is, no longer the compound offices of the Prayer Book), sold astonishingly well and continues to have its vigorous supporters.

Building on this success, the CW volume, *Daily Prayer*[40] maintains the shapes of the Morning Prayer, Evening Prayer, and Night Prayer of the Divine Office but, instead of Midday Prayer – the *ad horam mediam* office in *Liturgia Horarum* – attempts a versatile experiment with what it calls Prayer During the Day. The Office is cast in a fourfold shape, with Prayer During the Day at the beginning and Night Prayer at the end, thus providing two simple offices for private use. In between come Morning and Evening Prayer, with such optional 'cathedral' provision as 'The Acclamation of Christ at the Dawning of the Day' – a form of the invitatory – and 'The Blessing of Light' – a form of the *lucernarium*. The versatility of Prayer During the Day is that it can be used as a version of the Office of Readings as well as a minor office during the day. It is noticeable, however, that the duty and habit of reading long Old and New Testament readings at Morning and Evening Prayer persists even though it is perfectly proper for there to be only one long reading at each major office and, more than that, all the lengthy Bible reading that needs to be done can be consigned to Prayer During the Day, where there can be time for meditation, reflection, silence, and space. A very significant difference between CW *Daily Prayer* and the Roman Office is that, for Morning and Evening Prayer, though canticles are suggested, psalms and readings are not specified. These forms, therefore, can act as a framework for a number of different psalm and lesson schemes in *Daily Prayer* whereas in the Roman Office the *Psalterium* is integral to the Office.

---

39 London: Mowbray, 1992. Available both as *The Daily Office SSF* and *Celebrating Common Prayer* and, from 1994, in a simplified, pocket version.

40 London: Church House Publishing, 2005. See above, p. 142. For an introduction to the modern Church of England Office. See also Andrew Burnham, 2002, 'Introduction', in Jeremy Fletcher and Gilly Myers (eds), *Using Common Worship, Daily Prayer*, London: Church House Publishing, 2002.

The modern and rapid development of the Church of England Office[41] cannot be understood without reference to 'A Service of the Word', the introduction to which tells us what we really need to know: 'A Service of the Word is unusual for an authorized Church of England service. It consists almost entirely of notes and directions and allows for considerable local variation and choice within a common structure.'[42] It consists also of 'authorized' material, especially penitential and credal material, where there is acknowledged doctrinal sensitivity. Here, then, is a rather extreme version of what we called earlier 'the culture of choice'. The advantage is that most things – and in practice almost anything – can be made to fit into (or be omitted from) the agreed framework. The disadvantage is that any notion of commonality is imperilled. Also, in view of what we are saying about the contemporary revision of the Roman Office, it is interesting that Anglicans, from the starting point of the well-developed public Office of Cranmer's Prayer Book, have been keen to develop monastic shapes, and forms suitable for individual prayer and devotion, clerical and lay. In contrast, any examination – and reform – of the Roman Office starts with the given of well-developed monastic shapes and forms and, we would say, begins to look for more satisfactory ways of celebrating the Office communally, and especially parochially, even if, as seems likely, the social conditions for such celebrations may remain unpropitious.

Looking again at the Revisions of the 1970s

The monastic liturgy itself is not immune to the problems of choice: there is the same tension as elsewhere in the Church between the 1960s generation becoming accustomed and firmly wedded to comparatively new and progressive forms and the 1980s generation having a keen interest in what went on before they were born. It is easy to be critical of historicism, an excessive regard for what has gone before, but liturgy cannot be blind to, indeed must constantly look to, the tradition it seeks to maintain, if it is truly to be an expression of what unites worshippers through the ages. It is easy to sneer at what might be called 'medievalism with heating and sanitation' but the alternative, a disre-

---

41 For more information see Jeremy Fletcher and Gilly Myers (eds), *Using Common Worship, Daily Prayer*, and the essay by Paul Bradshaw and Simon Jones in Paul F. Bradshaw (ed.), *A Companion to Common Worship*, vol. 2, London: SPCK, 2006, Ch. 1.

42 See *Common Worship: Services and Prayers for the Church of England*, London: Church House Publishing, 2000, and *New Patterns for Worship*, London: Church House Publishing, 2002.

gard for what has gone before and a constant search for what is innova-
tory, risks fatal discontinuity and obsolescence.

In assessing the revisions of the 1971 Liturgy of Hours, a number
of questions present themselves. An obvious one is whether anything
of real importance has been discarded in these revisions. This question
is also the most urgent one if proper stewardship is to be exercised
and nothing of value permanently lost. We leave aside most calendrical issues, which are looked at in another chapter,[43] and questions of
language, assuming that any future version of the Divine Office would
be available in both Latin and the vernacular. It is enough to note that,
just as the translation policy of *Liturgiam authenticam* has led to the
replacing of the Roman Missal, produced by ICEL in 1973, so *The
Divine Office*, and *The Liturgy of the Hours*,[44] two closely related
versions of the Divine Office in English, will be replaced undoubtedly
by liturgical books with translations more closely following the Latin.
'Dynamic equivalence' – the theory that different languages say things
differently and best express each other's phrases and ideas in somewhat different words, phrases, and syntax – is giving way to 'literal
equivalence', where the words, phrases, and syntax of the vernacular
translation follow the Latin more closely. This is not a new idea for the
English liturgical tradition: the mainstream of biblical translation has
followed this principle.[45]

We leave aside here also hymns and music: inevitably a discussion of
the value of whatever is omitted would be complex and scholarly and
beyond the scope of our concern. Suffice it to say that the hymn texts
of the seventeenth-century pope, the accomplished Latinist Urban VIII,
have been replaced, partly by the texts they sought to improve, and
partly by additions to the repertoire necessary for the innovations of
1971.[46] Little is lost and much gained, as a glance through the plainsong hymn book, *Liber hymnarius*,[47] shows. (Most obviously, there are

---

43 There is a discussion of calendrical issues in Chapter 3, p. 86.

44 The title *The Divine Office* is used by the hierarchies of Australia, England and Wales,
Ireland, New Zealand, Scotland and certain other English-speaking countries. The title *The
Liturgy of the Hours* is used by the USA and certain other English-speaking countries. Some
countries permit either version to be used. Full details are given in the Bibliography.

45 See, for instance, the Revised Version of 1884 where the Revisers' Preface to the
Old Testament says 'the Authorised Version being either inadequate or inconsistent, and
sometimes misleading, changes have been introduced with as much uniformity as appeared
practicable or desirable' and cites as an example the use of 'tabernacle' and 'tent' to describe
one Hebrew word.

46 For a discussion of Pope Urban VIII's revisions, see Alcuin Reid, *The Organic
Development &c.*, pp. 37f. See also note 13, above.

47 *Liber hymnarius*, Solesmes, 1983.

two sets of ferial hymns, one for weeks one and three, the second for weeks two and four). It is almost certain that a new English version of the Liturgy of the Hours would seek to provide good translations of the Latin hymns – perhaps with others which are not direct translations in an appendix[48] – rather than the miscellany presently offered. Meanwhile, new hymn texts, much more so than new antiphon or respond texts, can be fitted where necessary to existing tunes, particularly since most office hymns are in long metre (that is, four lines of eight syllables, each line beginning with an anacrusis).[49]

Lost Ground in 1971

Fr Stanislaus Campbell gives us a blow-by-blow account of the work of the Pontifical Preparatory Commission on the Liturgy set up by Pope John in 1960, of the Consilium set up by the Second Vatican Council, and the nine *cœtus* (study groups) allocated to issues to do with the reform the breviary.[50] What were clearly lost in the Liturgy of Hours 1971 were: the office of Prime (suppressed by article 89 of *Sacrosanctum Concilium*),[51] the weekly recitation of the psalter, and some of the distinct provision for Holy Week and the *Triduum Sacrum*. Prime had been judged unnecessary as early as 1957 by Pope Pius XII's Commission,[52] as the Second Vatican Council was told, and was thought to be a duplication of Lauds. This view should not go entirely unchallenged. The problem with Lauds and Prime is not that they duplicate one another thematically: the one has a focus on thankfulness for the passing of darkness and the dawning of the light of a new day, a celebration, if you will, of the Resurrection; the other prepares for and consecrates the tasks of the day that lies ahead. Nor did the Benedictines fully agree, as we have seen: loyal to tradition they maintained Prime, which is arguably the most beautiful of the offices; loyal to the Council they made Prime optional. To lose Prime altogether means that

---

48 Such as those in *Hymns for Prayer and Praise*, compiled by the Panel of Monastic Musicians and edited by John Harper, Norwich: Canterbury Press, 1996.

49 The other metre, regularly used, if occasionally, is 11-11-11-5, permitting the use of such modern tunes as *Iste Confessor* (such as *English Hymnal* no. 435, *Catholic Hymn Book* no. 240) which originates in the Poitiers *Vesperale* of 1746 but does not seem to be known widely in the USA.

50 Stanislaus Campbell, *From Breviary &c.*, especially Chapters 3, 4 and 5.

51 The Second Vatican Council's *Constitutio de Sacra Liturgia*, Constitution on the Sacred Liturgy, 1964.

52 Stanislaus Campbell, *From Breviary &c.*, pp. 38f.

Iam lucis orto sidere – the hinge between thanksgiving for the daylight at Lauds and planning the day ahead – is almost lost,[53] as are the great orations *Domine . . . qui ad principium huius diei*[54] and *Dirigere et sanctificare.*[55] The real problem outside convents and monasteries is that, where Lauds immediately follows Matins, morning devotions, extended by Prime, are likely to be indigestibly long, and even run up to and collide with the hour of Terce.[56] The principle of *veritas horarum* (truth of the hours) was dear to the Council: everything had to be done to make it possible for the secular clergy to say the right office at the right time. This faithfulness to the appropriate timing of the hours is surely, and incontrovertibly, one of the finest fruits of the revision. Unfortunately, Prime became redundant: not only to lighten the load but also to tighten the timetable.

The perception that, when the Office is too burdensome, priests fail to maintain their canonical obligation to say it, or seek reasons for dispensations from saying it, no doubt lay behind the recasting of the psalter, so that the cycle became a monthly and not a weekly, still less a daily, one. Here again there is significant lost ground: to recite the psalter on a monthly basis is to gain passing familiarity with it; to recite the psalter on a weekly basis is to live with it as a constant inspiration and guide. And no question was more troublesome for the Consilium than the distribution of psalms. Article 91 of *Sacrosanctum Concilium* had specified that the psalter be distributed over a period longer than a week.[57] The revisers investigated various combinations of one-, two- and four-week cycles for the various offices before deciding on the four-week cycle for all the hours except Compline, with its weekly cycle (and with permission to use the Sunday Compline psalms on other days too). There were some casualties of this decision: one was the majority opinion of the Consilium that there should be five psalms for Lauds;

---

53 In *Liturgia Horarum* it continues to be used at Lauds on Thursdays in weeks 2 and 4.

54 In *Liturgia Horarum* it continues to be used at Lauds on Monday in week 2. It is used by Cranmer in the BCP as the third collect at Morning Prayer.

55 This oration appears as the collect for the Eighth Sunday after Trinity in Common Worship.

56 The Church of England compilers of *The BCP as proposed in 1928* (new edition, Norwich: Canterbury Press, 2008) clearly did not regard 'An Order for Prime' as a duplication of Morning Prayer: the rubrics make clear that the one may not supplant the other. Nor did the Benedictines, as we have seen, who, loyal to tradition clearly did not regard 'An Order for Prime' as a duplication of Morning Prayer: the rubrics make clear there that the one may not supplant the other.

57 Stanislaus Campbell, *From Breviary &c.*, pp. 137ff.

another was the unanimous opinion that there should be five psalms for Vespers, with provision for omitting two in celebrations with the people. We shall return to that but, suffice it to say that, had the number of psalms at Matins been reduced from nine to six,[58] and arranged as in the Ambrosian Rite over a two-week cycle, and had the psalms for monastic and individual celebration of Lauds and Vespers been kept at five, something more like the Benedictine *cursus* would have been possible, that is, a weekly cycle, albeit modified in accordance with *Sacrosanctum Concilium* article 91 to ease the burden of psalmody at Matins on the secular clergy and over-lengthy psalmody in public celebration of Lauds and Vespers.

There is not space here to discuss detailed revision of the Office. Though public liturgy needs to be clear and relatively easy to follow, much of the intricacy of the pre-conciliar breviary made it more devotionally rewarding for those bound to it. The 1971 revision emerged amidst an æsthetic of brutal simplicity – against the backdrop of the concrete, glass, and steel of the 1960s townscape – and much that was demolished, including in particular variations to the liturgy during Holy Week, and the Easter *Triduum*, removed much of the distinctiveness of the former season of Passiontide[59] and made the Office less interesting, memorable and pertinent for those bound canonically to its recitation. The office of Prime, which we have extolled, furnishes an example of interesting intricacy: midway through there is a *Benedicamus*[60] and, apparently, a new start. A rubric suggests the reading of the Martyrology of the day 'in choir and, where convenient, outside choir' and we imagine the monks in their stalls. We then gain a sense of the Communion of Saints in the prayer *Sancta Maria et omnes sancti intercedant pro nobis . . .*[61] as a very short, yet distinct, office, brings Prime to a conclusion and the day's work beyond the oratory and chancel begins. To lose all this – as with so much other detail – is to risk turning daily delight into daily drudgery.

---

58 The Benedictine *Schema A* has twelve psalms at Vigils, in addition to Psalm 3, the Invitatory (Ps. 94[95]) and three Old Testament canticles, that is, 17 pieces of psalmody.

59 Passiontide was attenuated but not quite abolished: references to the veiling of crosses and images and the possibility of using Holy Week hymnody in the week before Palm Sunday are examples of where a muted Passiontide reference has been maintained.

60 'Let us bless the Lord. Thanks be to God', a concluding formula.

61 'May holy Mary and all the saints pray for us . . .'

A Public Office?

In addition to looking at what of real importance has been discarded and may need to be recovered, we need to explore what unfinished business there is in the reform. The most urgent question remains how something more obviously suitable for 'town' use, a public Office, a 'people's Office', might evolve. A second question, as we intimated earlier, is how the Office of Readings, which we described as 'a brilliant idea, if as yet imperfectly executed', might further evolve.

As we saw earlier, with the Benedictine liturgical reform the monastic Office is in relatively good shape. As the Consilium and the nine *cœtus* proceeded with the reform of the breviary, few ideas were without their advocates and it is interesting to chase through some of the ideas which were not implemented and yet which had strong advocates, whether from individual liturgists or from large minorities within the Commission or Consilium, or, indeed, bishops at the Second Vatican Council. The 'town' question is a good example. It was put to *cœtus* 9 by Fr Juan Mateos SJ, a professor at the Pontifical Oriental Institute in Rome, a consultor rather than a member of a *cœtus*.[62] A specialist in Eastern liturgy, Fr Mateos saw the virtue of recapturing something of the vibrancy of the town liturgies of the early centuries. George Guiver enthusiastically describes the *akolouthia asmatike*, the old 'chanted' Office of Byzantium, 'the Office of all the secular churches of the empire, as well as the Orthodox churches of southern Italy, Sicily and Russia'.[63] This 'people's Office', replaced by the Byzantine Office as we now know it, survived in Byzantium until the Latins sacked the city in 1204, and in Thessalonica until 1430, when that city fell to the Turks. Guiver speculates that

> [the office's] most distinctive traits, especially the movement from narthex to nave and sanctuary, will have caught the popular imagination and endeared it to ordinary people. It has that feeling of the crowd bringing the ways of the street into the church which seems to characterise so many descriptions of the public office in the times of the Fathers.[64]

No doubt it was something of this atmosphere which inspired Fr Mateos's submission for the revival of Lauds and Vespers as public

---

62 Stanislaus Campbell, *From Breviary &c.*, pp. 78ff.
63 George Guiver, *Company of Voices*, pp. 73f.
64 George Guiver, *Company of Voices*, pp. 73f.

offices. When this proposal got nowhere, Mateos came up with a second suggestion: the revival of the 'cathedral Vigil of the Resurrection', to be celebrated on Sunday mornings before Lauds. This proposal for popular participation also failed to impress *cœtus* 9. It was thought sufficient that Lauds and Vespers had been declared to be the *duplex cardo*, the double hinge of the Office, and what Fr Mateos proposed for a 'cathedral Vigil' became, at Canon Martimort's suggestion, primarily a monastic Vigil for contemplatives, a very different thing indeed.

The Consilium went on to discuss whether there should be one unified Office or a double Office, a choral Office for contemplatives and another for those 'who lead an active life'.[65] A more pertinent question, also discussed, was whether different levels of obligation to, and participation in, the Divine Office might distinguish workers in different parts of the vineyard. This whole question can be examined historically, detailing the debate at the Second Vatican Council and looking earlier to historical precedent. It is encouraging, for example, to discover that, in the first millennium, *Ordo XII* provides for the minor hours to be joined together under one *Deus in adjutorium*, with one responsory, one versicle and the prayer concluding None.[66] It is also encouraging to look across to the Orthodox tradition, where it is recognized that no one person can take part in the whole of the Office for the day, especially when different observances coincide on the same day – the Annunciation and 'Great Friday' (Good Friday) is an extreme example – and the Orthodox practice is to celebrate both rather than move or suppress one in favour of the other.[67] Perhaps the West too needs to have an Office, maintained in full by the monastic tradition and in cathedrals but in which parochial clergy and laity participate to a greater or lesser extent, in prescribed ways but as godly circumstance dictates. This would be a huge cultural change in the meaning of the word 'obligation', a word which, as we have observed elsewhere,[68] derives from the same root as 'religion' and is about that to which one is bound rather than that which one is compelled to do.

---

65 George Guiver, *Company of Voices*, p. 85.
66 George Guiver, *Company of Voices*, p. 9.
67 See John Saward, *The Mysteries of March*, London: Collins, 1990, pp. xvff.
68 See p. 82.

The Future Development of the Divine Office

We have made several suggestions: restoring some of the riches of the pre-conciliar breviary (including the pre-1911 *cursus*); recovering the weekly cycle of the psalter for those for whom it is not burdensome; allowing some parts of the Office – especially Matins – to be governed, however, by a two-week psalm cycle, as in the Ambrosian Rite; developing a public Office with the possibility of 'a cathedral Vigil',[69] and public celebrations of Lauds and Vespers; introducing more flexibility to Prayer During the Day;[70] completing work on the Office of Readings. All of these, as was just seen, would be within a new framework of understanding of the notion of obligation, a new conceptual framework which, in its way, would be as revolutionary as the change in liturgical culture following the Second Vatican Council: the individual and community would be expected to participate appropriately and conscientiously in the Office of the day but would not be expected to accomplish every bit of it.

Any detailed working out of these suggestions is perforce hypothetical since the competence for dealing with liturgical reform lies entirely – and properly – elsewhere. And it might be argued reasonably that all these suggestions were addressed at the time of the conciliar reforms – and one or two of the unsuccessful ones had majority support. The difference now is that there has been a generation of liturgical worship in which the vehicles for celebration, rebuilt in the 1960s, have been extensively road-tested revealing – looking back – that some of the decisions underlying the 1971 Liturgy of the Hours were less astute than had been hoped.[71] Aware of a degree of self-indulgence, we make some concrete suggestions here, knowing that the opinion of any individual – let alone that of one writing presently as a bishop outside the Roman Communion – is an entirely speculative exercise, but conscious that a critical analysis which does not go on to suggest specific emendations falls well short as an analysis. Here then are seven principles

---

69 Such a 'cathedral Vigil' office has been celebrated, for instance before the televised Midnight Mass of Christmas in Westminster Cathedral 2001.

70 There is no space here to make specific suggestions about Prayer during the Day: obvious possibilities for reform would include simpler psalmody (which could be committed to memory, as with Compline) and the use of Lord's Prayer or an almost invariable collect appropriate to the time of day as the concluding prayer.

71 Some of the decisions are unsupported by views available from the widest consultation on the Office, authorized by Pius XII on 31 January 1956. This consultation included the entire episcopate and *praestantioribus sacerdotibus* (the more outstanding priests). See Stanislaus Campbell, *From Breviary &c.*, pp. 26–7.

for public celebration of a 'cathedral Office', that is, a 'cathedral Vigil', Lauds and Vespers, in aid of our project of re-enchantment:

1 Everything which is available in Latin (including perhaps the pre-conciliar form) should be available also in the vernacular, though vernacular alternatives, for instance hymns and poems composed in English, would not also be available in Latin.
2 Celebration of the Office in more than one language – for instance, Latin for the psalms and canticles and collects, and the vernacular for the readings and other prayers – should be encouraged.
3 Plainsong and, for the vernacular, modern tones adapted from plain-song, should be vigorously promoted for communal use. (There are a number of sets of these modern tones, such as the tones of Dom Gregory Murray OSB, still used at Downside Abbey, and the St Meinrad Psalm Tones).[72] These are startlingly simple to sing, compared with the difficulty of using the Gregorian tones with their varied intonations, mediations and cadences.
4 A weekly *cursus* based on the Benedictine *schema* A should be adopted,[73] with a two-week cycle for the Office of Readings and a fivefold section of psalmody (including the Old Testament canticle in the morning and, optionally, the New Testament canticle in the evening) at Lauds and Vespers.[74]
5 Provision should be made for the reduction of psalmody at Lauds and Vespers *ad libitum* from five portions to three when the office

72 St Meinrad Archabbey, 1973, 1993. In 2007, Liturgy Training Publications released the new *Mundelein Psalter* which provides complete Morning, Evening and Night Prayer orders, using the Grail Psalter and St Meinrad tones. The Murray tones best known in England are used at Mass and tend to be the ones least similar to the Gregorian tones, another example of the tendency to associate melodiousness, rather than plaintive simplicity, with durability and serviceability.

73 It might be helpful to note that on just over 100 of approximately 250 occasions each week the breviary of Pius V and *Schema* A prescribe the same psalm or portion of Ps. 118(119), that is about 40% of the time. On some 30 occasions, Pius V, Pius X and *Schema* A make common provision and on a similar number of occasions the Liturgy of the Hours 1971 makes the same provision as *Schema* A at some stage in the four week cycle, that is, about 3% of the time. See Appendix II for further details.

74 There are, broadly, two cycles of seven Old Testament canticles for Lauds in the pre-conciliar breviary: one set for Lauds I and the other for Lauds II. Liturgy of the Hours 1971 has four cycles of seven, of which the first two sets are an admirable modification of the 1911 provision, that is, most of them are the same provision, a few modify the verse selection and two or three are allocated to different days of the week. This shows admirable respect for continuity. The dozen extra canticles (for weekday ferias in weeks 3 and 4) are an innovation and therefore arguably mark a disregard for continuity. *Benedictus* (Lauds) and *Magnificat* (Vespers) would remain as before. Appendix II (see p. 167) provides tables showing the *cursus* of the *Breviarium Romanum* before 1911 and the Benedictine *Schema* A (as presented in 1977).

is sung in public. This might be done in such a way that those who attended regularly would experience some degree of variety.

6 More specific and authoritative provision should be made for such 'cathedral' elements as the *lucernarium*, the burning of incense, and processional modes of celebration, of which the old 'chanted' office of Byzantium, referred to earlier, is an example.[75]

7 Such 'cathedral' elements might include provision for Solemn Vigils – for instance, Matins celebrated in a cathedral or large town church before Christmas Midnight Mass or the Vigil Mass of Pentecost. The Paschal Vigil would then be perceived rightly as the Queen of Vigils and not, as it must seem to many, the only public Vigil of the liturgical year.

Plenty more could be said but we should find ourselves increasingly exploring detail and not principle. One specialized area, not covered by our recommendations of principles for public celebration, is the preservation of the pre-conciliar breviary. This should be available for use with its 1911 cursus – however regrettable the reforms of Pius X in this respect, the use of the breviary of 1911 will have political importance in the foreseeable future – and perhaps also in an edition with the Benedictine *schema A* cursus, recovering some of the richness of the pre-1911 breviary (for example the daily use of the *Laudate* Psalms (148–50) at Lauds, the omission of which in 1911 has been much lamented ever since).[76] This is of interest not only to monasteries of a traditional kind but to individuals exercising their right to use the Extraordinary Form for the Office. Incoming Anglicans bring with them their own riches in this respect: further groups of converts from the Anglican tradition might bring such splendid liturgical books as *Monastic Breviary: Matins according to the Holy Rule of Saint Benedict*,[77] *The Monastic Diurnal*,[78] and *The Anglican Breviary*[79] (a translation of the Breviary of Pius X) – which could be authorized with some directions as to their

---

75 See above, p. 157.

76 Alcuin Reid, *The Organic Development &c.*, p. 65, quotes Anton Baumstark saying that 'to the reformers of the *Psalterium Romanum* belongs the distinction of having brought to an end the universal observance of a liturgical practice which was followed, one can say, by the Divine Redeemer himself during his life on earth'.

77 *Monastic Breviary: Matins according to the Holy Rule of Saint Benedict*, Tymawr, Lydart, Monmouth: The Society of the Sacred Cross, 1961, reprinted Glendale: Lancelot Andrewes Press, 2007.

78 *The Monastic Diurnal*, London: Oxford University Press, last printed 1963.

79 *The Anglican Breviary*, 1955, reprinted 1998, Mt Sinai, Long Island, NY: Frank Gavin Liturgical Foundation Inc.

use[80] and eventually superseded by new editions on similar principles, perhaps using the Revised Standard Version and the revised thesaurus of patristic and hagiographical readings which has been half a century in the construction.

There is no reason, furthermore, why some of the rubrical simplifications of the Office which took place in 1971 should not be applied to the pre-conciliar breviary: there is nothing sacrosanct about the work of the Pian Commission (1945–60) or the *Codex Rubricarum* of 1960. The decision to abolish absolutions and blessings in the Office of Readings, for example, seems to have excited no controversy[81] and their omission from – or optional use in – pre-conciliar Matins, particularly in private recitation, seems therefore unimportant. Similarly, starting Lauds with a *Deus in adiutorium* when Lauds runs on from Matins might well be discontinued even in the pre-conciliar breviary: the few whom that suggestion would upset would ignore this modification, much as those who are appalled by the 1971 provision to conjoin the celebration of an office with the celebration of Mass simply don't do it!

The Office of Readings

The Office of Readings does seem to be unfinished business. The tying of the text of the responsories too closely to the lessons they surround, as László Dobszay suggests, is realizing 'the fictitious past in the future by creating responsories corresponding to each reading'.[82] And, more particularly, as he goes on to say, the large number of new responsories needed – amounting to hundreds – means that, to all intents and purposes, the corpus of responsories has become an anthology of study texts rather than a repertoire of musical compositions (even if the texts of that repertoire are more often read than sung). Dobszay speaks as a musicologist and makes the point that here

---

80 Such as dealing with the discrepancy between the similar but divergent Sarum/BCP and pre-conciliar schemes for the collects and readings on Sundays after Pentecost and omitting inappropriate insertions from the BCP Communion Service.

81 Stanislaus Campbell, *From Breviary &c.*, pp. 126ff.

82 László Dobszay, *The Bugnini-Liturgy and the Reform of the Reform*, Front Royal VA: Church Music Association of America, 2003, p. 66. Stanislaus Campbell is more forgiving: 'scholarship had no definitive conclusions on this matter at the time of the reform'. He does go on to say, however, that 'there is no evidence that [the reformers] even tired to ascertain their original meaning or function', Stanislaus Campbell, *From Breviary &c.*, p. 269. He makes a similar point earlier (p. 136).

is the first Office Book in the life of the Church without melodies
. . . it furthers the decadence of recent centuries and fosters the process by which the Office, earlier sung in common, is turned into . . .
private spiritual reading for priests.[83]

This is not an entirely fair point. A collection of plainsong responsories was published in the *Liber Hymnarius*,[84] and more may be learned
from *Antiphonale monasticum* IV.[85] It may be true that the tendency
in past ages has been to produce text and music together but there
has been much activity setting texts since 1971, evidenced by the rapid
production of monastic books. Other volumes of the new *Antiphonale
monasticum*[86] make it possible to sing the offices of Lauds and Vespers,
with antiphons for the *Benedictus* and *Magnificat*, which, if not the
same as the ones in *Liturgia Horarum*, at least conform to the Gospel of
the Day in the Lectionary. Meanwhile, a new *Antiphonale Romanum*
has been published (2010). All of this may have taken thirty years but,
considering the amount of work to be done, that does not seem to be
an excessively long period. Dobszay is certainly right in one important
respect: it is far from clear that those who composed new antiphons
and responsories knew how much musical work that would entail or
even understood that the work would have to be done. He is probably
right in another too: there are too many new texts. The ingenuity of
responsory texts is that they centonize different sentences of scripture,
revealing the complementariness of apparently disparate Old and New
Testament texts; this ingenuity is undiminished if none of the responsory texts is drawn from, or closely related to, the stories and themes of
the surrounding lessons. Thus one could argue that there was no need
for much more than the body of responsories for which music already
exists. The benefit of uncoupling of psalmody and lessons is that it is
not only possible to use either of the lectionary provisions that we have
seen gradually emerging for 1971 with the 1971 psalmody,[87] but also to
combine the lengthier psalmody of the 1911 *cursus*, or the Benedictine
Schema A, with modern lectionaries. The modern lectionaries, a dispas-
sionate look reveals, are surely fuller and richer than the pre-conciliar
provision and better suited to the task of formation, especially priestly
formation. Practically speaking, the responsories would run on, as we

---

83 László Dobszay, *The Bugnini-Liturgy &c.*, p. 64.

84 *Liber hymnarius*, Solesmes, 1983.

85 Unpublished as of 2009.

86 See above, p. 148, the three-volume edition produced in 2005–07.

87 The One-Year Cycle (as in the *Divine Office*) and the Two-Year Cycle as in *The CTS New Catholic Bible* (see above, p. 147).

suggested they might, as a set of semi-autonomous texts, with some interesting resonances with the readings, partly through coincidence and partly because the seasonal context makes such resonances all the more likely.

This does not quite meet every objection: though the texts of the magnificent corpus of plainsong responsories are not tied as directly to the lessons as the new texts are, they are tied somewhat to the ancient Office lectionary, which stayed with, for instance, the books of Moses from Septuagesima onwards, or the Catholic epistles during Eastertide, in contrast with the modern Office lectionaries which hop around every fortnight or so. Nevertheless, there is some painstaking work that could be done on harmonizing responsories and lectionaries and the substance of Dobszay's criticisms would be met if this work were done by liturgists and musicians in tandem. Meanwhile, the corollary of authorizing the conjoining of traditional psalm schemes with modern lectionaries would be authorizing the conjoining of the various psalm schemes, old and new, with the old Office lectionary.

The most propitious way to embody these various suggestions might be to publish Vigils in a couple of separate volumes, together with the traditional music of the responsorial repertoire as one version of the Office of Readings, primarily for communities, and to publish the Office of Readings similarly as another set of volumes, with an unashamed focus on private prayer, reflection and study. Here it would be a moot point whether responsorial texts would even be necessary. Orders for a less monastic form of Vigils, a 'cathedral Vigil', could be constructed from these provisions, bringing together whatever has been authorized and what best suits that kind of service. Meanwhile, the day hours, for those not using the choir books, could be gathered, as ever, into a diurnal, effectively a one-volume breviary. Finally, there would be a book for Parish Lauds and Parish Vespers, with music and the kind of ceremonial that suits a 'town' church.[88] The number of books suggested here is no greater than those presently available, and officially published, in support of the 1971 Liturgy of the Hours.

Re-enchantment of the Office

One of the perturbing features of the Church is the polarization of positions, liberal and conservative, and sometimes the malevolent tone

---

88 *Celebrating Sunday Evening Prayer*, Norwich: Canterbury Press, 2006, cautiously models something of what is possible though it includes very little Latin and no plainsong.

of the debate and the imputing of dishonest motives. The Office is not immune from this kind of discussion. At its best the Office – like the Church itself – is a deep sea in which all can swim, and little is achieved by enforced discontinuity. The completion of the reform of the Office, therefore, must not be a experienced as a disallowing of that which is nourishing people. Even the 1971 *cursus*, despite its own apparent discontinuity with what went before, has established itself in the affections of many of its users.

The 'town or country' analysis with which this chapter began is gradually and finally revealed to be inadequate as a description and as a prescription for development – for repairing the discontinuity and rupture. As a description it fails partly because the monastic celebration has its cathedral elements – a ceremony here, a solemnity there – and parish use has a monastic element, whether the priest alone, praying in the oratory, or the little group, coming together to pray, much as any community would. It fails partly because it is not possible entirely to attribute the collapse of cathedral celebrations of the Office to inadequate liturgical provision. Solemn Vespers and choral Evensong, as we have seen, are successful examples of the cathedral genre. It was interesting, moreover, that the Church of England Liturgical Commission, in the early 1990s, more than alive to the criticism of the Roman Office as persistently monastic, nonetheless was heavily influenced by its quasi-monastic shapes and by some of the decisions made by the Bugnini reform. Just as the Church of England found itself looking urgently for a more effective Office for use by individuals and small groups, so must the Roman Rite rediscover some of its lost riches in order to develop, against the odds sociologically, an effective public celebration of the Office which has roots and resonance. Re-enchantment of the Office is achieved partly by the implementation of the principles enumerated earlier. It is achieved more profoundly by a desire to experience the Prayer of the whole Church, united in space and time.

Appendix

I The Latin Psalter

The fourth-century version of the Bible, translated into Latin by St Jerome, was not the first Latin version of the Bible, indeed Jerome himself produced more than one translation. It is the second of Jerome's translations, later called the Clementine Vulgate, which remains the best known and most used version of the Latin Bible. The psalter of the Clementine Vulgate became known as 'the Gallican psalter' (it became the version most widely used in the West from the time of Charlemagne) and eventually this became the official text until the second half of the twentieth century.

A new Latin psalter, for optional use, was produced by Augustin Bea SJ in 1945, at the instigation of Pius XII. Unlike the Gallican psalter, which was based on the Septuagint, the Greek Old Testament, the Pian psalter was based on the Masoretic text, the Hebrew original of the Old Testament. There was a concern moreover to recover the cadences of classical Latin, a style more mellifluous than later Latin, and there are places where the Hebrew is direct – in its use of anthropomorphisms for God, for example – but the Greek less so. The Pian psalter was not adopted for the *Liturgia Horarum* in 1971 because its classical style and some of its startling changes – well-known phrases replaced, sometimes by phrases with an entirely different meaning, mood or tense – had not been persuasive.[89] Those who continue a generation later to publish and make use of the pre-conciliar breviary in its 1961 recension tend to use Jerome's Gallican psalter.

Pope Paul VI commissioned a new version of the Latin Bible, based on up-to-date scholarship, and the Neo-Vulgate is now the official Latin text, not only of the Bible but of the psalter. It is less stylistically eccentric, as regards ecclesiastical Latin, that is, than the Pian psalter but, because of its concern for accuracy, it inevitably departs from the text of the Gallican psalter, and emulates the Pian psalter. There is, therefore, a continuing conflict of interest between that what is known and that which is merely accurate. A final complication is that the Septuagint, the Greek Old Testament, which has been the basis of the Latin liturgical psalter for well over a millennium, is regarded by the Orthodox Church as the authentic Old Testament, a divinely inspired correction of the Hebrew original. Thus, departures from the Greek, even in the interest of better Hebrew scholarship, are, for some, departures from the Word of God as Christians have received it in Holy Scripture.

---

89 Alcuin Reid, *The Organic Development &c.*, p.120, quotes a French Canon who describes the Latin of the Pian psalter as 'the deliberate use of the Latin of Cicero-Caesar, of a Latin, consequently, anterior by nearly a century to Christianity . . . There is then a sort of historical absurdity in trying to translate, in a book of Christian prayers, the Latin of the Vulgate by the Latin of Cicero.'

II Traditional Psalm Cursus[90]

(i)   Cursus of Breviarium Romanum before 1911[91]

Office	Sun.	Mon.	Tues.	Weds.	Thurs.	Fri.	Sat.
Invitatory	94	94	94	94	94	94	94
Matins I	1–3 6–14	26–9 69–71	38–41 82, 83	52–56 101–103	68	80, 81	97–100
II	15–17	30–33	43–46	57–60	72–75	84–87	104–106
III	18–20	34–37	47–51	61, 63 65, 67	76–79	88, 93 95, 96	107–108
Lauds	92, 99, 62+66, OT 148 149–150	50, 5, 62+66 OT 148–50	50, 42 62+66 OT 148–50	50, 64 62+66 OT 148–50	50, 89, 62+66 OT 148–50	50, 142 62+66 OT 148–50	50, 91 62+66 OT 148–9 150
Prime	53, 117 118a 118b	53, 23, 118a 118b	53, 24 118a 118b	53, 25 118a 118b	53, 22 118a 118b	53, 21 118a 118b	53 118a 118b
Terce	118c 118d 118e	118c 118d 118e	118c 118d 118e	118c 118d 118e	118c 118d 118e	118c 118d 118e	118c 118d 118e
Sext	118f 118g 118h	118f 118g 118h	118f 118g 118h	118f 118g 118h	118f 118g 118h	118f 118g 118h	118f 118g 118h
None	118i 118j 118k	118i 118j 118k	118i 118j 118k	118i 118j 118k	118i 118j 118k	118i 118j 118k	118i 118j 118k
Vesp	109–113 119, 120	114–116 122–125	121, 126 128–130	127 134	131, 132 138–141	137 145–147	143–144 135, 136

---

90 For reasons of space, only the Septuagint numbering (generally one number lower than the Hebrew) is given in these tables. Also there is no space for details of canticles and seasonal variations, for instance provision for Lauds is modified for feasts and for penitential seasons.

    The New Testament Canticle at Vespers (as in the Liturgy of Hours 1971 and optional in *Schema A)* is omitted from the tables.

91 Numbers in bold are common to the Breviaries of Pius V (1568) and Pius X (1911).

Office	Sun.	Mon.	Tues.	Weds.	Thurs.	Fri.	Sat.
Compline	4	4	4	4	4	4	4
	30.1–6	30.1–6	30.1–6	30.1–6	30.1–6	30.1–6	30.1–6
	90	90	90	90	90	90	90
	133	133	133	133	133	133	133

(ii) Benedictine Schema A[92]

Office	Sun.	Mon.	Tues.	Weds.	Thurs.	Fri.	Sat.
Invitatory	**94***	**94***	**94***	**94***	**94***	**94***	**94***
Matins	**3***	32–34,	45–49,	59–61,	73, 74	85, 86,	101–103
	20	36, 37	51	65, 67	76–78	88,	**104***
		21–25					92, 93
	26–31	38–41	52–55,	68–72	79–80[93]	95–96	**105**[94]
		43–44	57, 58		81–84	97–98	**106**[95]
						99*	107–108
						100	
Lauds	50	50	50	50	50	50*	50
	117	5*	42*	63	87	75	142
	62*	35	56	**64**	**89**[96]	91	
	OT	OT	OT	OT	OT	OT	OT
	148	148–50	148–50	148–50	148–50	148–50	140–50
	149–50*						
Prime[97]	**118a**	1	7	9b	12	15	17b
	118b	2	8	10	13	16	18a
	118c	6	9a	11	14	17a	18b
	118d						19

---

92 Numbers in bold are common to the breviary of Pius V (1568) and *Schema A*. Numbers underlined are also in the *cursus* of Pius X (1911). Numbers asterisked occur at the hour in question in the Liturgy of Hours 1971 at one or more stages in the four-week cycle.

93 Psalms 79–80 are prescribed by the Liturgy of Hours for Thursday Lauds in Week 2.

94 Psalm 105 is prescribed by the Liturgy of Hours for Saturday Office of Readings in Week 2.

95 Psalm 106 is prescribed by the Liturgy of Hours for Saturday Office of Readings in Week 3.

96 Psalm 89 is prescribed by the Liturgy of Hours for Thursday Office of Readings in Week 3.

97 When Prime is not used, the psalms for Prime are redistributed.

Office	Sun.	Mon.	Tues.	Weds.	Thurs.	Fri.	Sat.
Terce[98]	**118e**	118n	119	119	119	119	119
	118f	118o	120	120	120	120	120
	118g	118p	121	121	121	121	121
Sext	**118h**	118q*	122	122	122	122	122
	118i	118r	123	123	123	123	123
	118j	118s	124	124	124	124	124
None	**118k**	118t	125	125	125	125	125
	118l	118u	126	126	126	126	126
	118m	118v	127	127	127*	127	127
Vespers	**109***	113	129	134	138	**141**	**144b**
	110*	114	130*	135	139	143	145
	111*	115	131	136	140	144a*	146
	112	116	128	132	137	147	
Compline	4	4	4	4	4	4	4*
	90*	90	90	90	90	90	90
	133	133	133	133	133	133	133*

---

98 The distribution of psalms for the minor hours is at the discretion of the abbot.

6

Mother or Maiden

For in this rose contained was
Heaven and earth in little space

There is no rose (c. 1420)

It is apt that we conclude this journey exploring the re-enchantment of
liturgy with a brief reflection on the honouring of the Blessed Virgin
Mary: the Mass itself is often followed by a Marian devotion and the
Office of the Day is not complete without a final anthem to the Virgin.
As with each of the stages of the journey, we begin with an apparent
antithesis and, as with earlier chapters, the 'or' turns out to be an 'and'
– and the lack of a question mark in the title an indication that this
will be so. Accordingly, we shall not be trying to decide whether Mary
is 'Mother or Maiden'. We are content with the medieval carol, 'As
Dew in Aprille', and with the whole orthodox Christian tradition, to
describe her as 'Mother and Maiden':

Moder and maiden
was never none but she:
well may such a lady
Goddes moder be.

Nonetheless, there is much to be pondered in the apparent antithesis, 'Mother or Maiden', and, as we weigh up this paradox, we shall
find that there are deep liturgical connections to be plumbed. Not only
that, though we are content with each, both descriptions, 'Mother' and
'Maiden', raise some questions. Sarah Jane Boss presents the problem
neatly:

It is evidently the case that Mary's physical motherhood does not
provide a visual focus for meditation or devotion in the iconography
of either Lourdes or Guadaloupe ... [T]he mediaeval representa-
tions of the Virgin as physical mother and bearer of God have been

gradually supplanted in Catholic devotion by images of a prayerful young woman whose body had no ostensible association with maternal functions.[1]

Is Boss's 'prayerful young woman' a goddess in the making, an idol in the Judaeo-Christian tradition, one to whom it would be dangerous to pray? Or is she the young girl, the 'Maiden', already fully graced and expectant on God's Word?

The anonymous piece of Middle English poetry[2] which inspired the book's title is not 'As Dew in Aprille', from which we draw 'Mother and Maiden', but the similarly popular carol text 'There is no rose'. The association of the rose with Mary is very ancient indeed.[3] The Rosary – usually five chaplets of one bead followed by ten beads, allowing the recitation of an Our Father, ten Hail Marys and (holding the chain before the next solitary bead) a Glory be – not only permits deep and imaginative contemplation of three sets of mysteries, joyful, sorrowful, and glorious, but, since these three sets of 50 add up to 150 Hail Marys, we have what amounts to a 'lay' or, at any rate, alternative psalter, a way of embracing the obligation of reciting the psalms without psalm texts, particularly helpful in ages and societies where literacy was and is low. The scheme was somewhat modified by an apostolic letter of Pope John Paul II in 2002,[4] the 25th anniversary of his pontificate, suggesting that five more mysteries – mysteries of light or luminous mysteries – should be added to the Rosary cycle.[5] The day suggested for these mysteries is

---

1 Sarah Jane Boss, *Empress and Handmaid: On Nature and Gender in the Cult of the Virgin Mary*, London and New York: Cassell, 2000, p. 40.

2 Anonymous if the text is not by John Dunstable, whose fifteenth-century setting was transcribed and edited by John Stevens, 1963, and was published by Stainer & Bell, Ltd., London, and thereafter in some carol anthologies. Stevens notes that this carol came from a manuscript roll of carols copied out in the early fifteenth century and now in the Library of Trinity College, Cambridge.

3 Tertullian (*Adv. Judaeos*, 9) and Ambrosius (*Exp. Gr. Luc.* II, 24) used the rose as a reference to the Davidic genealogy, the sprout or bush (*virga*) being Mary and the flower or rose Christ. In the fifth century Sedulius Caelius calls Mary a 'rose among thorns' (*Carmen paschale* II, 28–31). Theophanes Graptos in the ninth century uses the same phrase to express Mary's purity and her fragrance (*Oktoechos*, Friday of the sixth week). Frequent medieval references were made to the rose and rosebush inspired by Isaiah 11.1 ('There shall come forth a shoot from the stump of Jesse, and a branch shall grow out of his roots') and Ecclus. 24.14 ('like rose plants in Jericho').

4 *Rosarium Virginis Mariæ* is available (2009) on www.vatican.va

5 These mysteries are as follows:
   1 The Baptism in the Jordan.
   2 The Wedding at Cana.
   3 The Proclamation of the Kingdom.
   4 The Transfiguration.
   5 The Institution of the Eucharist.

Thursday, previously a day, like Monday, reserved for the joyful mysteries, but, if finding a day is no problem, the additional mysteries have nonetheless caused other problems: the lower basilica at Lourdes and the Anglican shrine church at Walsingham, each having fifteen chapels, have, in the case of the one, ingeniously added five mosaics to the West front of the lower basilica, depicting the mysteries of light, and in the case of the other, the Walsingham shrine, an outdoor altar of light. To retrieve – that is, to re-enchant – the lay psalter, it may be necessary – and this is no more than one suggestion – to gather together the Church's liturgical canticles into a formal anthology of 50.[6]

The Rosary is a garland of roses or the fragrant environment of a rose garden. 'Telling the beads', like looking at the great rose windows in the transepts of Gothic cathedrals, or following the labyrinth of the Cathedral of Chartres in France,[7] is being led inwards to the Mystical Rose herself, and thence to her child, the Blessed Babe, as this modern translation of what was been listed as a fourteenth-century German text, *Es ist ein Ros entsprungen*,[8] shows:

A spotless rose is growing,
sprung from a tender root,
of ancient seers' foreshowing,
of Jesse promised fruit;
its fairest bud unfolds to light
amid the cold, cold winter,
and in the dark midnight.

---

6 That this is possible is showed by Common Worship (CW) *Daily Prayer*, London: Church House Publishing, 2005, which, as well as 18 canticles derived from the psalms, has 58 canticles from elsewhere in the Bible and a further 11 post-biblical canticles.

7 See Sarah Jane Boss, 'Telling the Beads: The Practice and Symbolism of the Rosary', in Sarah Jane Boss (ed.), *Mary: The Complete Resource*, London and New York: Continuum, 2007, pp. 385ff.

The expression 'Mystical Rose' seems to have originated in the Dominican Rosary communities which influenced the Litany of Loreto (see note 80 below), first known in its present form in the middle of the sixteenth century. In the Marian apparition at Guadalupe, Mary had roses miraculously appear in the winter, to be taken by St Juan Diego to the bishop as a proof of the authenticity of the apparitions, and roses are associated with apparitions at other sites too. A miraculous image of the Mystical Rose has been venerated since 1739 at the sanctuary of Rosenberg, in Speyer, Germany. Pope John XXIII, in 1962, asked that all pray to the Mother of God as 'Mystical Rose' for the success of the Second Vatican Council (*Ancilla Domini* Magazine, 6 May 1962), and Pope Paul VI, on 5 May 1969, asked that the Rosary be prayed and that Mary be honoured with the title of 'Mystical Rose'.

8 This seems to be found first in the *Speier Gesangbuch* 1599, see *Songs of Syon* no. 214, London: Schott & Co., 1910. The well-known and very fine setting of the carol by Herbert Howells, London: Stainer & Bell, 1919, describes the text as fourteenth-century German but the source of the translation remains elusive.

The rose which I am singing,
whereof Isaiah said,[9]
is from its sweet root springing
in Mary, purest Maid;
through God's great love and might
the Blessed Babe she bare us
in a cold, cold winter's night.

It is in the 'Mother and Maiden', the 'rose', that we find the mystery of 'heaven and earth in little space'. It is a *res miranda*, a thing to be wondered at, as the macaronic text of 'There is no rose' goes on to say. There is an obvious symmetry – even synergy – in the God-bearing of the Holy Mother and the God-bearing of the Holy Eucharist. Both are divine gifts, not so much excited by the human instinct for prayer and sacrifice which preceded and precedes knowledge of the Gospel as exciting and enabling that prayer and sacrifice which God Incarnate offers in, for and through us. More simply: in the womb of the Virgin, and in the eucharistic elements, there is Emmanuel, God-with-us. Sacred womb and sacred liturgy are indeed 'heaven and earth in little space'. This is an insight developed by John Saward, with reference to poems by Gerard Manley Hopkins and St Thérèse of Lisieux on the subject.[10]

O Maria, Salvatoris Mater[11]

Only a century or two after the carol texts just quoted were written, the flowering of liturgical devotion – or rather 'extra-liturgical' devotion – is evident in Eton College Chapel. Here is the scene in the 1490s:

> The collegiate body – eventually including ten priest-fellows, 70 scholars, the master and the usher as well as the chaplains, clerks and choristers provided for by Henry VI's statutes – met in the quire, where most of the daily services took place but the nave, artificially enlarged by the moving east of the pulpitum, was the place for the singing of Vespers at 4pm and, at dusk, the daily Marian antiphon. Given that Vespers and the singing of the Marian antiphon were the public nave services, it is less surprising that the main contents of the

---

9 The primary reference is to Isaiah 11.1. Isaiah 35.1 in the AV has a 'rose' springing up in the desert. Later versions (for example Douay-Rheims, RSV) have 'lily' and modern versions (NRSV) 'crocus'.

10 John Saward, *Redeemer in the Womb*, San Francisco: Ignatius, 1993, pp. 112f.

11 'O Mary, Mother of the Saviour', a text set by John Browne in the Eton Choirbook.

Eton Choirbook[12] were its 24 settings of the *Magnificat* and more than 40 different settings of the Marian antiphons.

One might have expected late mediaeval *Salve* ceremonies to be collegiate – one is reminded of the way Benedictine communities still sing the *Salve* together intimately after Compline – but they were normally not a collegiate (that is, quire) activity at all but a public (nave) one. The 1444 College Statute required that the choir process reverently to the Chapel each evening, kneel at the crucifix to recite the Lord's Prayer, then rise and face the image of Our Lady and sing a *Salve* in her praise. Joining parishioners in the nave for the twilight antiphon would be fee-paying schoolboys – 'commensals' – almsmen and ancillary staff. Meanwhile, except in Lent and on vigils of feasts, the 70 Eton Scholars would not be in Chapel for the *Salve* but in their classrooms, reciting their own memorial, an antiphon with versicles, collects and Psalm 129(130) *de Profundis*.[13]

The valuable information here is not only the sheer size of the musical provision for the daily singing of the antiphon – 40 pieces of elaborate music, the finest of the period – but also the sense that this is a popular devotion – in an enlarged nave not in the quire – to conclude the public liturgy of the day, that is, to follow Vespers. The popular nature of the devotion may also be indicated by the absence of the 70 Eton Scholars, who have their own devotions, the examen-like and somewhat more cerebral *De Profundis*, recited (not sung), in classrooms (not in Chapel). Making allowances for changing times and circumstances, one is reminded of the contrast in pre-conciliar Catholicism between parishes where Sunday evening services were Sung Vespers and those where Rosary and Benediction better suited popular taste. Typically Anglo-Catholics of the period – and, where this is still feasible, to the present day – combined – and combine – Sunday night Evensong and Benediction bringing together office and extra-liturgical devotion, 'quire' and 'nave' elements.

It is not always realized how austerely the Western Rite manages devotion to the Virgin. In pre-conciliar Latin practice, with the exception of one or two texts on Marian feasts (such as *Beata es, Virgo*

12 Eton College Library MS 178.

13 Andrew Burnham, 'Our Lady of Eton and the Glory of the Eton Choirbook', Walsingham Assumptiontide Lecture, 2005. The information is gleaned from Magnus Williamson, *The Eton Choirbook* (DPhil. dissertation, University of Oxford, 1997), pp. 462f. See also Magnus Williamson, 'The Early Tudor Court, the Provinces and the Eton Choirbook', in *Early Music*, May 1997, and Magnus Williamson, '*Pictura et scriptura*: the Eton Choirbook in its Iconographical Context', in *Early Music*, August 2000.

Maria, 'Blessed are you Virgin Mary', the Offertorium on the Vigil of the Assumption), and invocation of the saints in the Litany of the Saints, public prayer to Mary was unknown during the pre-conciliar Mass. In the Office, again with the exception of hymns and antiphons on Marian feasts, in the *Officium sanctæ Mariæ in sabbato* (Office of St Mary on Saturday) and in 'the Little Office of the Virgin Mary',[14] public prayer to Mary played no part. An exception was *Sancta Maria, et omnes Sancti intercedant pro nobis* (May holy Mary and all the saints pray for us) at Prime, yet here is not a prayer but a pious expostulation in the form of the jussive subjunctive, bridging the reading of the Martyrology and the little monastic office added on to Prime, a focusing on the example and support of the saints as the work of the day beyond the monastic stalls begins, in which the community will still be surrounded by the company of heaven.

All but adoring love . . .

There was a similar reserve, liturgically, amongst Anglican Tractarians: loyal to the BCP, they were reluctant to utter Marian devotions aloud; whilst the *Angelus* was rung it was often the custom for those who knew the versicles and prayers to pray them silently. John Keble's poem for the Annunciation of the Blessed Virgin Mary,[15] part of which became a hymn, shows something of the scrupulousness of the Tractarians:

> Ave Maria! Thou whose name
> all but adoring love may claim,
> yet may we reach thy shrine;
> for he, thy Son and Saviour, vows
> to crown all lowly, lofty brows
> with love and joy like thine.

This poem of Keble began with six stanzas addressed to the Son of God before it addressed three stanzas to his Mother. The earlier Anglican tradition is even more cautious: Bishop Thomas Ken, the seventeenth-

---

14 'The Little Office of the Virgin Mary', derived from the Common of Our Lady in the Roman Breviary, has existed since the Middle Ages and has provided a form of the Office especially suitable for laity, tertiaries, and some religious communities engaged in an active apostolate. A Latin and English version conforming to the 1961 Roman Breviary was published by Baronius Press (London) in 2007.

15 John Keble, *The Christian Year*, London and New York: Frederick Warne and Co., 1827.

century non-juror and Bishop of Bath and Wells, had written about the joy of the Virgin, but it is notable both that he was not addressing her, and that when the verses of 'Her Virgin eyes saw God incarnate born' finally made it into the Tractarian hymn book, *Hymns Ancient and Modern*,[16] the words '*Next* to his throne her Son his Mother placed' were changed to '*Near* to his throne . . .', (my italics) a change which persists in *Common Praise*, the latest recension of the 'A & M' tradition.[17] There is a sense in which caution with regard to Marian devotion is endemic in Anglicanism: the discalced Carmelite bishop, Philip Boyce, comments extensively on the 'significant contribution to Catholic Mariology' of John Henry Newman, but it was only when Newman's spiritual journey had led him to Rome 'that he felt free to make his own all Roman Catholic practices, especially devotional and invocatory, of Marian piety'.

> Even during the period of the Oxford Movement, at least up until 1839, he considered the honours paid by Catholics to the saints, and in particular to Saint Mary, to be the very essence of Rome's corruption and theological error.[18]

If the once evangelical Newman struggled as an Anglican to accept Marian devotion and if, as a Catholic, he finds some devotions better suited to Italy than to England, he nonetheless concludes that it is countries that 'have lost their faith in the divinity of Christ, who have given up devotion to his Mother' and 'those on the other hand, who had been foremost in her honour' who 'have retained their orthodoxy'. As for the continental 'extravagances', Newman supposes that 'we owe it to national good sense, that English Catholics have been protected'.[19]

With the liturgical changes following the Second Vatican Council there was a risk that devotion to Mary would be almost entirely lost, and with it, if Newman was right, faith in the divinity of Christ and the experience of Emmanuel, God-with-us, on the altar and in the tabernacle. The decline in non-eucharistic worship being steep, some episcopal

---

16 *Hymns Ancient and Modern Revised*, no. 513, London: William Clowes & Sons, 1950.

17 See *Common Praise*, no. 239, Norwich: Canterbury Press, 2000.

18 Philip Boyce OCD, 'John Henry Newman and the Immaculate Mother of the Incarnate Word', in William McLoughlin and Jill Pinnock (eds), *Mary for Earth and Heaven: Essays on Mary and Ecumenism*, Leominster: Gracewing, 2002, p. 87.

19 Ian Ker, *John Henry Newman: A Biography*, Oxford, New York: Oxford University Press, 1988 (reissued 2009), p. 586. The primary source is Newman's *Certain Difficulties felt by Anglicans in Catholic Teaching*, vol. 2, pp. 92–3, 99–100.

conferences (England and Wales, for example) permitted a Hail Mary or other Marian devotion to be inserted towards the end of the Prayer of the Faithful at Mass, whilst others (Ireland, for example) continued to take the view that prayer to Mary should remain extra-liturgical. What had disappeared were the so-called 'Leonine Prayers' following Low Mass, including three Hail Marys, and the *Salve Regina* ('Hail, holy Queen').[20] There is no doubt that the falling away of popular devotion to the Virgin Mary was an accidental consequence in some quarters. Elsewhere it was no doubt more deliberate, a concession towards Protestant reticence on Mary: 'Mary is for Christmas not for life', one might say.[21] Meanwhile, Anglo-Catholics almost always insert a Hail Mary into the Prayer of the Faithful and continue to use – and sometimes sing – the *Angelus* (in Eastertide the *Regina cæli*) after the principal Mass on Sunday.[22] Some Catholic dioceses have introduced special provision too.[23] Ironically, it is not in the end the liturgy of the Church, nor her official provision of extra-liturgical devotion, that has safeguarded Marian devotion but the determination of clergy and lay people to persist: in August 2003 a poll conducted by the BBC Radio 4 programme 'Sunday' established that Walsingham, Norfolk, is England's favourite spiritual place,[24] mainly, it has to be said, amongst Anglicans, but Lourdes, in South West France, continues to draw massive and international crowds, including charabancs of Catholics from England and Wales, and the number of hotels in that little town

20 Originally introduced locally by Pope Pius IX in 1859 to seek the preservation of the Papal States, the prayers were extended for universal use by Pope Leo XIII in 1884 (hence 'Leonine'), including, from 1886, the Prayer to St Michael the Archangel. Pope St Pius X added a threefold petition to the Sacred Heart in 1904, and, in 1929, when the Lateran Treaty had dealt with the Roman question, Pope Pius XI directed that the intention should be henceforth for the Church in Russia. They were discontinued in 1964 but in practice remain optional since they are part of the Extraordinary Form.

21 Jaroslav Pelikan, *Mary Through the Centuries: Her Place in the History of Culture*, New Haven and London: Yale University Press, 1996, p. 13, shows how, in Lutheranism, for instance in the Bach *Christmas Oratorio* (1734–5), the emphasis is on Mary as the chosen one, rather than as the one who chooses to co-operate with God. *Euch ist ein Kindlein heut' geborn, /Von einer Jungfrau auserkoren*: ('To you this day is born a Child from an elect Virgin').

22 Somewhat ironically, the music used for the *Angelus* – for the Hail Marys and sometimes for the versicles and responses too – is, as regards musical structure, an Anglican chant. For the *Regina cæli*, 'Easter Hymn', *English Hymnal*, no. 133 (*English Hymnal*, new edition, London: Oxford University Press and Mowbray, 1933) is used and, often, in Ascensiontide, 'Llanfair' (*English Hymnal* no. 143).

23 The Catholic Archdiocese of Birmingham, England, for instance, specified the use of the Marian antiphon at the end of Lauds and Vespers.

24 BBC Radio 4, 10 August 2003, 7.10–7.55 am.

in the Hautes-Pyrénées is second only in France to the number of hotels in Paris.[25]

The *Pietà: Mater Dolorosa*

So far we have encountered Mary as the Immaculate One, Mary greeted by Gabriel, Mary as 'physical mother and bearer of God' (in Sarah Boss's phrase),[26] and Mary as the *Mater*, the Queen, who, as in Eton College Chapel, is greeted by her children with retiring *Salves*. We have not seen much of her as the one who shares our sufferings, though the sorrowful mysteries of the Rosary are themselves the events of the Passion. Perhaps the most powerful image of Mary of all, however, is the image of her compassion, symbolized by the *Pietà* and rehearsed in the *Stabat Mater dolorosa*. A programme of re-enchantment would include renewed devotion to the Seven Sorrows, popular in art but, in some places at least, a casualty of the decline of extra-liturgical devotion.[27] The same reintegration with the tradition, in many places, needs to happen with the Stations of the Cross, a journey with Mary, accompanying the Lord along the *Via Dolorosa*, to the singing of verses of the *Stabat Mater*, the sequence for the feast of the Seven Sorrows.[28] The image of Mary as the one who suffers the psychological onslaught of watching helplessly as her Son is harassed, arrested, tortured, paraded,

---

25 The (Anglican) Society of Mary undertakes regular pilgrimage to Lourdes and Nettuno. The pilgrimage to Lourdes in 2008, marking the 150th anniversary of the apparitions, was led by the Archbishop of Canterbury and homilies and talks from that pilgrimage may be found in *Mary: A Focus for Unity for all Christians? Sermons and Conference talks presented at Lourdes and Nettuno*, available (2009) from the Society of Mary: www.societyofmary.net/ The image at Nettuno is believed to have been that of Our Lady of Ipswich, rescued from a bonfire in Chelsea, and taken by ship to Nettuno.

26 See above, p. 170.

27 The Seven Sorrows (or Dolours) are:
  1 The Prophecy of Simeon over the Infant Jesus (Luke 2.34).
  2 The Flight into Egypt of the Holy Family (Matthew 2.13).
  3 The Loss of the Child Jesus for Three Days (Luke 2.43).
  4 The Meeting of Jesus and Mary along the Way of the Cross (Luke 23.26).
  5 The Crucifixion (where Mary stands at the foot of the Cross: John 19.25).
  6 The Descent from the Cross (where Mary receives the dead body of Jesus in her arms: Matthew 27.57).
  7 The Burial of Jesus (John 19.40).

28 See *English Hymnal*, no. 115; *Catholic Hymn Book*, no. 61, Leominster: Gracewing, 1998; *Adoremus Hymnal*, nos. 400 (Latin), 401 (English), San Francisco: Ignatius Press, 1997. The Orthodox *Staurotheotokion* (Russian *krestobogorodichen*) is similar to the *Stabat Mater* and is sung on Wednesdays and Fridays during the Office in place of the *Theotokion*, the canticle honouring the Virgin.

killed, pierced, and buried is – and should be – one of the most potent symbols of the Christian narrative and, though undeveloped in the Reformed tradition, is certainly fundamental in Catholic iconography. It is an image which is always wretchedly contemporary. The *Pietà*, the sixth of the Seven Sorrows and the 13th of the 14 Stations of the Cross, is the Mother holding on her lap the dead body of her Son. Before that comes the fourth sorrow and fourth station, when Jesus carrying the Cross meets his mother.

The affective text of the *Stabat Mater* has inspired some fine musical compositions. A double choir setting by Palestrina (1590), a couple of eighteenth-century settings – Pergolesi (1736) and Haydn (1767) – and a couple of nineteenth-century settings – Rossini (1832) and Dvořák (1876) – remain within the choral repertoire. It is a text which has inspired contemporary composers too: the Polish composer, Krzysztof Penderecki, has set the text (1971), and the Scottish composer, James Macmillan, incorporated it into his St John Passion (2007). The four-teenth-century sequence, attributed to Jacopone Da Todi OFM, is an imaginative – had it been written two hundred years later one would want to say Ignatian – meditation on the feelings of the mother, stand-ing at the foot of the Cross, praying that the worshipper of the Cruci-fied may learn something of the mother's bereavement and her love, and thus find companionship and a share in Paradise through her prayers. The first verse at least is scriptural – *stabat Mater dolorosa* ('the grieving mother was standing by the Cross') – and the singling out of the mother from the group of women at the Cross[29] is justified by the momentous exchange at the Cross, whereby Jesus entrusts the beloved disciple to his mother, 'Woman, behold, your son!' (John 19.26), and his mother to John, 'Behold, your mother!' (John 19.27). Those singing the *Stabat Mater* are the beloved disciples of Jesus and the one of whom, and to whom, they sing is his – and their – mother. It would prosify the story to exclude the sentiments expressed by the many verses of the sequence and it would work against the kenotic thrust of the Passion narrative to insist that at this point, whether during the Stations of the Cross or at the Cross, the one to be addressed must always be the Lord and not his grieving mother. The bereaved mother and the bereaved disciples can find consolation, for a time at least, only in addressing and supporting one another. The Son, the Master, is powerless, is dying, is dead. Such is the real experience of human bereavement, a paradoxically intense

---

29 *Stabant autem iuxta crucem Iesu Mater eius et soror matris eius Maria Cleopae et Maria Magdalene* ('Standing by the Cross of Jesus were his mother, and his mother's sister, Mary the wife of Clopas, and Mary Magdalene'), John 19.25.

experience of the absence of God: *un seul être vous manque et tout est dépeuplé* said the Catholic poet, Alphonse Marie Louis de Lamartine (1790–1869) in his *Élégie*, as he mourns the loss of Elvire.[30] This is a very different sentiment from Alfred de Vigny (1797–1863) who experiences the sheer indifference of heaven: *Mais le ciel reste noir, et Dieu ne répond pas.*[31] There is a different spirituality and theology that finds all this too emotional, too risky, and insists that the mysteries must be held together – the Cross must be empty because the Lord through his Resurrection has conquered death – but this is not the spirituality and theology of the Catholic celebration of the Passion, where there is the keenest experience of sorrow and loss, and the richest pæan of praise in the Easter alleluias.

In a longer exploration of the re-enchantment of liturgy there might have been a chapter to consider the revision and diminishment – and thus the need for further revision and recovery – of the rites of Holy Week. It is precisely in and through the liturgy – and the proclamation of the narrative which goes alongside it and is expressed through it – that the journey of faith takes place. The re-enactment is the ever deeper appropriation: an insight as apposite in the daily and weekly round of Office and Mass as in the yearly cycle of feast and fast. As we shall see, it is not entirely inappropriate to consider the celebration of Holy Week from a Marian perspective: to accompany Mary on the Stations of the Cross, to the singing of the *Stabat Mater*, is part of the re-enchantment we seek. So too is the re-discovery of the darkness of *Tenebræ*: not necessarily a re-instatement of what was there until 1955 – Matins and Lauds of Holy (that is, Maundy) Thursday, Good Friday and Holy Saturday, sung by anticipation the night before, amidst increasingly profound darkness as the fifteen candles of the 'herse'[32] are extinguished one by one – but something like it. The rubrics for the end of the Mass of the Lord's Supper on Maundy Thursday,[33] too,

---

30 'You lose one particular person and all is desolate' would be one translation of this phrase, so popular a cliché that it adorns mouse mats. Alphonse Marie Louis de Lamartine, 'Élégie', in Arthur G. Canfield, 1899, *French Lyrics*, is available (2009) through Project Gutenburg on www.gutenberg.org

31 'But the sky remains black, and God does not reply.' Alfred de Vigny, 'Le Mont des Oliviers', in William Rees (ed. with prose translations), *The Penguin Book of French Poetry: 1820–1950*, London: Penguin, 1992.

32 'Herse' or 'hearse' (*hercia*), a triangular frame containing the fifteen candles.

33 In the *Ceremonial of Bishops*, Collegeville: LP, 1989, 310:

At a suitable time the altar is stripped and, if possible, the crosses are removed from the church. It is desirable to cover any crosses that remain in the church, unless they have already been covered . . .

have turned a front of house liturgical ceremony – the stripping of the altars during the recitation of Psalm 21 (22), followed by the celebration of Compline amidst the desolation – into a backstage and rather functional preparation of the liturgical space for Good Friday, though, of course, the opportunity remains to keep a Gethsemane Watch at the altar of repose. It seems odd that the Roman Missal provides no fewer than three forms of celebration of the Lord's messianic entry on Palm Sunday – thus meeting the very different circumstances and needs of various liturgical communities – but only the simple ending of the Holy Thursday rite is provided.

Meanwhile, in the Anglican tradition, there are growing signs of recognition of the importance of the *Mater dolorosa*, the grieving mother, as provision for Holy Week continues to grow apace.[34] The Church of England's Common Worship (CW) *Times and Seasons*[35] anthology includes 'The Way of the Cross',[36] a set of stations based upon incidents which have scriptural support, but with the recommendation that 'it is traditional to use a verse from the hymn *Stabat Mater* to conclude each station'.[37] 'Liturgical resources' are offered 'only for scriptural stations, because those churches which have non-scriptural tableaux in place will probably have the resources already'.[38] There is, however, a list of the traditional stations.[39] Ironically, there is also somewhat richer provision than the modern Roman Rite for Maundy Thursday: though there is no mention of the Transfer of the Holy Eucharist, which arguably would contravene the Thirty-nine Articles,[40] there is a Watch, with 'a procession and a hymn or psalm', and a list of readings and psalms for the Watch.[41] Since the Liturgy of Good Friday has 'The Liturgy of the Sacrament', at the beginning of which 'the holy table is covered with a fair linen cloth and the consecrated elements are placed on it in silence',[42] the inference is that the Maundy Thursday procession was a

---

Unlike some of the rubrics in the *Ceremonial of Bishops*, this takes us no further than the corresponding rubric in the Roman Missal.

34 *Lent, Holy Week, Easter: Services and Prayers*, London and Cambridge: Church House Publishing, Cambridge University Press, SPCK, 1986, the first official provision in the Church of England, acknowledged its indebtedness to the Book of Common Prayer, According to the Use of the Episcopal Church of the USA (1979).

35 CW, *Times and Seasons*, London: Church House Publishing, 2006.

36 CW, *Times and Seasons*, pp. 236ff.

37 CW, *Times and Seasons*, note 5, p. 237.

38 CW, *Times and Seasons*, 'The Way of the Cross, A Brief History', p. 236.

39 CW, *Times and Seasons*, p. 256.

40 See Article XXVIII *Of the Lord's Supper*. The Thirty-nine Articles are printed at the back of the Book of Common Prayer 1662.

41 CW, *Times and Seasons*, p. 304.

42 CW, *Times and Seasons*, p. 319.

procession of the Blessed Sacrament and that the Watch too may focus on the eucharistic elements. Much of this is keeping up with, and recognizing, the richness of the Latin Holy Week Liturgy, but not only are there extra resources here but also, for 'the Stripping of the Sanctuary' at the conclusion of the Maundy Thursday Liturgy, provision is made for this to happen as part of the public rite: 'Psalm 88 . . . or another psalm, or these or other verses from Lamentations may be used.'[43] The reference to Lamentations is as clearly evocative of *Tenebræ* as the mention earlier of the *Stabat Mater* is evocative of the spirituality of the *Pietà*, the *Mater dolorosa*, the grieving mother.

Mary, Seat of Wisdom[44]

Detailed examination of the liturgical nuancing of Mary in the Eastern Rite is beyond our competence and would extend the scope of this present reflection too far. However, one can venture to make one or two general observations, not least that prayer to the Virgin is very ancient indeed: the oldest prayer we seem to have is *Sub Tuum Præsidium*, a Greek text found on a third-century Egyptian papyrus:

> We turn to you for protection,
> holy Mother of God.
> Listen to our prayers
> and help us in our needs.
> Save us from every danger,
> glorious and blessed Virgin.[45]

The *Akathistos* ('Standing') Hymn, popular since it became a prayer for protection for Byzantium in the sixth century, has this prayer:

---

43 CW, *Times and Seasons*, p. 303. Psalm 88 in the Vulgate numbering is Psalm 87.

44 *Sedes sapientiæ* ('Seat of Wisdom') from the Litany of Loreto, see note 80, below.

45 The *Sub Tuum Præsidium* (here in an ICEL version) is in many popular collections in various translations. See *Saint Benedict's Prayer Book*, Leominster: Gracewing and Ampleforth Abbey Press, 1993, p. 147; Seán Finnegan (comp.), *A Book of Hours and Other Catholic Devotions*, Norwich: Canterbury Press, 1998, p. 20; *Handbook of Prayers*, Princeton, New Jersey: Scepter and Chicago: Midwest Theological Forum, sixth edition, 2001, p. 434. Anglican sources include Andrew Burnham (comp.), *A Manual of Anglo-Catholic Devotion*, Norwich: Canterbury Press, 2001, p. 371; and Andrew Burnham (comp.), *A Pocket Manual of Anglo-Catholic Devotion*, Norwich: Canterbury Press, 2004, p. 303.

Our most gracious Queen, our hope, O *Theotokos*,[46] who receivest
the orphaned and art the intercessor for the stranger; the joy of those
in sorrow, protectress of the wronged, see our distress, see our afflic-
tion! Help us, for we are helpless. Feed us, for we are strangers and
pilgrims. Thou knowest our offences; forgive them, and resolve them
as thou dost will. For we know no other help but thee, no other intercessor, no gracious comforter, only thee, O *Theotokos* to guard and
protect us for ages of ages. Amen.

We are not so very far, devotionally, in this Eastern prayer from the
Memorare, the Western prayer, some six hundred years later, attributed
to St Bernard of Clairvaux (1090–1153):

Remember, O most blessed Virgin Mary, that never was it known
that anyone who fled to your protection, implored your aid, or sought
your intercession was left unaided. Filled, therefore, with confidence
in your goodness, I fly to you, Virgin of virgins, my Mother. To you
I come, before you I stand, sinful and sorrowful. O Mother of the
Word incarnate, despise not my petition, but in your mercy hear and
answer me.[47]

What is distinctly Eastern about the *Akathistos* Hymn, however, is
that the priest goes on to make this and similar invocations: 'Wisdom,
Most Holy *Theotokos*, save us.'[48] Amidst an extravagance of theological ideas in the *Akathistos* Hymn, therefore, we find ourselves with
more than one difficulty. First there is the immense topic of whether
the Virgin and Holy Wisdom may be identified as one and the same.
Aficionados of Margaret Barker will know her chapter, 'Wisdom, the
Queen of Heaven',[49] which, perhaps too daringly, brings many themes
together, not least the Wisdom (Sophia) language, such as we find it

---

46 *Theotokos* means 'God-bearer' and is usually translated by Catholics as 'Mother of
God'.

47 The *Memorare* is in many popular collections, such as *Saint Benedict's Prayer Book*,
p. 146; Seán Finnegan (comp.), *A Book of Hours and Other Catholic Devotions*, p. 345;
and *Handbook of Prayers*, p. 473. Anglican sources include Andrew Burnham (comp.),
A Manual of Anglo-Catholic Devotion, p. 371; and Andrew Burnham (comp.), *A Pocket
Manual of Anglo-Catholic Devotion*, p. 303.

48 See, for example, www.fatheralexander.org/booklets/english/m_akathist_e.htm.
See also Kallistos Ware and Roger Green, *The Akathistos Hymn in Two translations with
Introductions*, Ecumenical Society of the Blessed Virgin Mary, 1987, available from the
Publications Secretary. The ESBVM website address is: www.esbvm.org

49 Margaret Barker, *The Great High Priest*, London and New York: T&T Clark
International, 2003, pp. 229ff.

in the *Akathistos* Hymn and the identification of Mary and Wisdom in icons. The same identification is evident, similarly daringly, in the work of Orthodox theologians such as Sergius Nikolaevich Bulgakov, whose 1926 study, *The Burning Bush*, was not published in English until 2009: 'The Mother of God, personally sinless and cleansed of original sin, was the expression of Ever-virginity in a creature, the full revelation of Sophia in a human being.'[50] 'The divine maternal principle is symbolized by the blue of church vestments, by heavenly azure', he says. 'The Mother of God is the exalted, glorified, divinized creature: the darkness of creaturely non-existence is overcome and illuminated by Divine Sophia and it has lighted up in feminine blue.'[51] We note the careful use of the word 'creature' and are mindful of the theological tradition in Orthodoxy expounding Deification, the transforming effect of grace, of becoming 'partakers of the divine nature' (2 Pet. 1.4).[52] Bulgakov himself tells us that the 'idea of sophianic reverence for the Mother of God, which crowns orthodox theologizing about her as with a cupola, by liturgically connecting the celebration of Sophia with the commemoration of the Mother of God' is Russian. 'This differs from the *Byzantine* church where the Christological aspect was singled out in Sophiology and sophianic festivals were united with dominical ones (Nativity of Christ, Resurrection)',[53] and he attempts to show how, in Orthodox understanding, these insights merge and complement one another. He also goes to some lengths to show us when we cry out 'most holy *Theotokos save* us', 'it is indicated perfectly clearly that this power of the Mother of God is derivative, conditioned by her "holy and almighty prayers"', and that she 'is only *the first* in a series of holy intercessors . . .'[54] Bulgakov was heavily censured at the time by the Moscow Patriarchate, and called a heretic by the Russian Orthodox Church outside Russia, and it is not for us to pursue the doctrinal dis-

---

50 Sergius Nikolaevich Bulgakov, (tr.) Thomas Allan Smith, *The Burning Bush: On the Orthodox Veneration of the Mother of God*, Grand Rapids, Michigan and Cambridge: Eerdmans, 2009, p. 69. Bulgakov signs off Chapter 4, 'The Glorification of the Mother of God' with the apostrophe 'Most Holy *Theotokos*, save us!' (p. 114). In three excursuses he grounds his argument on the Glory of God in the Old Testament (pp. 117ff.), the Old Testament Doctrine of the Wisdom of God (pp. 131ff.), and the Doctrine of the Wisdom of God in St Athanasius the Greet and Other Church Fathers (pp. 143ff.).

51 Sergius Nikolaevich Bulgakov, *The Burning Bush*, p. 105.

52 'Deification' is explained simply in Jaroslav Pelikan, *Mary Through the Centuries*, pp. 107f.

53 Sergius Nikolaevich Bulgakov, *The Burning Bush*, p. 107: italicized emphasis *Byzantine* as in the published translation.

54 Sergius Nikolaevich Bulgakov, *The Burning Bush*, p. 76: italicized emphases *save* and *the first* as in the published translation.

cussion here. We are content to allude to the difficulties that liturgical texts can cause.

There are at least some parallels in the West too: Sarah Boss shows us the liturgical links between Mary and Wisdom, first made by Alcuin of York, compiling votive mass propers in the ninth century. This association proved popular and, later, we find Ecclesiastes 24.14–16[55] used in the Vigil Mass of the Assumption, and Proverbs 8.22–31 for the Nativity and Conception of the Virgin. Here Boss makes the interesting point that, whereas the RSV translates Proverbs 8.24 as 'when there were no depths I was brought forth', the Vulgate's translation of the Hebrew is 'when there were no depths, already was I conceived'.[56]

Following this first difficulty, whether Mary and Holy Wisdom may be identified as one and the same,[57] we must consider the second. The second difficulty is that with the liturgical petition 'Holy *Theotokos* save us' we are dangerously close to C. G. Jung's perception, admittedly that of a mystic rebelling against the stern patriarchy of the Protestant presbytery in which he had been brought up, that a complete doctrine of Mary transforms a masculine trinity into a fully gendered quaternity, an observation in *Antwort auf Hiob* (*Answer to Job*) in 1952,[58] about the promulging of the doctrine of the Assumption by Pope Pius XII in 1950, achieved, he thought, by overwhelming popular demand, what the Church calls the *sensus fidelium* (consensus of the faithful). In Jung's view:

> the quaternity is the *sine qua non* of divine birth and consequently of the inner life of the trinity. Thus circle and quaternity on one side and the threefold rhythm on the other interpenetrate so that each is contained in the other. [59]

In the 1960s, Harvey Cox, writing as a Baptist and a professor at Harvard, wrote about America's cult of 'The Girl', 'the omnipresent icon of consumer society' and symbol and consequence of the masculinist Christianity Jung had rejected in the Swiss Calvinism of his upbringing:[60]

55 vv. 9–12 in Hebrew and English bibles.

56 Sarah Jane Boss, *Empress and Handmaid*, pp. 139f.

57 See Richard Rutt, *Mary, Disciple of the Lord: Changes in the Use of Scripture in Marian Masses since 1970*, Ecumenical Society of the Blessed Virgin Mary, 2002, ISBN 1 869927 39 7, pp. 3f., 8, and 22.

58 C. G. Jung, G. Adler, M. Fordham and H. Read (eds) (tr.) R. F. C. Hull, *Collected Works*, 9ii, 142, (21 volume set), New Jersey: Princeton University Press, 2000.

59 C. G. Jung, *Collected Works*, 11, 125.

60 Harvey Cox, *The Secular City*, New York: Macmillan, and London: SCM Press, 1965, pp. 204ff.

Just as the Virgin appears in many guises – as our Lady of Lourdes or of Fatima or of Guadalupe – but is always recognisably the Virgin, so with The Girl.

If men sometimes sought to buy with gold the Virgin's blessings on their questionable causes, so The Girl now dispenses her charismatic favour on watches, refrigerators, and razor blades – for a price.

'The Girl' needed to be rumbled for what she was, an idol. She was the unattainable temptress, displaying her unpurchasable wares in the *Playboy* magazine. 'The Girl' had taken hold on society because Protestantism, a very masculine form of Christianity, had banished the Virgin and all devotion to her. As Cox says,

> [The Girl] reverses most of the values traditionally associated with the Virgin – poverty, humility, sacrifice . . . The Girl has nothing to do with filling the hungry with 'good things', hawking instead an endless proliferation of trivia on TV spot commercials. The Girl exalts the mighty, extols the rich, and brings nothing to the hungry but added despair.

Though for Jung the promulging of the doctrine of the Assumption was clearly the most significant religious event since the Protestant Reformation, Catholics would have to say that the notion of the quaternity is straightforwardly heretical from a Christian point of view, articulating, however cleverly and positively, the basic Protestant neurosis about honouring Mary.[61]

Nonetheless, in contemplating Jung's view, and Cox's rumbling of the sexism fuelled by American evangelicalism, we are not too far from understanding the underlying anxiety over such phrases in the *Akathistos* hymn as 'thou knowest our offences, forgive them, and resolve them' and 'we know no other help but thee, no other intercessor, no gracious comforter, only thee' and, most startling of all to Western sensibilities, 'save us'. We have been looking here at translations, an important *caveat*, but we notice that, whereas the *Sub Tuum Præsidium* has 'save us from every danger' (other translations say 'deliver us')

---

61 In his essay 'Devotion to the Mother of God', in E. L. Mascall (ed.), *The Mother of God: A Symposium by Members of the Fellowship of St Alban and St Sergius*, London: Dacre Press, 1949, p. 74, the Anglican historian of the English Reformation, Tom Parker, recounts that 'Frederick the Great once said that but for the Reformation the Roman Church would have made the Blessed Virgin a Fourth Person of the Trinity.' He also said (p. 66) that 'to forget her in the choric functions of worship which we perform in the play is like ignoring Jocasta in *Œdipus Rex*'.

which is asking for the kind of protection which devotion to angels and saints has always asked for, the 'save us' of the *Akathistos* Hymn is more radically redemptive in character. The West never comes closer to this in a liturgical formulation than in the collect associated with the *Regina cæli*, the Marian antiphon for Eastertide, and here we must look at the Latin. The Latin phrase, *per eius Genetricem Virginem Mariam perpetuæ capiamus gaudia vitæ*, is often translated 'through the intercession of the Virgin Mary, his Mother, we may obtain the joys of everlasting life'[62] or 'with the help of his Mother the Virgin Mary'.[63] Both 'the intercession of' and 'the help of', however, are manifestly interpolations,[64] softening the implication that the Virgin Mother might be viewed otherwise not only as 'co-redemptrix' or 'co-mediatrix', about which there continues to be legitimate and stimulating debate, but as sole mediatrix of 'the joys of everlasting life', which no one would want to say. With the possible exception of this prayer – and the traditional orations anyway have been omitted from the post-conciliar Marian antiphons (though one can but hope for their restoration) – the careful hierarchy in Western theology (albeit using Greek terms) of *latria*, the worship of God, *hyperdulia*, the special honour due to the Mother of God, and *dulia*, the honour due to angels and saints seems to have been preserved in the *lex orandi*, the rule about what should be prayed.

By contrast, the devotional language of the East, as it developed, has not had to survive either the polemical threshing floor of the Reformation or the doctrinal mills of Catholicism, seeking to assert both its authority and salvific assurance in the midst of the difficult political circumstances of nineteenth-century Italy and twentieth-century Europe, as the evolving focus of the 'Leonine Prayers' indicated.[65] In part this is because we are in a popular and essentially extra-liturgical area which has not been so heavily policed. Within the Divine Liturgy of St John Chrysostom the *Theotokos* is greeted and given an honoured place – the choir chanting this, or some other similar text, during the last part of the Eucharistic Prayer:

It is truly right to call you blessed, who gave birth to God, ever-blessed and most pure, and Mother of our God. Greater in honour than the Cherubim and beyond compare more glorious than the Sera-

---

62 See *Handbook of Prayers*, p. 56.

63 As in Andrew Burnham (comp.), *A Manual of Anglo-Catholic Devotion*, p. 669 and Andrew Burnham (comp.), *A Pocket Manual of Anglo-Catholic Devotion*, p. 442.

64 No such interpolation is made in Seán Finnegan (comp.), *A Book of Hours and Other Catholic Devotions*, p. 343.

65 See note 20.

phim, without corruption you gave birth to God the Word, truly the Mother of God, we magnify you.[66]

Immediately, once we have got beyond the startling interpolation of a 'mini-magnificat', sung to the Mother of God, at a liturgical moment where, in the West, only God himself is addressed, we notice the careful theological language of this doxology. Anglicans have picked up exactly these sentiments, whether enthusiastically or unwittingly, in the popular hymn 'Ye watchers and ye holy ones' written by Athelstan Riley (1858–1945).[67] Riley himself, something of an expert on Oriental Christianity, especially the Assyrian Christians of the Middle East, knows exactly what seams he is mining, and what sentiments he is encouraging.[68] He was an enthusiast for the English Hymnal project and was sharply criticized for providing for it a translation of the *Ave maris stella*, 'Hail, O Star that pointest'.[69] It was he who, with his preference for the 'English Use' and his interest in Orthodox and Oriental Christianity, rather tellingly wrote *A Guide to the Divine Liturgy in the East, Being a Manual for the Use of English Churchmen* (1922):[70]

O higher than the Cherubim,
more glorious than the Seraphim,
lead their praises, alleluya!
Thou Bearer of the eternal Word,
most gracious, magnify the Lord,
Alleluya, alleluya, alleluya, alleluya, alleluya.[71]

Much more typical of Anglican treatment of the Blessed Virgin Mary is the reticence of the no less popular hymn 'Tell out my soul', a paraphrase of the *Magnificat*, published in 1962 by the evangelical bishop

---

66 Η ΘΕΙΑ ΛΕΙΤΟΥΡΓΙΑ ΤΟΥ ΕΝ ΑΓΙΟΙΣ ΠΑΤΡΟΣ ΗΜΩΝ ΙΩΑΝΝΟΥ ΤΟΥ ΧΡΥΣΟΣΤΟΜΟΥ *The Divine Liturgy of our Father among the Saints John Chrysostom*, Oxford: Oxford University Press, 1995, p. 35.

67 *English Hymnal*, no. 519.

68 A pious Anglo-Catholic layman and a rich benefactor, Riley's story is told in Michael Yelton, *Outposts of the Faith*, Norwich: Canterbury Press, 2009, pp. 51ff.

69 *English Hymnal*, no. 213.

70 Earlier, Riley wrote *A Guide to High Mass Abroad, Being a Manual for the Use of English Churchmen Attending the Celebration of the Eucharist in Roman Catholic Countries*, London: Mowbray, 1906. The 1924 edition is available (2009) on Project Canterbury, founded in 1999, anglicanhistory.org/

71 *English Hymnal*, no. 519. Riley's wife, Andalusia, said of him that whenever he could not think of a rhyme for one of his hymns, he ended the line with an alleluia, Michael Yelton, *Outposts of the Faith*, p. 60. She perhaps had this hymn in mind.

Timothy Dudley-Smith.[72] How many realize, as they sing it, that the one verse omitted from the paraphrase is 'All generations shall call me blessed'? This is not dissent from Holy Scripture but nervousness about Mariolatry,[73] the same nervousness that allows CW, slightly more bravely, to refer to the 'God-bearer' but not to the 'Mother of God':

> May the Holy Spirit,
> by whose overshadowing Mary became the God-bearer,
> give you grace to carry the good news of Christ.[74]

Mother of the Church or Symbol of the Church

Something like the 'Mother or Maiden' apparent antithesis of this chapter is contained in the tension between the notions of Mary as Mother of the Church – that is, as distinct from the Church as a mother is from her child – and Mary as Symbol of the Church, the symbol of all who respond to the call of Christ, bearing through the Holy Eucharist, and thus within themselves, his presence and the marks of his suffering and glory. Sometimes the floribundance of the liturgy takes us in the first direction; significantly, the *Benedictus* antiphon at Lauds on 15 September, Our Lady of Sorrows, in the (post-conciliar) Divine Office calls Mary *universorum regina*, Queen of the universe. On the other hand, the pre-conciliar feast of the Seven Sorrows of the Blessed Virgin, on the same date, is more restrained: *Venite, ascendamus ad montem Domini, et videte, si est dolor, sicut dolor meus.* We are called, with the Mother of the Lord, to ascend the hill of his Cross and see if there is any sorrow like 'my' – is that his or her? – sorrow.

The Dutch theologian, Edward Schillebeeckx,[75] recounts, from his own somewhat liberal standpoint, some of the Mariological tensions in the Second Vatican Council. One was whether the topic of Mary

---

72 First published in the *Anglican Hymn Book*, no. 439, London: Church Book Room Press, [Church Society]), 1965, and thereafter in *Ancient and Modern*, no. 422, New Standard Edition, Norwich: Canterbury Press, 1983, and *New English Hymnal*, no. 186, Norwich: Canterbury Press, 1985.

73 For an overview of the place of the Virgin Mary in Anglican history, see Paul Williams, 'The English Reformers and the Blessed Virgin Mary' (pp. 238ff.), and 'The Virgin Mary in Anglican Tradition' (pp. 314ff.), in Sarah Jane Boss (ed.), *Mary: The Complete Resource*.

74 Christmas Blessing, CW: *Times and Seasons*, London: Church House Publishing, p. 87.

75 Edward Schillebeeckx and Catharina Halkes, (tr.) John Bowden, *Mary Yesterday, Today, Tomorrow*, London: SCM Press, 1993, pp. 12ff.

– Mother of the Church – should be the subject of a discrete dogmatic constitution, or whether, as happened, the Church's reflections on Mary – Symbol of the Church – should be included in *Lumen Gentium*, the dogmatic constitution on the Church. In fact what became known as the 'Suenens Amendment' was the narrowly gained addition to *Lumen Gentium* 8:65 of an explicit acknowledgement of the pre-eminence of the *Beatissima* – the most blessed one – and her role as the paradigm of discipleship.[76] At the same time, in a vote on 29 October 1964 the Council fathers declined the use of the title 'Mary, Mother of the Church', a title used in medieval times but unknown in the first thousand years of Church history. One factor, certainly, was that the Council was sensitive to the wider ecumenical context and keen to avoid further developments in Marian doctrine: it was less than fifteen years, after all, since the controversial pronouncement of the doctrine of the Assumption. Declining the use of the title is not the same, however, as rejecting its theological content. So *Lumen Gentium*,[77] picking up a theme of St Augustine, does say of Mary:

> She is 'the mother of the members of Christ . . . having cooperated by charity that faithful might be born in the Church, who are members of that Head'.[78] Wherefore she is hailed as a pre-eminent and singular member of the Church, and as its type and excellent exemplar in faith and charity. The Catholic Church, taught by the Holy Spirit, honours her with filial affection and piety as a most beloved mother.

Nonetheless, it was one of those occasions on which the Pope, as guardian of the whole tradition, thought it necessary to overrule the temporary – and here that means the understated – consensus of a present age and, on his own authority, Paul VI, on 21 November 1964 – that is, only three weeks later than the Council vote – decided himself to declare Mary 'Mother of the Church'. In so doing he not only satisfied the conservative minority – not least by implicitly reinforcing the quotation from St Augustine – but also, it could be argued, demonstrated the balance between papal and conciliar authority, complementing the conciliar emphasis of the Second Vatican Council with the monarchical

---

76 Marie Farrell RSM, 'Evangelization, Mary and the "Suenens Amendment" of *Lumen Gentium* 8', in William McLoughlin and Jill Pinnock (eds), *Mary for Earth and Heaven*, Leominster: Gracewing, 2002, pp. 146ff.

77 *Lumen Gentium*, 53. *Lumen Gentium*, 1963, the Second Vatican Council Dogmatic Constitution on the Church, is available (2009) on www.vatican.va

78 St Augustine, *De Sancte Virginitate*, 6: PL 40, 399.

emphasis of the First. That is not quite Schillebeeckx's take on things but he does give us two insights which are particularly useful to our discussion. The first is that

> (though) it is not Mary but the Holy Spirit who is 'the mother of all believers', the true 'mother of the church', . . . Mariological titles of honour are a second level transference. They are transferred from the Holy Spirit to the Church, and from this ecclesiological transference 'transferred' once again, specifically to Mary, the mother of Jesus, the first and pre-eminent member in faith of the Church's community of faith.[79]

We are not as far away here from liturgical considerations as it might seem: Schillebeeckx reaches his conclusion not least by noticing how the various Marian titles in the Litany of Loreto[80] are derived from the Holy Spirit – and therefore, one might say, from his overshadowing – and we are helped, though we have neither the skill in dogmatics nor the space here to consider such matters further – to see that any unease we might feel about the confusion of Holy Wisdom, a *Theotokos* who can save (that is co-redeem and co-mediate), guard and protect – with the Sovereign Spirit can be set aside, at least at a popular level, provided that due vigilance is shown by those who supervise the rites of the Church. As we have seen, the Latin Rite is particularly economical and judicious in these respects.

As for the second insight of help to us here, Schillebeeckx infers from the notion of Abraham as 'the father of all who believe' (Rom. 4.11; see also Heb. 11.8–12, Rom. 4.1, James 2.21–23) that 'alongside Abraham, Mary – as the believing mother of Jesus, confessed by Christians as Christ, God's Son, our Lord – is the mother of all believers'.[81] Pelikan makes the same point, saying that if Eve is 'the mother of all living' (Gen. 3.20) and 'if there were to be a "mother of all them that believe",

---

79 Edward Schillebeeckx and Catharina Halkes, *Mary Yesterday, Today, Tomorrow*, pp. 28f. See also St Augustine's phrase which we mention slightly later (p. 425): 'She is a holy member of the Church; she is the holy member; she is the member above all members; but she is still one member of the whole body.'

80 The Litany of Loreto (also called the Litany of the Blessed Virgin Mary) is in many popular collections, such as *Saint Benedict's Prayer Book*, pp. 166ff., and *Handbook of Prayers*, pp. 435ff. Anglican sources include Andrew Burnham (comp.), *A Manual of Anglo-Catholic Devotion*, p. 394; and Andrew Burnham (comp.), *A Pocket Manual of Anglo-Catholic Devotion*, pp. 333ff.

81 Edward Schillebeeckx and Catharina Halkes, *Mary Yesterday, Today, Tomorrow*, p. 42.

the prime candidate would have to be Mary'.[82] This is not a new idea for we are reminded of yet another medieval carol, the fifteenth-century *Nova, nova: Ave fit ex Eva* ('News, news: *Ave* has been made from *Eva*'). This is not an exclusively Catholic conclusion: as Pelikan points out, the redoubtable seventeenth century Protestant, John Milton, describes the Virgin as 'blest Marie, second Eve'.[83] Not only are we not detracting from the honour and glory that belong to God alone – 'the careful hierarchy of *latria*, the worship of God, *hyperdulia*, the special honour due to the Mother of God, and *dulia*, the honour due to angels and saints' to which we have already referred – but we are seeing in Mary's belief, response and prayers the archetype of the belief, response and prayers of all Christian disciples, individually and collectively. She is Mother of the Church and Symbol of the Church: how appropriate it is that the cathedral – 'mother church' of the diocese – is so often dedicated to the Blessed Virgin Mary. It is there that her children gather. It is there where her Son is present *par excellence* in the 'local church', the centre of the diocese. It is there where all disciples in Christ wait in prayer, wait in obedience, and follow her supreme example: to learn and study his will and, pondering these things, to have them in mind (Phil. 2.5) and keep them in the heart (Luke 2.19; 2.51), not being conformed to this world but transformed (Rom. 12.2) thus, like Mary, predestined and called (Rom. 8.30), and fulfilling – each one – his and her individual, unique and providential vocation.

Fellow Disciple or Sign of Discipleship

So Mary is at once fellow disciple and model or sign of discipleship. An extract from a sermon of St Augustine, set for the Office of Readings on the Presentation of the Blessed Virgin Mary, 21 November,[84] says of Mary that 'indeed she did the Father's will' but, he goes on to say, 'it is a greater thing for her that she was Christ's disciple than that she was his mother'. 'She is a holy member of the Church; she is the holy member; she is the member above all members; but she is still one member of the whole body.'

---

82 Jaroslav Pelikan, *Mary Through the Centuries*, p. 20.

83 Jaroslav Pelikan, *Mary Through the Centuries*, p. 45. The reference is to *Paradise Lost* V.385–7.

84 Sermon 25, 7–8, an exegesis of Matt. 12.46–50 and parallels.

In a homily for the Assumption,[85] Max Kramer recalls C. S. Lewis's book, *The Great Divorce*,[86] in which Lewis's day-trippers catch sight

> of an enormous procession of angels accompanying a woman who walks upon the rose petals that cherubim scatter before her feet. She is dazzlingly beautiful clothed at once in the glorious nakedness of the garden of Eden and in the sumptuous finery of the kingdom of heaven. On her head she wears a crown that is so much part of her identity that, as Lewis says, you cannot tell where the head ends and the crown begins.

The identity that springs to mind, of course, is that she is Mary . . . 'a woman, adorned with the sun, standing on the moon, and with the twelve stars on her head for a crown'. However, as the story progresses we learn that this woman is, in fact, an ordinary humble girl from a poor part of an industrial city, who had used up her life in love.

Kramer goes on to say:

> we think of Mary as an example of how Christians should behave . . . but God's plan for Mary is so much greater than this. For it is God's plan that Mary not only models Christian behaviour but that she is a model, a 'sign' . . . of what a Christian is.
>
> And so the whole of the Christian story of Mary becomes God's way of teaching us not only how to behave, but what we are. For, in her immaculate conception Mary is a 'sign' of the freedom from sin that Christians have through Baptism into the sacrificial death of her Son, in the virgin birth she becomes a sign of God's taking the first move to reconcile the human race to himself, and of his power to do even that which seems impossible, and in her Assumption . . . Mary is the sign of the glory of the eternal future that is promised to all the faithful.

In a fairly straightforward way, then, the prayers of Mary are the prayers of a fellow disciple, a fellow Christian, the first disciple of her Son,[87] and the prayers of the one who is both the sign and the model of what it is to pray in faith, in obedience, and in trust: 'Behold I am the handmaid of the Lord; let it be to me according to your word'

---

85 The homily was preached at the Parish Church of St John the Evangelist, New Hinksey, Oxford, on 16 August 2009. It has not been published otherwise.

86 C. S. Lewis, *The Great Divorce*, 1946, London: G. Bles, reprinted by London: HarperCollins, 1997, and New York: HarperCollins, 2001.

87 John Paul II, *Redemptoris Mater*, n.20, 1987, www.vatican.va

(Luke 1.38) and 'Do whatever he tells you' (John 2.5). She is archetype and ensample. However devoutly we greet her within the liturgy, or in extra-liturgical devotion, we are always looking beyond her – she is always pointing beyond herself – to her Divine Son, cradled on her lap or enthroned upon the Cross. This is the meaning of the *Hodegetria*, the icon of Mary, in which 'the child Christ sits cradled by his mother's left arm while she points to him with her right'.[88] In *Mary for All Christians*, the fruit of several talks to the Ecumenical Society of the Blessed Virgin Mary, splendidly readable and, a generation later, still the most accessible introduction of the topic of Mary to the diffident, the Anglican theologian John Macquarrie quotes St Louis Grignon de Montfort (1673–1716),[89] of whom Macquarrie says, 'There have been few devotees of Mary so enthusiastic.' These are de Montfort's words:

> I avow, with all the Church, that Mary, being a mere creature that has come from the hands of the most High, is in comparison with his infinite majesty less than an atom; or rather, she is nothing at all, because only he is He Who Is . . . Jesus Christ, our Saviour, true God and true Man, ought to be the last end of our devotions, else they are false and delusive. If then we establish solid devotion to our blessed Lady, it is only more perfectly to establish devotion to Christ. . .When we praise her, love her, honour her or give anything to her, it is God who is praised, God who is loved, God who is glorified and it is to God that we give, through Mary and in Mary.

Though the emphasis on God being glorified is central to most Marian iconography, there will be those who find the medieval representation of the Virgin – the Walsingham image – more helpful than Boss's 'prayerful young woman', the Immaculate Lady of Lourdes or the crowned Empress of Fatima. One expects perhaps to have to wrestle with these matters at Marian shrines,[90] but at Lourdes, as one experiences it, the Virgin at the Grotto of Massabielle is no goddess. As we attend on her, having ourselves walked in the steps of St Bernadette, the Lady herself

---

88 Rowan Williams, *Ponder these Things: Praying with Icons of the Virgin*, Norwich: Canterbury Press, 2002, p. 3.

89 John Macquarrie, *Mary for All Christians*, London; Collins, 1990, p. 133.

90 The question of why Marian apparitions have been such a feature of Christian history, Catholic and Orthodox, is discussed, and a bibliography given, in Chris Maunder, 'Apparitions of Mary', in Sarah Jane Boss (ed.), *Mary: The Complete Resource*, pp. 424ff. See also Richard Rutt, 'Why should he send his Mother? Some reflections on Marian apparitions?', in William McLoughlin and Jill Pinnock (eds), *Mary is for Everyone*, p. 274.

stands beside the Church in every sense. She is the first of the redeemed standing beside the congregating crowds of her fellow disciples, to whom she is saying, as she said at Cana, 'Do whatever he tells you'; beside the Calvary she stands not as 'Maiden' but as 'Mother', Mother not only of the beloved disciple but of all beloved disciples. She stands as 'Mother' beside the very basilicas – upper, lower, and underground – in which her Son, her own flesh and blood, is present in the Holy Eucharist. We find her kneeling with us as a disciple in the Cenacle, the upper basilica, as it were, expectant that the gifts of the Spirit poured out on the apostles will be poured out afresh on all those made apostolic by baptism. Indeed as Pope John Paul II has said, 'Devotion to Our Lady . . . is not opposed to devotion to her Son. Rather it can be said that by asking the beloved disciple to treat Mary as his Mother Jesus founded Marian devotion.'[91] Those who see such devotion as a wandering away from the doctrines that Christ alone is our sole Advocate, Mediator and Redeemer – which in the most important of senses he is – have never been enthralled by the music of Tomás Luis de Victoria's double choir *Ave Maria* (1585), Claudio Monteverdi's Vespers of 1610, Anton Bruckner's *Ave Maria* (1861), or Henryk Górecki's *Totus tuus* (1987).[92]

Gate of Heaven and Earthly Rose[93]

There are balances between the Lord and Israel, the Lord and the faithful Daughter of Zion, the Bridegroom and the Bride, Christ and the Church, Jesus and Mary.[94] There is the filial relationship between the Mother and the Beloved Disciple solemnized at the Cross and drawing us in. As Rowan Williams reminds us, there is also the ancient image of 'The Virgin of the Sign – The *Orans*', the woman with hands outstretched in prayer, 'on her breast . . . a roundel or medallion in which Christ is depicted'. As he explains:

---

91 Quoted in Arthur Burton Calkins, 'Mary's Spiritual Maternity', in William McLoughlin and Jill Pinnock (eds), *Mary is for Everyone*, p. 79.

92 These composers represent the finest flowering of music in the deeply Catholic countries of Spain, Italy, Austria and Poland.

93 *Ianua cæli* (Gate of Heaven) is from the Litany of Loreto, see note 80 above. As 'earthly rose' Mary lends her name to varieties of rose, as in the rose gardens of such Marian shrines as that in Knock, Ireland.

94 For further exploration of these ideas, see, for example, Cardinal Angelo Scola, (tr.) Michelle Borras and others, *The Nuptial Mystery*, Grand Rapids, Michigan and Cambridge: Eerdmans, 2005.

Since very early on, Christians had imagined the Church in the form of a woman; and the *orans* figure, the woman praying with hands extended and head covered, stood for the whole believing community considered as Christ's bride.[95]

So, what use is Mary, what use is the Church, if she is not my mother too, as I try to be a beloved disciple? And how else is this relationship pursued and sustained other than within the life of Christian prayer, the celebration of the Liturgy, as those who 'have no lasting city' on earth (Heb. 13.14), 'come to Mount Zion and to the city of the living God, the heavenly Jerusalem, and to innumerable angels in festal gathering, and to the assembly of the first-born who are enrolled in heaven' (Heb. 12.22–23a)?[96] *The Catechism of the Catholic Church*, in the final section on prayer, quoting *Lumen Gentium*, says that

> From the most ancient times the Blessed Virgin has been honoured with the title of 'Mother of God', to whose protection the faithful fly in all their dangers and needs . . . This very special devotion . . . differs essentially from the adoration which is given to the incarnate Word and equally to the Father and the Holy Spirit, and greatly fosters this adoration.[97]

It is this last point – that devotion to the Mother of Jesus, far from detracting from the worship of God, 'greatly fosters this adoration' that needs to be worked at and understood anew in this project of re-enchantment. If lay folk paused at morning, noon, and night for the *Angelus*, if the Rosary became part of the daily rhythm of prayer, and if the Marian antiphon at the end of the day were to become once more a nocturnal habit, Christian daily life would again be Christocentric; there is no adequate Christology without an adequate Mariology, as the Council of Ephesus (AD 431) insisted, as it declared Mary *Theotokos*, Mother of God. As Pope John Paul II said:

> With the Rosary, the Christian people sits at the school of Mary and is led to contemplate the beauty on the face of Christ and to experience the depths of his love. Through the Rosary the faithful receive

---

95 Rowan Williams, *Ponder these Things*, pp. 43f.

96 This paragraph and some of the material elsewhere in the chapter began as a paper given by the author in April 2001 to the Society of Mary and the Ecumenical Society of the Blessed Virgin Mary, 'Mary and Christian Prayer'. The paper was published privately by the Society of Mary.

97 *The Catechism of the Catholic Church*, para. 971.

abundant grace, as though from the very hands of the Mother of the Redeemer.[98]

If these devotions were revived, we should see once more signs of the everyday piety which Christianity knew in its fifteenth century of development, and which Islam still has in its fifteenth century. In each of the Christians devotions the Mother points to her Son, whether we are saying 'The Word became flesh and dwelt among us' (John 1.14) in the *Angelus*, or recalling that 'those whom [God] foreknew he also predestined to be conformed to the image of his Son' (Rom. 8.29) in the Paschal *Regina Cæli*. The macaronic text of the medieval carol, *There is no rose*, the starting point of our quest for re-enchantment, begins with an *alleluia* refrain, and then speaks of a *res miranda*, a thing to be wondered at. That leads us on to a pondering of *pares forma*: 'God in persons three', 'equal in form'. The *Gloria in excelsis* of the angels takes us thereafter both with the shepherds to Bethlehem and with the saints throughout the ages into Mass. So, *gaudeamus*, 'let us rejoice', and *'transeamus'* 'let us follow'.

In the English tradition, who could not pray with the *Gaude flore Virginali*, especially as it is sung to the music of Hugh Kellyk in the Eton Choirbook:[99]

> Rejoice that you are so united in the bond of will
> and the embrace of love with the Most High
> that you obtain the promise of whatever virgin prayer you make of
> your sweetest Jesus.

Or, indeed, with John Browne's setting of O *Maria Salvatoris Mater* from the same source?

> We have a mother ready at those times to help us:
> lo! how graciously Mary ever stands by us.
> let us make our prayer also to Frideswide,
> to Magdalene, to Catherine learned in philosophy . . .

If music is not how we pray, there is always the prayer of Erasmus as printed in *The Walsingham Pilgrims' Manual*:[100]

---

98 Introduction to *Rosarium Virginis Mariæ* (2002).

99 The translation of this and the following piece is from *The Flower of All Virginity*, Music from the Eton Choirbook, Vol. IV, The Sixteen, Harry Christopher, Collins Classics 13952 © 1993 Lambourne Productions Ltd.

100 *The Walsingham Pilgrims Manual* is an Anglican publication, available from the Walsingham College Trust Association, The Shrine Office, Walsingham, Norfolk, NR22

What shall I call thee, O Full of Grace?
Heaven, for of thee arose the Sun of Righteousness;
Paradise, for thou hast budded forth
the Flower of Immortality;
Virgin, for thou didst hold in thy embrace
the Son who is God of all:
pray thou to him that he will save our souls.

Mother of God, we fly to you,
our shade and shelter on our pilgrim's way.
Look kindly on our prayers,
and turn not from us in our time of need.
But free us from the dangers that beset us, radiant and holy Virgin.

O alone of all women, Mother and Virgin,
Mother most happy, Virgin most pure,
now we, impure as we are,
come to see thee who art all-pure; we salute thee;
we worship thee as how we may
with our humble offerings.
May thy Son grant us, that
imitating thy most holy manners,
we also, by the grace of the Holy Ghost,
may deserve spiritually to conceive
the Lord Jesus in our inmost soul,
and once conceived, never to lose him. Amen.

It would be very bad form – and entirely incorrect – to try to claim that Erasmus of Rotterdam was an Anglican, though many would know what one meant were one to say that Erasmus was a kind of Anglican. But Erasmus's Prayer to Our Lady of Walsingham in 1511 has a typically Anglican moderation. 'What shall I call thee, O Full of Grace?' is very Anglican in its diffidence. The conclusion of the prayer too is rather Anglican: by now the energy of the prayer is entirely focused on Mary's Son and the prayer is that 'we also, by the grace of the Holy Ghost, may deserve spiritually to conceive the Lord Jesus in our inmost soul'.

Prayer to Mary through the antiphons, hymns, motets, prayers, and responsories which the Church provides both austerely within the

---

6EE. It is regularly re-published and Erasmus's Prayer is on p. 66 of the current (2009) undated edition.

liturgy, and sometimes more luxuriantly in extra-liturgical devotions, is not a doctrinally hazardous affair. The mysteries of the Catholic religion appeal to the whole person, emotional, intellectual, sensory and spiritual. All ends in pilgrimage: heaven and earth in little space was the hypostatic union – the union of divine and human – in the person of Jesus, the baby in Mary's womb. Heaven and earth in little space is the place of the liturgy, the sanctuary of God, Mount Zion, a place of peace and stillness amidst the bustle of ordinary roads and thoroughfares, beside businesses and factories, alongside homes and restaurants, near hospitals and hospices, schools and shops. Heaven and earth in little space is the Angel, Christ himself, amidst the chanting of psalms and the burning of incense, which is the prayer of the saints, bearing up the eucharistic gifts to the altar on high of the Divine Majesty.[101] Heaven and earth in little space is the Body and Blood of Christ in the bellies of the baptized, in the lives of believers, and in the dignity of the dispossessed. Heaven and earth in little space is the Marriage Supper of the Lamb, when at the end of time the Bridegroom will be fully at one with the Bride. As we look towards that final *parousia*, the life of the world to come, may we experience with greater intensity, in a re-enchanted liturgy, the *sacrum convivium*, that holy feast and sacrifice in which Christ is received and the memory of his passion renewed. Through the prayers of Our Lady St Mary, as the medievals called her, may our lives be filled with grace, as we receive both a foretaste and pledge of future glory.

There is no rose of such virtue
as is the rose that bare Jesu;
alleluia.

For in this rose contained was
heaven and earth in little space;
res miranda.

By that rose we may well see
that he is God in persons three,
pares forma.

The angels sungen the shepherds to:
Gloria in excelsis Deo:
gaudeamus.

---

101 The reference here is to the *Supplices* in the Roman Canon. The notion of Christ himself as 'Angel' is not an undisputed reading: see p. 15, note 49.

Leave we all this worldly mirth,
and follow we this joyful birth;
transeamus.

Alleluia, res miranda,
pares forma, gaudeamus,
transeamus.

Bibliography

A General Note

In a book for the general reader which visits several topics, providing a comprehensive bibliography is difficult. Many of the specialized books listed here, however, have recent and well-stocked bibliographies. The list of articles, books and resourced below are such as are referred to in – or needed in the understanding of – the main text.

The bibliography is chapter by chapter. Several books are germane to more than one chapter: duplications in the bibliography, therefore, are to provide readers with the convenience of needing to refer only to the bibliography of the particular chapter they are reading. Increasingly material is available online. This is indicated particularly when searching the internet is the only – or the only convenient – way of access.

Every attempt has been made to avoid infringement of copyright. The author apologizes and seeks pardon for any unwitting transgression.

Introduction

Articles and books

Baker, Jonathan, 'Seeking Holiness: Eliot, Auden, Betjeman', in *Literature & Aesthetics: The Journal of the Sydney Society of Literature and Aesthetics*, June 2008.

Bartlett, Alan, *A Passionate Balance: The Anglican Tradition*, London: Darton, Longman & Todd, 2007.

Chadwick, Henry, *Augustine of Hippo: A Life*, Oxford: Oxford University Press, 2009.

Dormor, Duncan, McDonald, Jack and Caddick, Jeremy, *Anglicanism: The Answer to Modernity*, London: Continuum, 2003.

Hemming, Laurence, *Worship as a Revelation: The Past, Present and Future of Catholic Liturgy*, London: Continuum, 2008.

Horne, Brian, review of *Worship as a Revelation*, *International Journal for the Study of the Christian Church*, Volume 9 Number 4, Routledge, 2009.

Jeanes, Gordon P., *Signs of God's Promise: Thomas Cranmer's Sacramental Theology and the Book of Common Prayer*, London: T&T Clark, 2008.

Lamb, Matthew L. and Levering, Matthew (eds), *Vatican II: Renewal within Tradition*, Oxford: Oxford University Press, 2008.

Leachman OSB, James G. (ed.), *The Liturgical Subject: Subject, Subjectivity and the Human Person in Contemporary Liturgical Discussion and Critique*, London: SCM Press, 2008.

Mascall, E.L., *The God-Man*, London: Dacre Press, 1940.

McCullough, Peter (ed.), *Lancelot Andrewes: Selected Sermons & Lectures*, Oxford: Oxford University Press, 2005.

Norman, Edward, *Anglican Difficulties: A New Syllabus of Errors*, London: Morehouse 2004.

Pecklers SJ, Keith, *The Genius of the Roman Rite*, London: Burns & Oates, 2009.

Pusey, Edward Bouverie, 'Thoughts on the Benefits of the System of Fasting, Enjoined by our Church' *Tracts for the Times*, Number 18.

Shanks, Andrew, *Anglicans Reimagined: an honest church?*, London: SPCK, 2010.

Torevell, David, *Losing the Sacred: Ritual, Modernity and Liturgical Reform*, London: T&T Clark, 2000.

Williams, Rowan, *Anglican Identities*, London: Darton, Longman & Todd, 2004.

Liturgical Books and Reports and Documents

Anglican

The Eucharist: Sacrament of Unity (2001) (GS Misc 632).

Ecumenical

Growing Together in Unity and Mission: Building on 40 years of Anglican-Roman Catholic Dialogue. An Agreed Statement of the International Anglican-Roman Catholic Commission for Unity and Mission, London, 2007.

Chapter 1 Catholic or Reformed

Articles and Books

Avis, Paul, *The Identity of Anglicanism: Essentials of Anglican Ecclesiology*, London: T&T Clark, 2008.

Bailey, Simon, *A Tactful God*, Leominster: Gracewing, 1995.

Beckwith, Roger, 'The Anglican Eucharist: from the Reformation to the Restoration', in Cheslyn Jones, Geoffrey Wainwright, Edward Yarnold, SJ, and Paul Bradshaw (eds), *The Study of Liturgy*, revised edition, London: SPCK, 1992.

Beckwith, R. T. and Tiller, J. E. (eds), *The Service of Holy Communion and its Revision*, Abingdon: Marcham Manor Press, 1972.

Botte OSB, Bernard, (tr.) John Sullivan OCD, *From Silence to Participation*, Washington: The Pastoral Press, 1988.

Buchanan, Colin, *The New Communion Service – Reasons for Dissent*, London: Church Society, 1966.

Buchanan, Colin (ed.), *Modern Anglican Liturgies 1958–1968*, London: Oxford University Press, 1968.

Buchanan, Colin (ed.), *Further Anglican Liturgies 1968–1975*, Bramcote: Grove Books, 1975.

Buchanan, Colin, *What did Cranmer think he was doing?* Bramcote: Grove Liturgical Study 7, 1976; republished in Buchanan, Colin, *An Evangelical Among the Anglican Liturgists*, London: SPCK, Alcuin Club Collections 84, 2009.

Buchanan, Colin, *The End of the Offertory*, Bramcote: Grove Liturgical Study 14, 1978; republished in Buchanan, Colin, *An Evangelical Among the Anglican Liturgists*, 2009.

Cuming, Geoffrey (ed.), *The Durham Book*, London: Oxford University Press, 1961.

Cuming, Geoffrey, 1983, *The Godly Order*, London: Alcuin Club-SPCK, 1983.

Dickens, A. G., *The English Reformation*, London: Fontana, 1964; second edition, London: B. T. Batsford, 1991.

Dix, Gregory, *The Shape of the Liturgy*, London: Dacre Press, 1945; new edition, London: Continuum, 2005.

Dudley, Martin (comp. and ed.), *The Collect in Anglican Liturgy, Texts and Sources 1549–1989*, Collegeville: Liturgical Press, 1994.

Duffy, Eamon, *The Stripping of the Altars: Traditional Religion in England c1400–c1580*, New Haven: Yale University Press, 1992.

Duffy, Eamon, *Fires of Faith*, New Haven & London: Yale University Press, 2009.

Dugmore, C. W., *The Mass and the English Reformers*, London: Macmillan, 1958.

Franklin, R. William (ed.), *Anglican Orders, Essays on the Centenary of Apostolicæ Curæ*, London: Mowbray, 1996.

Gamber, Klaus, (tr.) Klaus D. Grimm, *The Reform of the Roman Liturgy: Its Problems and Background*, San Juan Capistrano, California: Una Voce Press, 1993.

Gordon-Taylor, Benjamin and Jones, Simon, 2005, *Celebrating the Eucharist*, Alcuin Liturgy Guides 3, London: SPCK, 2005.

Gordon-Taylor, Benjamin and Jones, Simon, *Celebrating Christ's Appearing: Advent to Candlemas*, Alcuin Liturgy Guides 5, London: SPCK, 2008.

Gordon-Taylor, Benjamin and Jones, Simon, *Celebrating Christ's Appearing: Ash Wednesday to Trinity*, Alcuin Liturgy Guides 6, London: SPCK, 2009.

Hill, Christopher and Yarnold SJ, Edward (eds), *Anglicans and Roman Catholics: The Search for Unity*, London: SPCK, Catholic Truth Society, 1994.

Hill, Christopher and Yarnold SJ, Edward, *Anglican Orders: The Documents in the Debate*, Norwich: Canterbury Press, 1997.

Hunwicke, John, 'Which one this morning?', *New Directions*, March 2005.

Irvine, Christopher (ed.), *The Use of Symbols in Worship*, Alcuin Liturgy Guides 4, London: SPCK, 2007.

Jasper, R. and Cuming, G. (eds), *Prayers of the Eucharist: Early and Reformed*, third edition, Collegeville: Liturgical Press, 1990.

Jungmann, SJ, Joseph, *The Mass of the Roman Rite: Its Origins and Development (Missarum Sollemnia)*, two vols, New York: Benziger Brothers Inc., 1951, replica edition, Dublin: Four Courts Press, 1986.

King, Archdale A., *Liturgy of the Roman Church*, London: Longmans, 1957.

MacCulloch, Diarmaid, *Thomas Cranmer*, New Haven and London: Yale University Press, 1996.

Mascall, Eric, *Corpus Christi*, London: Longmans, 1953.

Mazza, Enrico, *The Eucharistic Prayers of the Roman Rite*, New York: Pueblo, 1986.

Nichols OP, Aidan, *The Panther and the Hind*, London: T&T Clark, 2000.

Nichols OP, Aidan, *The Realm*, Oxford: Family Publications, 2008.

Nichols, Bridget, 'An Anglican experiment in Appreciating the Liturgy: the Easter Day Collect (First Holy Communion) in the First Prayer Book of Edward VI', in James G. Leachmann OSB and Daniel P. McCarthy OSB (eds), *Appreciating the Collect*, Farnborough: St Michael's Abbey Press, 2008.

Nichols, Bridget, 'F. E. Brightman', in Christopher Irvine (ed.), *They Shaped Our Worship, Essays on Anglican Liturgists*, London: SPCK, 1998.

Nockles, Peter, *The Oxford Movement in Context: Anglican High Churchmanship, 1760–1857*, Cambridge: Cambridge University Press, 1997.

Nockles, Peter, 'Survivals or New Arrivals?', in Platten, Stephen (ed.), *Anglicanism and the Western Christian Tradition*, Norwich: Canterbury Press, 2003.

Oberman, Heiko A., *The Dawn of the Reformation; Essays in Late Medieval and Early Reformation Thought*, Edinburgh: T&T Clark, 1986.

Pius XII, Encyclical, *Mediator Dei*, London: Catholic Truth Society, 1947, available (2009) on www.vatican.va

Platten, Stephen (ed.), *Anglicanism and the Western Christian Tradition*, Norwich: Canterbury Press, 2003.

Pocknee, Cyril E., *The Parson's Handbook, the Work of Percy Dearmer*, London: Oxford University Press, 1965.

Podmore, Colin, *Aspects of Anglican Identity*, London: Church House Publishing, 2005.

Procter, F. and Frere, W. H., The Book of Common Prayer, London: Macmillan, 1901; third impression with corrections and alterations, 1961.

Ramsey, Michael (posthumous), (ed.) Dale Coleman, *The Anglican Spirit*, London: SPCK, 1991.

Stringer, Martin D., *A Sociological History of Christian Worship*, Cambridge: Cambridge University Press, 2005.

Sykes, Stephen W., *The Integrity of Anglicanism*, London: Mowbray, 1978 (reprinted 1984).

Sykes, Stephen, Booty, John and Knight, Jonathan (eds), *The Study of Anglicanism*, revised edition, London: SPCK, 1998.

Wetherell, John, *Lex Orandi, Lex Credendi*, Cambridge: The Saint Joan Press, 2005.

Wigan, Bernard (ed.), *The Liturgy in English*, London: Oxford University Press, 1962.

Williams, Rowan, *Anglican Identities*, London: Darton, Longman and Todd, 2004.

Yelton, Michael, *Anglican Papalism: An Illustrated History 1900–1960*, Norwich: Canterbury Press, 2005.

Liturgical Books and Reports and Documents

Anglican

The Alternative Service Book 1980, jointly published by (1) Oxford: Oxford University Press and Mowbray, and (2) Cambridge: Cambridge University Press, Colchester: William Clowes, and London: SPCK.

The Anglican Breviary, 1955, Mt Sinai, Long Island, NY: Frank Gavin Liturgical Foundation Inc., reprinted 1998.

The Book of Common Prayer 1662, Standard Edition, Cambridge: Cambridge University Press.

The Book of Common Prayer, according to the Use of The Episcopal Church 1979, New York: Church Publishing Incorporated.

The Book of Common Prayer, according to the Use of the Protestant Episcopal Church in the United States 1928, New York: Harper and Brothers, 1928.

The Book of Common Prayer, as proposed in 1928, Norwich: Canterbury Press, 2008 (new edition).

The Canons of the Church of England, London: Church House Publishing. The current edition (sixth edition, 2009) and additions and corrections are available online through the Church of England website.

The Commemoration of Saints and Heroes of the Faith in the Anglican Communion; the Report of a Commission appointed by the Archbishop of Canterbury, London: SPCK, 1957.

Common Worship: Services and Prayers for the Church of England, London: Church House Publishing, 2000.

Common Worship: Ordination Services, London: Church House Publishing, 2007.

English Missal, The fifth and last edition of the altar edition, London: W. Knott & Son, 1958, republished Norwich: Canterbury Press, 2001.

The First and Second Prayer Books of Edward VI, London: Dent, 1910 (reprinted in 1968).

Milner-White, Eric, *My God, my Glory*, London: SPCK, 1954 (republished 1994).

Monastic Breviary: Matins according to the Holy Rule of Saint Benedict, Tymawr, Lydart, Monmouth: The Society of the Sacred Cross, 1961 (reprinted Glendale, Colorado: Lancelot Andrewes Press, 2007)

The Monastic Diurnal, last printed London: Oxford University Press, 1963.

The Shorter Prayer Book, London: Oxford University Press; London: Eyre and Spottiswoode Ltd; London: Cambridge University Press, all 1948; reprinted Cambridge University Press, 1992.

Catholic

Catechism of the Catholic Church (revised edition), London: Geoffrey Chapman, 1999.

The Code of Canon Law in English Translation, London: Collins Liturgical Publications, 1983.

The Revised Standard Version of the Bible, Second Catholic Edition, San Francisco: Ignatius Press, 2006.

Ecumenical

Baptism Eucharist and Ministry (39th printing), Faith & Order Paper 111, Geneva: World Council of Churches, 1992, 2007; also available (2009) as: *Baptism, Eucharist and Ministry* (Faith and Order Paper no. 111, the '*Lima Text*').

The Church of the Triune God – The Cyprus Agreed Statement, London: Anglican Communion Office, 2006.

English Language Liturgical Consultation (ELLC), *Praying Together*, Norwich: Canterbury Press, 1988.

The English Language Liturgical Consultation (ELLC) was the ecumenical successor of the International Consultation on English Texts (ICET) whose work is used and acknowledged in the English version of the Roman Missal of 1975.

Chapter 2 Extraordinary or Ordinary

Articles and Books

Baldovin SJ, John F., *Reforming the Liturgy: A Response to the Critics*, Collegeville: Liturgical Press, 2008.

Barker, Margaret, *The Great High Priest: The Temple Roots of Christian Liturgy*, London and New York: T&T Clark International, 2003.

Bonneterre, Didier, *The Liturgical Movement: from Dom Gueranger to Annibale Bugnini*, Kansas City: Angelus Press, 2002.

Botte OSB, Bernard, (tr.) John Sullivan, *From Silence to Participation*, Washington: The Pastoral Press, 1988.

Bouyer, Cong. Orat., Louis, *Liturgy and Architecture*, Indiana: University of Notre Dame Press, 1967.

Bradshaw, Paul F. (ed.), *A Companion to Common Worship*, vol. 1, London: SPCK, 2001.

Bradshaw, Paul F. (ed.), *A Companion to Common Worship*, vol. 2, London: SPCK, 2006.

Bugnini CM, Annibale, (tr.) Matthew J. O'Connell, *The Reform of the Liturgy 1948–1975*, Collegeville: Liturgical Press, 1990.

Cekada, Anthony, *The Problems with the Prayers of the Modern Mass*, Rockford, Ill.: TAN Books, 1991.

Crouan STD, Denis, (tr.) Marc Sebanc, *The Liturgy Betrayed*, San Francisco: Ignatius Press, 2000.

Crouan STD, Denis, (tr.) Michael Miller, *The History and the Future of the Roman Liturgy*, San Francisco: Ignatius Press, 2005.

Deiss CSSp, Lucien, (tr.) Jane M.-A. Burton, (ed.) Donald Molloy, *Visions of Liturgy and Music for a New Century*, Collegeville: Liturgical Press, 1996.

Dobszay, László, *The Bugnini-Liturgy and the Reform of the Reform*, vol. 5 of *Musicæ Sacræ Meltemata*, Front Royal VA: Church Music Association of America, 2003.

Elliott, Peter J., *Ceremonies of the Modern Roman Rite*, San Francisco: Ignatius Press, 1995.

Elliott, Peter J., *Liturgical Question Box*, San Francisco: Ignatius Press, 1998.

Elliott, Peter J., *Ceremonies of the Liturgical Year*, San Francisco: Ignatius Press, 2002.

Elliott, Peter J., 'A Question of Ceremonial', in Thomas M. Kocik, *The Reform of the Reform? A Liturgical Debate: Reform or Return*, San Francisco: Ignatius Press, 2003.

Flanagan, Kieran, *Sociology and Liturgy: Re-presentations of the Holy*, New York: St Martin's Press, 1991.

Gamber, Klaus, (tr.) Simone Wallon, *La Réforme Liturgique en Question*, Paris: Éditions Sainte-Madeleine, 1992. The English edition is as below.

Gamber, Klaus, (tr.) Klaus D. Grimm, *The Reform of the Roman Liturgy: Its Problems and Background*, San Juan Capistrano, California: Una Voce Press, 1993.

Gamber, Klaus, (tr.) Henry Taylor, *The Modern Rite: Collected Essays on the Reform of the Liturgy*, Farnborough: St Michael's Abbey Press, 2002.

Giles, Richard, *Re-Pitching the Tent: Reordering the Church Building for Worship and Mission*, revised and expanded edition, Norwich: Canterbury Press, 1997.

Hahn, Scott, *Letter and Spirit: From Written Text to Living Word in the Liturgy*, London: Darton, Longman and Todd, 2006.

Harrison OS, Brian W. 'The Post-conciliar Eucharistic Liturgy: Planning a Reform of the Reform', printed serially in editions of *Adoremus* Bulletin from November 1995 to January 1996. Reprinted in Kocik, Thomas M., *The Reform of the Reform? A Liturgical Debate: Reform or Return*, San Francisco: Ignatius Press, 2003.

Hemming, Laurence P., 'The Liturgical Subject: Introductory Essay', in Leachman OSB, James G. (ed.), *The Liturgical Subject: Subject, Subjectivity and the Human Person in Contemporary Liturgical Discussion and Critique*, London: SCM Press, 2008.

Hemming, Laurence P., *Worship as a Revelation: The Past, Present and Future of Catholic Liturgy*, London: Burns & Oates, 2008.

Hill, Christopher and Yarnold SJ, Edward (eds), *Anglicans and Roman Catholics: the Search for Unity*, London: SPCK and Catholic Truth Society, 1994.

Hitchcock, James, *The Recovery of the Sacred*, New York: Seabury, 1974.

Jasper, Ronald C. D. and Bradshaw, Paul F. (eds), *A Companion to the The Alternative Service Book 1980*, jointly published by (1) Oxford: Oxford University Press and Mowbray, and (2) Cambridge: Cambridge University Press, Colchester: William Clowes, and London: SPCK, 1986.

Jasper, Ronald C. D. and Cuming, Geoffrey (eds), *Prayers of the Eucharist: Early and Reformed*, third edition, Collegeville: Liturgical Press, 1990.

Kavanagh OSB, Aidan, *On Liturgical Theology*, New York: Pueblo, 1984.

King, Archdale A., *Liturgy of the Roman Church*, London: Longmans, 1957.

Kocik, Thomas M., *The Reform of the Reform? A Liturgical Debate: Reform or Return*, San Francisco: Ignatius Press, 2003.

Kwasniewski, Peter A., 'St Thomas on Eucharistic Ecstasy', in Leachman OSB, James G. (ed.), *The Liturgical Subject: Subject, Subjectivity and the Human Person in Contemporary Liturgical Discussion and Critique*, London: SCM Press, 2008.

Lang Cong. Orat., Uwe Michael, *Turning Towards the Lord: Orientation in Liturgical Prayer*, San Francisco: Ignatius Press, 2004 (foreword by Joseph, Cardinal Ratzinger).

Lang Cong. Orat., Uwe Michael (ed.), *Ever Directed Towards the Lord: The Love of God in the Liturgy of the Eucharist, Past, Present, and Hoped For*, London: T&T Clark, 2007.

Lewis, C. S., *Letters to Malcolm, Chiefly on Prayer*, London: G. Bles, 1964.

Mannion, M. Francis, 'The Catholicity of the Liturgy: Shaping a New Agenda', in Caldecott, Stratford (ed.), *Beyond the Prosaic: Renewing the Liturgical Movement*, Edinburgh: T&T Clark, 1998.

Piero Marini, Mark R., Francis, John R. Page and Pecklers, Keith F. (eds), *A Challenging Reform: Realizing the Vision of the Liturgical Renewal*, Collegeville: Liturgical Press, 2007.

Mazza, Enrico, (tr.) Matthew J. O'Connell, *The Eucharistic Prayers of the Roman Rite*, New York: Pueblo, 1986.

Nichols OP, Aidan, *Looking at Liturgy: A Critical View of Its Contemporary Form*, San Francisco: Ignatius Press, 1996.

Nichols OP, Aidan, 'Salutary Dissatisfaction: An English View of "Reforming the Reform", in Kocik, Thomas M., *The Reform of the Reform? A Liturgical Debate: Reform or Return*, San Francisco: Ignatius Press, 2003.

Pecklers SJ, Keith, *The Genius of the Roman Rite: The Reception and Implementation of the New Missal*, London: Burns & Oates, 2009.

Pickstock, Catherine, 'Liturgy and Language: The Sacred Polis', in Paul Bradshaw and Bryan Spinks (eds), *Liturgy in Dialogue*, London: SPCK, 1993.

Pickstock, Catherine, 'A Short Essay on the Reform of the Liturgy', in *New Blackfriars* 78, 912 (1997).

Pickstock, Catherine, *After Writing: On the Liturgical Consummation of Philosophy*, Oxford: Blackwell, 1998.

Ratzinger, Joseph, *Eschatology*, Washington DC: Catholic University of America Press, 1988.

Ratzinger, Joseph, (tr.) John Saward, *The Spirit of the Liturgy*, San Francisco: Ignatius Press, 2000.

Reid, Alcuin, *The Organic Development of the Liturgy*, Farnborough: St Michael's Abbey Press, 2004.

Reid, Scott M. P. (ed.), *A Bitter Trial: Evelyn Waugh and John Carmel Cardinal Heenan on the Liturgical Changes*, Curdridge, The Saint Austin Press, 1996.

Robinson Cong. Orat., Jonathan, *The Mass and Modernity: Walking to Heaven Backwards*, San Francisco: Ignatius Press, 2005.

Robinson Cong. Orat., Jonathan, 'The Mass and Modernity', in Lang, Uwe Michael (ed.), *Ever Directed Towards the Lord: The Love of God in the Liturgy of the Eucharist, Past, Present, and Hoped For*, London: T&T Clark, 2007 (The title of the paper is the same as the title of the book referred to above).

Schönborn, Christoph, (tr.) John Saward, *Loving the Church: Spiritual Exercises Preached in the Presence of Pope John Paul II*, San Francisco: Ignatius Press, 1998.

Smolarski SJ, Dennis C., *The General Instruction of the Roman Missal: A Commentary, 1969-2002*, Collegeville: Liturgical Press, 2003.

Society of St Pius X, *The Problem of the Liturgical Reform: A Theological and Liturgical Study*, Kansas City, Angelus Press, 2001.

Stancliffe, David, 'Creating Sacred Space', in Brown, D. and Loades, A. (eds), *The Sense of the Sacramental: Movement and Measure in Art and Music, Place and Time*, London: SPCK, 1995.

Stancliffe, David, *The Lion Companion to Church Architecture*, Oxford: Lion Hudson, 2008.

Stephenson, Colin, *Merrily on High*, London: Darton, Longman and Todd, 1972; republished by London: SCM-Canterbury Press, 2008.

Stringer, Martin D., *A Sociological History of Christian Worship*, Cambridge: Cambridge University Press, 2005.

Torevell, David, *Losing the Sacred: Ritual, Modernity and Liturgical Reform*, Edinburgh: T&T Clark, 2000.

Turner, Victor, 'Ritual, Tribal and Catholic', *Worship* 50 (1976), pp. 504–26.

Vagaggini OSB, Cipriani, (ed. and tr.) Peter Coughlan, *The Canon of the Mass and Liturgical Reform*, London: Geoffrey Chapman, 1967.

Wilkes, Paul, *Excellent Catholic Parishes: The Guide to Best Places and Practices*, New York: Paulist Press, 2001.

Liturgical Books and Reports and Documents

Anglican (see also 'Catholic or 'Reformed')

The Alternative Service Book 1980, jointly published by (1) Oxford: Oxford University Press and Mowbray and (2) Cambridge: Cambridge University Press, Colchester: William Clowes, and London: SPCK.

The Book of Divine Worship, 2003, Mt Pocono: Newman House Press, at the time of writing out of print but available (2009) online.

Common Worship, *Services and Prayers for the Church of England*, 2000, London: Church House Publishing.

English Missal, fifth and last edition of the altar edition, 1958, London: W. Knott & Son, 1958, republished 2001, Norwich: Canterbury Press.

Monastic Breviary: Matins according to the Holy Rule of Saint Benedict, Tymawr, Lydart, Monmouth: The Society of the Sacred Cross 1961; reprinted Glendale, Colorado: Lancelot Andrewes Press, 2007.

The Monastic Diurnal, last printed London: Oxford University Press, 1963.

Mission-shaped Church: Church Planting and Fresh Expressions of Church in a Changing Context, GS 1523, London: Church House Publishing, 2004.

Catholic

Missale Romanum, 1962, *editio typica Vaticanis*.

Roman Missal, 1962, London: and Oil City, PA: Baronius Press.

Missale Romanum . . . Pauli PP. VI, 1971, *editio typica Vaticanis*.

Missale Romanum . . . Pauli PP. VI 1975, *editio typica secunda* (second edition).

Missale Romanum . . . Pauli PP. VI . . . Ioannis Pauli PP. II . . . editio typica tertia, (third edition), published also under licence as a study edition by Woodridge, Illinois: Midwest Theological Forum, 2002.

The Roman Missal, Dublin: Liturgical Books: Talbot Press Ltd and Glasgow: Wm Collins Sons & Co, both 1975. Also published in hand-missal size as:

Saint Luke's Daily Missal, Alcester and Dublin: C. Goodliffe Neale Ltd., 1975.
The translation produced, 1969–74, by the International Commission on English in the Liturgy (hereafter ICEL), officially approved for use in Australia, England and Wales, Ireland and Scotland. Psalm verses for Propers are mainly from the 1963 Grail Psalms and Scripture texts are from the Jerusalem Bible.

The Sacramentary, New York: Catholic Book Publishing Co., 1985.
Revised to conform to the second typical edition of the *Missale Romanum* (1975), the translation is that produced, 1969–74, with material produced between 1975 and 1985, by ICEL, officially approved for use in the United States, and includes three 'Eucharistic Prayers for Masses with Children' and two 'Eucharistic Prayers for Masses of Reconciliation'. Scripture texts are from the New American Bible.

English translation of *The Order of Mass I* © 2006, 2008, ICEL. At the time of writing, the English translation of *The Order of Mass I* is available (2009) on the ICEL website www.icel/web.org/ but not yet in print.

Catechism of the Catholic Church, revised edition, London: Geoffrey Chapman, 1999.

Congregatio de Cultu Divino et Disciplina Sacramentorum, 'Editoriale: Pregare "ad orientem versus"', *Notitiæ* 29 (1993): 245–9.

Catholic Bishops' Conference of England and Wales, *Celebrating the Mass: A Pastoral Introduction*, London: Catholic Truth Society, 2005.

Congregation for Divine Worship and the Discipline of the Sacraments, Liturgiam authenticam: *On the Use of Vernacular Languages in the Publication of the Books of the Roman Liturgy*, London: Catholic Truth Society, 2001; also available (2009) at www.vatican.va

2002 *General Instruction of the Roman Missal* (GIRM), Catholic Bishops' Conference of England and Wales, London: Catholic Truth Society, 2005.

Benedict XVI, Address to the Curia of 22nd December 2005, *Acta Apostolicæ Sedis*, Vatican, vol. 98 (2006), pp. 44–5, also available (2009) at www.vatican.va

Benedict XVI, Post-Synodal Exhortation, *Sacramentum Caritatis*, London: Catholic Truth Society, 2007; also available (2009) at www.vatican.va

Benedict XVI, *motu proprio*, *Summorum Pontificum* (and accompanying explanatory letter to the bishops), London: Catholic Truth Society, 2007; also available (2009) at www.vatican.va

Sacrosanctum Consilium, 1963, the Second Vatican Council Dogmatic Constitution on the Liturgy, is available (2009) on www.vatican.va

A Group of Roman Theologians, *A Critical Study of the New Order of the Mass (Novus Ordo Missae)*, *Lumen Gentium* Foundation, 1970; copies were available (at least at the time) from the Latin Mass Society.

Chapter 3 Fast or Feast

Articles and Books

Atwell, Robert (comp.), *Celebrating the Seasons: Daily Spiritual Readings for the Christian Year*, Norwich: Canterbury Press, 1999.

Atwell, Robert (comp.), *Celebrating the Saints: Daily Spiritual Readings to accompany the Calendars of the Church of England, the Church of Ireland, the Scottish Episcopal church and the Church in Wales*, Norwich: SCM Press; 2004 (enlarged edition).

Bugnini CM, Annibale, (tr.) Matthew J. O'Connell, *The Reform of the Liturgy 1948–1975*, Collegeville: Liturgical Press, 1990.

Burleigh, Michael, *Sacred Causes: Religion and Politics from the European Dictators to Al Qaeda*, London: Harper Collins, 2006.

Chryssavgis, John, 'The Spiritual Way', in Cunningham, Mary B. and Theokritoff, Elizabeth (eds), *The Cambridge Companion to Orthodox Christian Theology*, Cambridge: Cambridge University Press, 2008.

Daniélou SJ, Jean, '*La Théologie du dimanche*', in *Le Jour du Seigneur*, Paris: R Laffont, 1948.

Douglas, Mary, 'The Contempt of Ritual', in *New Blackfriars* 49, nos. 577–8: pp. 475–82; 528–39, 1968.

Douglas, Mary, *Natural Symbols: Explorations in Cosmology*, London: Routledge, 1970.

D'Souza, Dinesh, 'Created Equal: How Christianity Shaped The West,' *Imprimis* 37, no. 11, November 2008, pp. 1–5.

Duffy, Eamon, *The Stripping of the Altars: Traditional Religion in England c1400–c1580*, New Haven: Yale University Press, 1992.

Hemming, Laurence P., *Worship as a Revelation: The Past, Present and Future of Catholic Liturgy*, London: Burns & Oates, 2008.

Hunwicke, John, *Fr Hunwicke's Liturgical Notes*, 1 June 2009, 'Paschaltide?' http://liturgicalnotes.blogspot.com/

MacCulloch, Diarmaid, *Thomas Cranmer*, New Haven and London: Yale University Press, 1996.

Lang Cong. Orat., Uwe Michael (ed.), *Ever Directed Towards the Lord: The Love of God in the Liturgy of the Eucharist, Past, Present, and Hoped For*, London: T&T Clark, 2007.

Linden, Ian, *Global Catholicism: Diversity and Change since Vatican II*, London: Hurst & Co., 2009.

Martimort, Aimé-Georges and others (eds), (tr.) Matthew J. O'Connell, *The Church at Prayer*, Vol. IV: *The Liturgy and Time*, London: Geoffrey Chapman, 1986.

Nichols OP, Aidan, *Looking at the Liturgy: A Critical View of Its Contemporary Form*, San Francisco: Ignatius Press, 1996.

Plekon, Michael, 'The Russian Religious Revival and its Theological Legacy', in Cunningham, Mary B. and Theokritoff, Elizabeth (eds), *The Cambridge Companion to Orthodox Christian Theology*, Cambridge: Cambridge University Press, 2008.

Schmemann, Alexander, *Introduction to Liturgical Theology*, Leighton Buzzard: Faith Press, second edition, 1975.

Taft SJ, Robert, *The Liturgy of the Hours in East and West*, second revised edition, Collegeville: Liturgical Press, 1993.

Walsh, Michael (ed.), *Butler's Lives of the Saints*, Tunbridge: Burns & Oates, and North Blackburn, Victoria: Collins Dove, revised edition 1991.

Walsh, Michael, *A New Dictionary of Saints: East and West*, Collegeville: Liturgical Press, 2007.

Liturgical Books and Reports and Documents

The Alternative Service Book 1980, jointly published by (1) Oxford: Oxford University Press and Mowbray and (2) Cambridge: Cambridge University Press, Colchester: William Clowes, and London: SPCK.

The Commemoration of Saints and Heroes of the Faith in the Anglican Communion; the Report of a Commission appointed by the Archbishop of Canterbury, London: SPCK, 1957.

Common Worship: Services and Prayers for the Church of England, London: Church House Publishing, 2000.

The Code of Canon Law (in English translation), London: Collins, 1983.

The Revised Common Lectionary: The Consultation on Common Texts, Norwich: The Canterbury Press, 1992.

Paul VI, Apostolic Exhortation, *Evangelii nuntiandi*, London: Catholic Truth Society, 1975. Also available (2009) at www.vatican.va

Chapter 4 Said or Sung

Articles and Books

2002 *General Instruction of the Roman Missal* (GIRM), Catholic Bishops' Conference of England and Wales, London: Catholic Truth Society, 2005.

Berry, Mary, *Plainchant for Everyone*, RSCM Handbook, third edition 1996.

Crocker, Richard L., *An Introduction to Gregorian Chant*, New Haven: Yale University Press, 2000.

Day, Thomas, *Why Catholics Can't Sing*, New York: Crossroad, 1990.

Dobszay, László, *The Bugnini-Liturgy and the Reform of the Reform*, vol. 5 of *Musicæ Sacræ Meltemata*, Front Royal VA: Church Music Association of America, 2003.

Dobszay, László, *The Restoration and Organic Development of the Roman Rite*, London: T&T Clark, 2009.

Fassler, Margot, *Gothic Song: Victorine Sequences and Augustinian Reform in Twelfth-Century Paris* (Cambridge Studies in Medieval and Renaissance Music), Cambridge: Cambridge University Press, 1993.

Göschl OSB, Johannes Berchmans, 'One Hundred Years of the *Graduale Romanum*', in *Sacred Music*, Summer 2008, vol. 135, no. 2, pp. 8ff., Richmond VA: Church Music Association of America, 2008.

Harper, John, *The Forms and Orders of Western Liturgy from the Tenth to the Eighteenth Century: A Historical Guide for Students and Musicians*, Oxford: Clarendon Paperbacks, 1991.

Hemming, Laurence P., *Worship as a Revelation: The Past, Present and Future of Catholic Liturgy*, London: Burns & Oates, 2008.

Hiley, David, *Western Plainchant: A Handbook*, Oxford: Oxford University Press, 1993.

ICEL, 2009, *Music for the English*, www.icelweb.org/ICELMusicIntroduction. pdf

Jungmann SJ, Joseph, *The Mass of the Roman Rite: Its Origins and Development (Missarum Sollemnia)*, two vols, New York: Benziger Brothers Inc., 1951; replica edition Dublin: Four Courts Press, 1986.

Kruckenberg, Lori, 'Neumatizing the Sequence: Special Performances of Sequences in the Central Middle Ages,' *Journal of the American Musicological Society*, Summer 2006, vol. 59, No. 2, pp. 243–317.

Leaver, Robin A. and Zimmerman, Joyce A. (eds), *Liturgy and Music*, Collegeville: Liturgical Press, 1998.

Leaver, Robin A., 'Liturgical Music as Anamnesis', in Leaver, Robin A. and Zimmerman, Joyce. A. (eds), *Liturgy and Music*, Collegeville: Liturgical Press, 1998.

McKinnon, James W., *Music in Early Christian Literature* (Cambridge Readings in the Literature of Music), Cambridge: Cambridge University Press, 1987.

Merkley, Paul A. and Merkley, Lora L. M., *Music and Patronage in the Sforza Court*, Turhout, Belgium: Brepols, 1999.

Molloy, Michael J., 'Liturgical Music as Corporate Song 3', in Leaver, Robin A. and Zimmerman, Joyce A. (eds), *Liturgy and Music*, 1998, p. 328.

Oost-Zinner, Arlene and Tucker, Jeffrey, 'An Idiot's Guide to Square Notes', *Crisis*, May 2006.

Otto, Rudolf, *The Idea of the Holy*, Oxford: Oxford University Press, 1923 (English translation of German original).

Pius X, *motu proprio* (a statement made by the Pope 'at his own initiative'), *Tra Le Sollecitudini* (On Sacred Music), 22 November 1903; available (2009) on www.adoremus.org

Pius XII, Encyclical, *Musicæ Sacræ*, 25 December 1955; available (2009) on www.vatican.vaBibliography: Said or Sung (3)

Poterack, Kurt, 'The Strange Rejection of the *Roman Gradual*', in *Sacred Music*, Summer 2008, vol. 135, no. 2, pp.91f., Richmond VA: Church Music Association of America, 2008.

Quitslund, Beth, *The Reformation in Rhyme: Sternhold, Hopkins and the Metrical Psalter, 1547–1603* (St Andrews Studies in Reformation History), Aldershot: Ashgate Publishing, 2008.

Reid, Alcuin, *The Organic Development of the Liturgy*, Farnborough: St Michael's Abbey Press, 2004.

Saulnier OSB, Daniel, (tr.) Mary Berry, *Gregorian Chant for Musicians: A Complete Guide to the History and Liturgy*, Brewster, Mass.: Paraclete Press, 2007.

Schmemann, Alexander, *Introduction to Liturgical Theology*, Leighton Buzzard: Faith Press, second edition 1975.

Ratzinger, Joseph, (tr.) John Saward, *The Spirit of the Liturgy*, San Francisco: Ignatius Press, 2000.

Tucker, Jeffrey, 'Music at St Peter's: The Transformation', *New Liturgical Movement*, 10 August 2009, www.newliturgicalmovement.org

Zon, Bennett, *The English Plainchant Revival*, Oxford: Oxford University Press, 1999.

Plainsong Resources, Hymnals, Reports and Documents

Latin Chant (the Use of Salisbury)

Sandon, Nicholas (ed.), *The Use of Salisbury*, Newton Abbot, 1984 onwards. A project to retrieve and republish the treasury of Sarum chant, that is, the chant of the Use of Salisbury which was prevalent in England before the Reformation. The volumes so far (2009) are:

1　The Ordinary of the Mass.
2　The Proper of the Mass in Advent.
3　The Proper of the Mass from Septuagesima to Palm Sunday.
4　The Masses and Ceremonies of Holy Week.
5　The Proper of the Mass from Easter to Trinity.
6　The Proper of the Mass from Trinity to Advent.

Latin Chant (Vatican)

For the 'bruising' relationship between Solesmes and Vatican editions, see Hiley (pp. 624ff.). Since the Second Vatican Council, Solesmes has been entrusted with producing the necessary liturgical chant books (see below). The exception, however, is:

Graduale simplex, Rome: *Libreria Editrice Vaticana*, 1999.

Latin Chant (Solesmes: Abbaye Saint-Pierre de Solesmes)

There are several books published for particular purposes, which are selections from the main books. The main resources are as follows and dates, where known, are given:

Pre-conciliar (Vulgate text)

- *Antiphonale monasticum*, 1934, for the hours of the day.
- *Liber Usualis*, 1961, 1963, the largest Solesmes plainsong anthology, of particular interest to musicologists, is also available (2009) online.
- *Processionale monasticum*, 1893, reprinted.
- *Propers from the ancient Processionale monasticum with neumes taken from the manuscript of the Antiphonaire de Hartker (St Gall).*

Post-conciliar (neo-Vulgate text)

- *Antiphonale monasticum I, 2005, de tempore, for the hours of the day.*
- *Antiphonale monasticum II, 2006, Psalterium, for the hours of the day.*
- *Antiphonale monasticum III, 2007, de sanctis, for the hours of the day.*
- *Antiphonale monasticum IV (unpublished as of 2009), for the office of vigils.*

- *Antiphonale monasticum V de sanctis (as used by the Solesmes Congregation).*
- *Antiphonale Romanum I, 2009 (unpublished at the time of writing).*
- *Psalterium monasticum, 1981, monastic psalter including psalms for vigils, with hymns, versicles and short readings.*
- *Liber hymnarius, 1983, 1985, hymns and invitatories for the Liturgy of the Hours with a selection of responsories and also the monastic Propers.*
- *Graduale Romanum, 1974, the Roman Gradual: chants for the Ordinary and the Proper of the Mass of 1970.*
- *Graduale triplex. Here the usual notation is accompanied by neumes from the manuscripts of Laon, Einsiedeln and those of the St Gall family.*

English Plainchant

Merbecke, John, *The Booke of Common Praier Noted*, 1550 (The Merbecke settings still used are in *New English Hymnal*, no. 542).

The Ordinary of the Mass, Plainsong and Mediæval Music Society, 1896, revised edition 1937.

Burgess, Francis, *The English Gradual Part I, The Plainchant of the Ordinary*, London: Plainchant Publications Committee, seventh edition 1961 (enquiries to the RSCM).

Palmer, G. H. and Burgess, Francis (eds), *The Plainchant Gradual*, Wantage: St Mary's Press, revised edition 1962 (enquiries to the RSCM).

Allan CR, Peter (ed.), *An English Kyriale*, Mirfield: Community of the Resurrection, and London: HarperCollins Religious, 1991.

Burt, C. David (adaptor and ed.), *The Anglican Use Gradual*, Mansfield, Mass.: Partridge Hill Press, 2007. *The Anglican Use Gradual* is available (2009) online as an Adobe Acrobat file.

Ford, Bruce E. (adaptor and ed.), *The American Gradual*, second edition, Hopkinsville, KY, 2008. *The American Gradual* is also available (2009) online: www.musicasacra.com/books/americangradual1.pdf

Ford, Paul F. (arr.), *By Flowing Waters* (*Graduale Simplex* in English), Collegeville: Liturgical Press, 1999.

Mundelein Psalter, Collegeville: Liturgy Training Publications, 2007. Complete Morning, Evening and Night Prayer orders, using the Grail Psalter and St Meinrad tones.

Other Internet Resources

Adoremus www.adoremus.org provides downloadable files of the music from *Jubilate Deo* (in plainsong and modern notation) and MP3 files.

Church Music Association of America, 12421 New Point Drive, Richmond, Virginia 23233, USA, can be reached (2009) at www.musicasacra.com

The Gregorian Association Web Page and lists of chant resources can be reached (2009) through hyperlinks at www.beaufort.demon.co.uk

Rice, Richard, *Simple Choral Gradual: Entrance, Offertory, and Communion Antiphons for Parish Choirs* is available (2009) online: www.musicasacra.com/books/simplechoralgradual.pdf

St Thomas Aquinas, St Thomas's *Introduction* to his *Exposition of the Psalms of David*, Hugh McDonald (tr.), Latin Text according to the Venice Edition MDCCLXXV available (2009) The Aquinas Translation Project htttp://www4.desales.edu/~philtheo/loughlin/ATP/index.html)

The Royal School of Church Music, Sarum College, 19 The Close, Salisbury, Wiltshire, SP1 2EB, UK, www.rscm.com

Hymnals

Adoremus Hymnal, San Francisco: Ignatius Press, 1997.

Catholic Hymn Book, Leominster: Gracewing, 1998.

Celebration Hymnal for Everyone, Great Wakering: McCrimmons, 1995.

Common Praise, Norwich: Canterbury Press, 1986.

English Hymnal, London: Oxford University Press and Mowbray, new edition, 1933.

Laudate, Mildenhall, Suffolk: Decani Music, 1999.

Hymns for Prayer and Praise, Canterbury Press: Norwich, 1996.

New English Hymnal, Norwich: Canterbury Press, 2000.

New English Praise, Norwich: Canterbury Press, 2006.

20th Century Folk Hymnal, Great Wakering: Mayhew-McCrimmon, 1974.

Chapter 5 Town or Country

Articles and Books

Barry OSB, Patrick, *A Rule of Saint Benedict*, Leominster: Gracewing, 1997.

Bradshaw, Paul F. and Jones, Simon, 'Daily Prayer', in Bradshaw, Paul F. (ed.), *A Companion to Common Worship*, vol. 2, SPCK 2006.

Bugnini CM, Annibale, (tr.) Matthew J. O'Connell, *The Reform of the Liturgy 1948–1975*, Collegeville: Liturgical Press, 1990.

Burnham, Andrew, 'Introduction', in Fletcher, Jeremy and Myers, Gilly (eds), *Using Common Worship, Daily Prayer*, London: Church House Publishing, 2002.

Campbell FSC, Stanislaus, *From Breviary to Liturgy of the Hours*, Collegeville: Liturgical Press, 1995.

Dobszay, László, *The Bugnini-Liturgy and the Reform of the Reform*, vol. 5 of *Musicæ Sacræ Meltemata*, Front Royal VA: Church Music Association of America, 2003.

Fletcher, Jeremy and Myers, Gilly (eds), *Using Common Worship, Daily Prayer*, London: Church House Publishing, 2002.

Guiver CR, George, *Company of Voices*, Norwich: Canterbury Press, revised edition 2001.

Hemming, Laurence P., *Worship as a Revelation: The Past, Present and Future of Catholic Liturgy*, London: Burns & Oates, 2008.

Pius X, Apostolic Constitution, *Divino Afflatu* (on the reform of the Roman Breviary), 1 November 1911; available (2009) on the unofficial website www.papalencyclicals.net

Pius X, *motu proprio, Abhinc duos annos*, October 1913. For the text see AAS 5 (1913), pp. 449–551.

Reid, Alcuin, *The Organic Development of the Liturgy*, Farnborough: St Michael's Abbey Press, 2004.

Saward, John, *The Mysteries of March*, London: Collins, 1990.

Taft SJ, Robert, *The Liturgy of the Hours in East and West*, second revised edition, Collegeville: Liturgical Press, 1993.

Liturgical Books and Reports and Documents

Catholic

Pre-conciliar Resources

Breviarum Romanum, 1961 (implementing *Codex Rubricarum*, 1960), two vols, Holy Apostolic See and Sacred Congregation of Rites (Vatican), 1961 [incorporating the revised Latin Psalter of Pius XII, 1945 (the 'Pian Psalter')].

Breviarum Romanum, 1961 (implementing *Codex Rubricarum*, 1960), two vols, Bonn: nova & vetera, 2008 [incorporating the Vulgate Psalter].

Post-conciliar Resources

Liturgia horarum, four volumes, 1971, 1985–87, *Libreria editrice Vaticana*:
I   *Tempus Adventus* (Advent), *Tempus Nativitatis* (Christmas).
II *Tempus Quadragesimæ* (Lent), *Sacrum Triduum Paschale* (Easter Triduum), *Tempus Paschale* (Eastertide).
III *Tempus Per Annum Hebdomadæ* I–XVII (Weeks 1–17).
IV *Tempus Per Annum Hebdomadæ* XVIII–XXXIV (Weeks 18–34).

The Liturgy of the Hours in English
Two versions exist, based on the Latin *editio typica* of 1971:

1 *The Divine Office*, three vols, London: Collins, 1974, reprinted 2005–2006
I   Advent, Christmastide and Weeks 1–9 of the Year
II   Lent and Eastertide
III Weeks of the Year 6–34
This translation was not the ICEL translation but is officially approved for use in Australia, England and Wales, Ireland, Scotland, and for individual dioceses in Africa and Asia, New Zealand and the West Indies. The Psalter is from the 1963 Grail Psalms and canticles and readings are from various versions of the Bible, including the Revised Standard Version, the Jerusalem Bible, the Knox Bible, the Good News Bible, and the New English Bible.

Shorter editions:
• *Daily Prayer* (that is, a diurnal, the Divine Office omitting the Office of Readings)
• *Morning and Evening Prayer*, 1974, (that is, omitting the Office of Readings and Prayer during the Day but including Night Prayer)
• *Shorter Morning and Evening Prayer* (that is, the Psalter for Morning, Evening and Night Prayer and a selection of texts from the *Sanctorale* and *Temporale*)

2 *The Liturgy of the Hours*, four vols, New York: Catholic Book Publishing Company, 1975

I   Advent Season, Christmas Season
II   Lenten Season, Easter Season
III Ordinary Time, Weeks 1–17
IV   Ordinary Time, Weeks 18–34

The version, produced by ICEL, is officially approved for use in the USA, Canada, New Zealand, and various Asian and African countries. The Psalter is mainly from the 1963 Grail Psalms and the canticle and readings and canticles are from the New American Bible.

Shorter editions:

• *Christian Prayer: Liturgy of the Hours*, Daughters of St Paul, and Catholic Book Publishing Company, is a one-volume version (a diurnal)
• *Shorter Christian Prayer*, New York: Catholic Book Publishing Company, 1988 (a pocket-sized version: the Psalter for Morning, Evening and Night Prayer and a selection of texts from the *Sanctorale* and *Temporale*)

Celebrating Sunday Evening Prayer, Norwich: Canterbury Press, 2005.
Solesmes resources, see Bibliography for Chapter 4
The Second Vatican Council, *Constitutio de Sacra Liturgia*, Constitution on the Sacred Liturgy, 1964.
The CTS New Catholic Bible, London: Catholic Truth Society, 2007.
General Instruction on the Liturgy of the Hours, see The Divine Office 1972.
Thesaurus Liturgiæ Horarum Monasticæ (Thesaurus of the Monastic Liturgy of the Hours) was approved in 1977 by a decree of the Sacred Congregation of Sacraments and Divine Worship, *Operi Dei*, 10 February 1977.

Anglican

Morning and Evening Prayer (Alternative Services Series 1 and Series 2). The proposals to the Convocations and the Church Assembly were published by the Society for Promoting Christian Knowledge (London) and issued in booklet form on various dates in the later part of the 1960s.
The Alternative Service Book 1980, jointly published by (1) Oxford: Oxford University Press and Mowbray, and (2) Cambridge: Cambridge University Press, Colchester: William Clowes, and London: SPCK.
Celebrating Common Prayer, London: Mowbray, 1992. Available both as *The Daily Office SSF* and *Celebrating Common Prayer* and, from 1994, in a simplified, pocket version.
Church of England, *Daily Prayer*, London: Church House Publishing, 2005.
Common Worship: Services and Prayers for the Church of England, London: Church House Publishing, 2000.
New Patterns for Worship, London: Church House Publishing, 2002.

Unofficial Liturgical Books

Catholic

A Short Breviary for Religious and Laity, Collegeville: Liturgical Press, 1941.

The Monastic Diurnal, Farnborough: St Michael's Abbey Press, 2004.

Johnson, Maxwell E. *et al.* (comp.), *Benedictine Daily Prayer*, Dublin: The Columba Press, 2005.

Stravinskas, Peter (ed.), *Lauds and Vespers: Per annum*, Princeton, NJ: Scepter Publishers and Mt Pocono, Penn.: Newman House Press, both 2001.

Stravinskas, Peter (ed.), *Lauds and Vespers:* Enlarged edition, Princeton, NJ: Scepter Publishers and Mt Pocono, Penn.: Newman House Press, both 2006.

Anglican and Ecumenical

The Anglican Breviary, Mt Sinai, Long Island, NY: Frank Gavin Liturgical Foundation Inc., 1955, reprinted 1998.

Burnham, Andrew (comp.), *A Manual of Anglo-Catholic Devotion*, second edition, Norwich: Canterbury Press, 2001.

Burnham, Andrew (comp.), *A Pocket Manual of Anglo-Catholic Devotion*, Norwich: Canterbury Press, 2004.

Monastic Breviary: Matins according to the Holy Rule of Saint Benedict, Tymawr, Lydart, Monmouth: The Society of the Sacred Cross, 1961; reprinted by Glendale: Lancelot Andrewes Press, 2007.

The Monastic Diurnal, London: Oxford University Press, last printed 1963.

The Monastic Diurnal Noted, vol. I, 1952, vol. II, 1961, Kenosha, Wisconsin: Community of St Mary; reprinted in one volume by Glendale: Lancelot Andrewes Press, 2005.

Pitchford, John (comp.), *Discovering Prayer with the Church*, Norwich: Tufton Books, 2006.

Chapter 6 Mother or Maiden

Articles and Books

St Augustine, *De Sancte Virginitate*, 6: PL 40, 399.

Barker, Margaret, *The Great High Priest*, London and New York: T&T Clark International, 2003.

Boss, Sarah Jane *Empress and Handmaid: On Nature and Gender in the Cult of the Virgin Mary*, London and New York: Cassell, 2000.

Boss, Sarah Jane, 'Telling the Beads: The Practice and Symbolism of the Rosary', in Boss, Sarah Jane (ed.), *Mary: The Complete Resource*, London and New York: Continuum, 2007, pp. 385ff.

Boyce OCD, Philip, 'John Henry Newman and the Immaculate Mother of the Incarnate Word', in McLoughlin, William and Pinnock, Jill (eds), *Mary for Earth and Heaven: Essays on Mary and Ecumenism*, Leominster: Gracewing, 2000, p. 87.

Bulgakov, Sergius Nikolaevich, (tr. Thomas Allan Smith), *The Burning Bush: On the Orthodox Veneration of the Mother of God*, Grand Rapids, Michigan and Cambridge: Eerdmans, 2009.

Burnham, Andrew, Paper given to the Society of Mary and the Ecumenical Society of the Blessed Virgin Mary, 'Mary and Christian Prayer', 2001. The paper was published privately by the Society of Mary.

Burnham, Andrew, 'Our Lady of Eton and the Glory of the Eton Choirbook', Walsingham Assumptiontide Lecture, 2005.

Calkins, Arthur Burton, 'Mary's Spiritual Maternity', in McLoughlin, William and Pinnock, Jill (eds), *Mary is for Everyone*, Leominster: Gracewing, 1997, p. 79.

Catechism of the Catholic Church, London: Geoffrey Chapman, 1999 (revised edition).

Cox, Harvey, *The Secular City*, New York: Macmillan, and London: SCM Press, 1965.

Farrell R. S. M., Marie, 'Evangelization, Mary and the "Suenens Amendment" of *Lumen Gentium* 8', in McLoughlin, William and Pinnock, Jill (eds), *Mary for Earth and Heaven*, Leominster: Gracewing, 2002.

John Paul II, *Redemptoris Mater*, 1987, is available (2009) on www.vatican.va

John Paul II, *Rosarium Virginis Mariæ*, 2002, is available (2009) on www.vatican. va

Jung, C. G., (eds) G. Adler, M. Fordham and H. Read, (tr. R. F. C. Hull), *Collected Works*, 9ii, 142, and 11, 125 (21 volume set), New Jersey: Princeton University Press, 2000.

Ker, Ian, *John Henry Newman: A Biography*, Oxford, New York: Oxford University Press, 1998 (reissued 2009). The primary source is Newman's 'Certain Difficulties felt by Anglicans in Catholic Teaching', vol. 2, pp. 92–3, 99–100.

Lamartine, Alphonse Marie Louis de, 'Élégie', in Canfield, Arthur G., *French Lyrics*, 1899; available (2009) through Project Gutenburg on www.gutenberg. org

Lewis, C. S., *The Great Divorce*, London: G. Bles, 1946; reprinted by London: HarperCollins, 1997, and New York: HarperCollins, 2001.

Lumen Gentium, the Second Vatican Council Dogmatic Constitution on the Church, 1963, is available (2009) on www.vatican.va

Macquarrie, John, *Mary for All Christians*, London: Collins, 1990.

Mary: A Focus for Unity for all Christians? Sermons and Conference talks presented at Lourdes and Nettuno, 2008, available (2009) from the Society of Mary: www.societyofmary.net/

Maunder, Chris, 'Apparitions of Mary', in Boss, Sarah Jane (ed.), *Mary: The Complete Resource*, London and New York: Continuum, 2007, pp. 424ff.

Parker, Thomas M., 'Devotion to the Mother of God', in Mascall, E. L. (ed.), *The Mother of God: A Symposium by Members of the Fellowship of St Alban and St Sergius*, London: Dacre Press, 1949.

Pelikan, Jaroslav, *Mary through the Centuries: Her Place in the History of Culture*, New Haven: Yale University Press, 1996.

Rutt, Richard, 'Why should he send his Mother? Some reflections on Marian Apparitions?', in McLoughlin, William and Pinnock, Jill (eds), *Mary is for Everyone*, Leominster: Gracewing, 1997, p. 274.

Rutt, Richard, *Mary, Disciple of the Lord: Changes in the Use of Scripture in Marian Masses since 1970*, Ecumenical Society of the Blessed Virgin Mary, 2002, ISBN 1 869927 39 7.

Saward, John, *Redeemer in the Womb*, San Francisco: Ignatius, 1993.

Schillebeeckx, Edward and Halkes, Catharina, (tr.) John Bowden, *Mary Yesterday, Today, Tomorrow*, London: SCM Press, 1993.

Scola, Angelo, Cardinal, (tr. Michelle Borras and others), *The Nuptial Mystery*, Grand Rapids, Michigan and Cambridge: Eerdmans, 2005.

Vigny, Alfred de, 'Le Mont des Oliviers', in Rees, William (ed. and tr), *The Penguin Book of French Poetry: 1820–1950*, London: Penguin, 1992.

Williams, Paul, 'The English Reformers and the Blessed Virgin Mary', in Boss, Sarah Jane (ed.), *Mary: The Complete Resource*, London and New York: Continuum, 2007, pp. 238 ff.

Williams, Paul, 'The Virgin Mary in Anglican Tradition', in Boss, Sarah Jane (ed.), *Mary: The Complete Resource*, pp. 314ff.

Williams, Rowan, *Ponder these Things: Praying with Icons of the Virgin*, Norwich: Canterbury Press, 2002.

Williamson, Magnus, 'The Early Tudor Court, the Provinces and the Eton Choirbook', in *Early Music*, May 1997.

Williamson, Magnus, *The Eton Choirbook*, D.Phil. Thesis, University of Oxford, 1997.

Williamson, Magnus, '*Pictura et scriptura*: the Eton Choirbook in its Iconographical Context', in *Early Music*, August 2000.

Yelton, Michael, *Outposts of the Faith*, Norwich: Canterbury Press, 2009.

Devotional and Liturgical Resources

Anglican

The Book of Common Prayer, According to the Use of the Episcopal Church of the USA (1979).

Burnham, Andrew (comp.), *A Manual of Anglo-Catholic Devotion*, Norwich: Canterbury Press, 2001.

Burnham, Andrew (comp.), *A Pocket Manual of Anglo-Catholic Devotion*, Norwich: Canterbury Press, 2004.

Common Worship, *Daily Prayer*, London: Church House Publishing, 2005.

Common Worship, *Times and Seasons*, London: Church House Publishing, 2006.

Keble, John, *The Christian Year*, London and New York: Frederick Warne and Co., 1827.

Lent, Holy Week, Easter: Services and Prayers, London and Cambridge: Church House Publishing, Cambridge University Press, SPCK, 1986.

Project Canterbury: founded in 1999, available (2009) on http://anglicanhistory.org/

The Walsingham Pilgrims Manual, available from the Walsingham College Trust Association, The Shrine Office, Walsingham, Norfolk, NR22 6EE.

Catholic

Ceremonial of Bishops, Collegeville: Liturgical Press, 1989.

Finnegan, Seán (comp.), *A Book of Hours and Other Catholic Devotions*, Norwich: Canterbury Press, 1998.

Handbook of Prayers, Princeton, New Jersey: Scepter and Chicago: Midwest Theological Forum, sixth edition 2001.

The Little Office of the Blessed Virgin Mary, London: Baronius Press, 2007.

Saint Benedict's Prayer Book, Leominster: Gracewing and Ampleforth Abbey Press, 1993.

Orthodox

Akathistos Hymn: www.fatheralexander.org/booklets/english/m_akathist_e.htm

The Akathistos Hymn in Two translations, with Introductions by Kallistos Ware and Roger Green, Ecumenical Society of the Blessed Virgin Mary, 1987, available from the Publications Secretary. The ESBVM website address (2009) is: www.esbvm.org

Divine Liturgy of St John Chrysostom:

Η ΘΕΙΑ ΛΕΙΤΟΥΡΓΙΑ ΤΟΥ ΕΝ ΑΓΙΟΙΣ ΠΑΤΡΟΣ ΗΜΩΝ ΙΩΑΝΝΟΥ ΤΟΥ ΧΡΥΣΟΣΤΟΜΟΥ *The Divine Liturgy of our Father among the Saints John Chrysostom*, Oxford: Oxford University Press, 1995.

Hymn Books and Musical Resources

Adoremus Hymnal, San Francisco: Ignatius Press, 1997.

Anglican Hymn Book, London: Church Book Room Press Ltd (Church Society), 1965.

Catholic Hymn Book, Leominster: Gracewing, 1998.

Common Praise, Norwich: Canterbury Press, 1986.

English Hymnal, London: Oxford University Press and Mowbray, new edition 1933.

Eton Choirbook: Eton College Library MS 178.

Hymns Ancient and Modern New Standard Edition, Norwich: Canterbury Press, 1983.

Hymns Ancient and Modern Revised, London: William Clowes & Sons, 1950.

New English Hymnal, Norwich: Canterbury Press, 1985.

Songs of Syon, London: Schott & Co., 1910.

'The Flower of All Virginity', *Music from the Eton Choirbook*, Vol. IV', The Sixteen, Harry Christopher, Collins Classics 13952 © 1993 Lambourne Productions Ltd.

Index